A 52-Week Bible Journey

ROUTE 52

Follow
Jesus

52 Bible Lessons from the
Life of Christ for Ages 6–8

Carol A. Jackson

Standard
PUBLISHING

Cincinnati, Ohio

Published by Standard Publishing, Cincinnati, Ohio
www.standardpub.com

16 15 14 13 12 11   9 10 11 12 13 14 15 16 17

ISBN-13: 978-0-7847-1328-0   ISBN-10: 0-7847-1328-6

This book is a revision of *Jesus and Me* (42031).

Project Editors: Ruth Frederick, Christine Spence
Cover Design: Malwitz Design
Inside Illustrations: Becky Radtke
Page Design: Andrew Quach

▼ Table of Contents ▲

Unit Title	Scripture	Application	Memory Verse
Unit 1 — **Jesus' Birth Helps Me Worship**	**Isaiah 9; Micah 5; Luke 1; Matthew 3** *(prophecy)* **Luke 1** *(Mary)* **Luke 2** *(Jesus is born)* **Luke 2** *(shepherds)*	Worship God because He kept His promise.	Isaiah 25:1 Challenge: Luke 2:20
Unit 2 — **Jesus Was a Child Just Like Me**	**Luke 2** *(Simeon and Anna)* **Matthew 2** *(wise men)* **Matthew 2** *(to Egypt)* **Luke 2** *(boy Jesus at temple)*	Tell about Jesus' childhood.	Luke 2:51, 52 Challenge: Luke 2:40
Unit 3 — **Jesus Wants Me to Follow Him**	**Matthew 3** *(Jesus' baptism)* **Matthew 4** *(Jesus is tempted)* **Matthew 4; Mark 1; Luke 5** *(fishermen follow)* **John 1; Luke 6; Mark 2, 3** *(the twelve)* **John 2** *(Jesus and God's house)*	Use the Bible verse to remember ways to follow Jesus.	Names of twelve apostles Challenge: Ephesians 6:1; Philippians 2:14; Ephesians 4:25; Hebrews 13:16; Luke 10:36, 37; Matthew 6:9
Unit 4 — **Jesus Teaches Me to Have His Attitude**	**Matthew 20; Mark 10** *(serving)* **Matthew 4, 5** *(overcome evil with good)* **Matthew 5** *(love your enemies)* **John 13, Luke 22** *(washing feet)*	Follow Jesus by changing their attitudes to be like His.	Philippians 2:5, 7 Challenge: 1 Thessalonians 5:15
Unit 5 — **Jesus' Stories Help Me Follow Him**	**Matthew 7; Luke 6** *(wise builder)* **Luke 10** *(good Samaritan)* **Luke 12** *(rich farmer)* **Matthew 18** *(unforgiving servant)* **Luke 15** *(loving father)*	Choose to do what Jesus taught in His stories.	Matthew 27:24, 26 Challenge: Matthew 27:24-27
Unit 6 — **Jesus Helps Me Worship**	**Matthew 6; Luke 11** *(pray)* **Mark 12; Luke 21** *(give)* **Luke 22; Acts 20** *(remember)* **Matthew 21; Psalm 8** *(sing)*	Joyfully worship God and Jesus.	Isaiah 12:4, 5 Challenge: Psalm 8:1, 2

	Unit Title	Scripture	Application	Memory Verse
Unit 7	Jesus Helps Me Be a Friend	**John 3** (Nicodemus) **Luke 7** (sinful woman) **Luke 10** (Mary and Martha) **Matthew 19; Mark 10; Luke 1** (Jesus and children) **Luke 19** (Zacchaeus)	Follow Jesus by being a friend.	3 John 11 Challenge: 2 John 9; 1 Corinthians 11:1
Unit 8	Jesus Helps Me Bring Friends to Him	**John 4** (Samaritan woman) **Matthew 9; Mark 2; Luke 5** (four friends) **Matthew 8; Luke 7** (centurion's servant) **Mark 7** (man who can't hear)	Bring friends to Jesus.	John 4:28-30 Challenge: John 4:42
Unit 9	Jesus Helps Me Love My Family	**Mark 1; Matthew 8; Luke 4** (Peter's mother-in-law) **John 4** (official's son) **Luke 7** (widow's son) **Matthew 9; Mark 5** (Jairus's daughter)	Follow Jesus by showing love to people in their families.	1 John 3:18 Challenge: 1 Thessalonians 5:11; Philippians 2:14
Unit 10	Jesus' Power Helps Me Worship Him	**Matthew 8; Mark 4** (stops storm) **Luke 17** (heals lepers) **Matthew 14; Mark 6; John 6** (water walk) **John 9** (heals blind)	Worship Jesus.	Revelation 15:3 Challenge: Revelation 15:4
Unit 11	Jesus' Miracles Help Me Tell About Him	**Mark 5; Luke 8** (Gadarene) **Matthew 14; Mark 6; Luke 9;** **John 6** (feeds 5,000) **John 5** (heals man at pool) **John 11** (Lazarus alive)	Tell about Jesus.	Luke 8:38, 39 Challenge: John 20:30, 31
Unit 12	Jesus' Resurrection Is Good News for Me to Tell	**Matthew 26, 27; John 18, 19** (crucifixion) **Matthew 28; Mark 16** (resurrection) **Luke 24** (Emmaus road) **John 21** (appears by Lake Galilee) **Matthew 28; Mark 16; Luke 24; Acts 1** (Jesus' command to go, tell)	Tell Jesus' Good News!	Mark 16:15 Challenge: Matthew 28:18-20

Follow Jesus

There are many books to help you recite the facts of Jesus' life. Knowing what Jesus did and said are prerequisites to being able to follow Him. This course places a strong emphasis on learning.

But knowing what Jesus did and said is an empty end product. The value of knowing what Jesus did and said comes from letting it affect our lives. For example, Jesus' birth is more than a story about shepherds and a star and the first Christmas gifts. Jesus' birth is the fulfillment of a promise made 2,000 years ago. When we look at Jesus' birth as a reason to worship God, we have made a tangible connection between what the Bible says and what we will do about it.

Each unit in this course looks at a specific area of Jesus' life or teaching. In addition to teaching children what Jesus did and said, each unit helps children relate what they learn to their own lives.

What's Unique About *Follow Jesus?*

• **It suggests group projects that help the children carry out the application of the Scriptures.**

Each unit has a group project that will be accomplished by the end of the unit. The group will work on the project during each lesson, with the guidance of the adult leaders. Many Bible school curriculums focus on individual applications. But there are also things we can do together to worship, follow, and tell about Jesus. The project time during each lesson is designed to help the children do something in response to Scripture, as a group. The project time is a good opportunity to informally evaluate what the children have learned. But the greatest value is how it helps the children think and reflect on what they know and how that helps them to worship, follow Jesus, and tell about Jesus.

• **The learning activities in this course reflect three important ways children learn new information.**

Some learn more easily by seeing information. So *Follow Jesus* includes flash cards, matching games, puzzles, worksheets, charts, pictures, posters, wall strips, and ideas for using video cassettes. Some learn more easily by being told information. So the course includes songs, rhythm raps, rhythm instruments, read-aloud items, and ideas for audio cassettes. Some learn more readily by touching things and moving around. So there are games, models to make, dramas, and many projects that take the learner out of the classroom. Most people have a preferred way to learn, but everyone can benefit from using all three styles: seeing, hearing, and doing.

Even adults have preferences toward one of these ways of learning, usually the visual. When teaching, it is easier for teachers to use the way of learning they enjoy the most. But some children will learn more easily in a way that is not the teacher's favorite one to prepare. Our goal is to help every child learn. In each unit, *Follow Jesus* provides for a balance of all three styles of learning. This will help the teacher guide children to reach their potential for worshiping, following Jesus, and telling about Jesus.

• **Reproducible pages follow the lesson plan sheets in each unit.**

Some learning activities involve puzzles, writing, things to make, or games to play. These are printed on the reproducible pages. You may photocopy these for your classroom use.

• **The materials can be non-consumable, so originals can be filed and reused.**

You may also want to keep a copy of the changes you made to tailor the lesson to your children. A simple filing system requires twelve file folders. Label the folders with the names of the twelve units. When you finish a lesson, drop the materials you have used into the file folder for that unit.

• **This series of lessons builds on what the children know Jesus did and said.**

Knowing Jesus is more than mastering the facts of His earthly life. The lessons guide the children to think about and use that information in a project. Primary age learners relate in concrete ways to Jesus, so the projects are concrete things the learners can do. Each unit focuses on one major application. For example, Unit 1 lessons are about Jesus' birth. The children will learn and/or review what they know about Jesus' birth. Then they will use what they know: They will worship God because of all the promises He kept when Jesus was born. Each unit follows this same pattern. The Bible stories establish what we know Jesus did and said. The unit application works on a way to help the child use that information with a biblical response to Jesus.

How Is *Follow Jesus* Organized?

Each unit in *Follow Jesus* has a knowledge aim, an attitude aim, and an action aim. These three aims tell what the learners should be able to do by the end of the unit. The goals for each lesson will help the learners reach the unit aims. Every *Follow Jesus* lesson has six learning activities to accomplish the goals for that lesson. Each activity will take approximately ten minutes. The Bible Story and Bible Project may take a little longer. The Bible Search and Bible Verse activity may take a little less time.

Bible Search (5-10 minutes) begins each lesson with an opportunity for the children to dig out some Bible facts. The learners are involved in using the Bible to learn facts from the Bible story.

Bible Story (10-15 minutes) uses a common object either to introduce or help illustrate the story. Often the learners will report what they found in their Bible Search activity. Each story is told from the perspective of one of the characters, and it seeks to illustrate the application of the lesson. The stories have been carefully written to be interesting, detailed, and informative. At the end of the story, the learners will talk about the story in a review activity and in the summary questions.

Bible Verse (5-10 minutes) allows the learner to see, hear, and say or sing the verse repeatedly, in a fun way. It provides an opportunity for children to do the verse when possible.

Bible and Me (10 minutes) helps learners to think about and begin doing the application part of the lesson. This is where learners choose what to do and how they will respond to the facts they have learned about Jesus.

This builds from week to week in a helpful cycle:
1. Tell what we will do in this unit and why it is important.
2. Compare examples and tell which is and which is not doing the application.
3. Plan how and then practice doing the application in the classroom.
4. Tell what you did or said when you tried it on your own (report).
5. Do the application in a group project.

Bible Project (10-15 minutes) helps the entire group accomplish the unit action aim. Each week the learners will add to the project so that it can be completed by the end of the unit. Bible Project ideas are explained in detail in the introduction to each unit.

Bible Sharing (10 minutes) allows the children to talk about and answer questions about lesson goals while they share a lesson-related snack. This activity provides closure to the lesson and allows the leaders to evaluate how well the lesson goals were accomplished.

▼ Verse Activity Ideas ▲

This list suggests ideas for helping children memorize, understand, and use or do what Bible verses say. If you feel the activity in a lesson will work well for your children, try one of these ideas. You can see examples of some activities on the pages in parentheses.

Verse Activities According to Learning Goals

To help children memorize verses, use
* audio tapes, to hear the verse and then say key words in pauses (page 65)
* chalkboard, to erase words or phrases each time they say the verse (page 206)
* rap, to say the verse with a helpful rhythm (page 14)
* read-aloud, to say the verse aloud to the group or to themselves (page 116)
* songs, to sing, to play musical chairs (page 95)
* stop watch, to time how fast a child or team can put a verse in order (pages 203, 295)
* wall strips, to put in order, or sort out strips that don't belong (page 17)
* word cards, to put in order on a wall, clothesline, table, cookie sheet (magnetic tape), flannel board or floor (page 221)

To help children understand verses, use
* designated spot in a (circular) path, to decide who will explain the verse each time the group sings or raps the verse while walking on the path (page 180)
* item on string or item to pass around circle, to choose who will tell what the verse means when the timer rings or music stops (pages 122, 150)
* motions, to help show what a verse is saying as they say it (page 44)
* murals, to illustrate the action or content of the verse (page 206, option)
* pictures, to substitute for key words in verse (pages 101, 125)
* worksheets, to mark parts of a verse or answer questions about a verse (page 92)

To help children do what a verse says, use
* board games (page 230)
* spinner games (page 301)
* verse cubes (pages 23, 269)
* mini-dramas (pages 128, 206)
* knocking down two-liter bottles with choices of how to do the verse (page 278)

Games require good questions to ask the children about what they would do to use the verse you are applying. For examples of questions, see pages 168 or 248.

The Night That Jesus Was Born

Traditional "Skip to My Lou"

Mary Ann McPherson

1. The inn - keep - er said, "Go down to the sta - ble," The
2. A star shone down on Beth - le - hem, A
3. Shep - herds watched their flocks that night,
4. The an - gel said, "Do not be a - fraid," The
5. The an - i - mals shared their man - ger hay, The
6. Ma - ry wrapped the ba - by in warm, soft cloth,
7. God sent to us His on - ly Son,

inn - keep - er said, "Go down to the sta - ble," The
star shone down on Beth - le - hem, A
Shep - herds watched their flocks that night,
an - gel said, "Do not be a - fraid," The
an - i - mals shared their man - ger hay, The
Ma - ry wrapped the ba - by in warm, soft cloth,
God sent to us His on - ly Son,

inn - keep - er said, "Go down to the sta - ble," The
star shone down on Beth - le - hem,
Shep - herds watched their flocks that night,
an - gel said, "Do not be a - fraid,"
an - i - mals shared their man - ger hay,
Ma - ry wrapped the ba - by in warm, soft cloth,
God sent to us His on - ly Son,

the night that Je - sus was born.

© 1989 Mary Ann McPherson. Used by permission.

Jesus, Jesus Born Today

Traditional "Twinkle, Twinkle Little Star"

Mary Ann McPherson

Je - sus, Je - sus born to - day lies up - on the man - ger hay.

Up a - bove the an - gels sing prais - es to the new - born King.

Je - sus, Je - sus born to - day lies up - on the man - ger hay.

© 1989 Mary Ann McPherson. Used by permission.

Use these words for Lesson 3:

Jesus, Jesus born today
Lies upon the manger hay.
Mary holds the promised One,
Jesus, Jesus, God's own Son.
Jesus, Jesus born today
Lies upon the manger hay.

Jesus' Birth Helps Me Worship

Unit Memory Block
"Lord, you are my God. I honor you and praise you. You have done amazing things. You have always done what you said you would. You have done what you planned long ago" (Isaiah 25:1).

Memory Challenge
"Then the shepherds went back to their sheep, praising God and thanking him for everything that they had seen and heard. It was just as the angel had told them" (Luke 2:20).

1 God Makes a Promise
Isaiah 9:6; Micah 5:2; Luke 1:5-17; Matthew 3:1-4
God's prophets said Jesus would be a son, born in Bethlehem.
We worship God because we know He kept this promise.

2 God Sends a Message to Mary
Luke 1:26-56
Mary worshiped God when Gabriel said 1) she would have a son,
2) she would name Him Jesus, and 3) Jesus would be the Son of God.
We worship God because He kept His promise that Jesus would come.

3 God Keeps His Promise
Luke 2:1-7
God kept His promises when Jesus was born in Bethlehem.
We worship God because He kept His promise.

4 The Shepherds See Jesus
Luke 2:8-20
The angels and shepherds worshiped God when Jesus was born.
We worship God because He kept His promise.

By the end of the unit, the leaders and learners will
KNOW details of God's promises and how it came true.
FEEL a sense of awe because God kept His promise.
DO Worship God because He kept His promise.

Unit Value
   The story of *Follow Jesus* began hundreds of years before Jesus was born when God's prophets foretold what would happen. In Lesson 1, the children will discover two details of Jesus' birth foretold by Isaiah and Micah. The next three stories of the unit illustrate how God's promises came true.

   This unit will help the learners know what worship is, understand why we worship, and prepare a group worship time to share with parents and friends. Mary's song and the shepherds telling what they had seen God do are biblical examples of worship. The Bible verse to memorize gives the children another example of worship. Children who learn to worship will get a head start toward a mature relationship with their Promise-Keeper.

▼ Bible Project ▲

A Worship Time

Help children worship God because He kept His promise to send Jesus. Guide them to sing worship songs, pray worship prayers, write worship poems, and draw worship pictures. Plan a worship time that children can lead.

Before the first class session, make a tentative decision about what will be included in the worship time. Then you will be able to give children choices and direct their decisions. It is important to meet with church leaders to schedule a time for the children to share their worship project.

Week 1: Choose worship activity.
Week 2: Assign work spaces for each group; plan worship activity.
Week 3: Complete activities.
Week 4: Practice the worship program.

Worship Activity Ideas

Worship pictures: pictures that illustrate the promise God kept or pictures that illustrate the Bible stories. Captions should describe what God did. (God promised Mary she would have a son. God kept His promise!).

Worship prayers: prayer sentences that worship God for keeping His promise. Use these phrases to complete: Dear God, You are special because… Dear God, Only You can… Dear God, You are great! You…

Illustrated Bible verse: Students can learn Isaiah 25:1 and illustrate it (enlarge pictures from page 30); or recite the verse with motions.

Worship songs: Practice some of the students' favorite praise songs. Put worship words to a familiar tune (see page 32).

Worship poems: Write unrhymed couplets that tell what God said and did, or have children fill in the blanks of this poem.

God always does what He says,
Here's what God said He would do: _____
And God kept that promise too.

Choral speaking: Use a Scripture and divide it into parts. Or say ways God kept promises, and have the entire group say, "God kept His promise," between each sentence.

Materials

Provide materials to help children create worship pictures, prayers, and poems or learn worship songs:
paper (drawing, shelf, lined, construction)
pencils, markers, crayons, colored pencils
music (CDs or audio cassettes and CD or cassette player or music to sing or play on a keyboard)

Verse Rhythm

Lord, You are my God._____ I hon - or You___ and praise You. You have done a - maz - ing things. You have al - ways done what You said You would._____ You have done what you planned long a - go._____ I - sai - ah twen - ty five, one.

12

God Makes a Promise

Isaiah 9:6; Micah 5:2; Luke 1:5-17; Matthew 3:1-4

Lesson Goals
- Name four people who spoke God's message about Jesus' coming.
- Name one thing each person told about Jesus' coming.
- Begin to memorize Isaiah 25:1.
- Tell what it means to worship God.
- Worship God because He kept His promise.

Memory Block
"Lord, you are my God. I honor you and praise you. You have done amazing things. You have always done what you said you would. You have done what you planned long ago" (Isaiah 25:1).

▼ Bible Search ▲

Two prophets, an angel, and a preacher told people that Jesus was coming. The two prophets spoke about Jesus' coming a long time before Jesus was born. Let's look in our Bibles to find out who told about God's promise to send Jesus.

Small groups will work together to find out about one person who spoke about Jesus' coming. Group children into four teams. Each child will need the card (from page 25) for the person his team is researching. Guide the children to find the Bible book in the table of contents of their Bibles. Locate the page the book begins on, then the big number for the chapter and the small number for the verse. Encourage the children to do as much as possible by themselves. Read each team's verse with them. Help them complete their cards.

Who spoke God's message about Jesus' coming? (Each team can report one: Isaiah, Micah, Gabriel, John the Baptist.) **Which one was an angel?** (Gabriel) **Which one preached in the desert?** (John the Baptist) **Which two were prophets who spoke for God?** (Isaiah, Micah)

Purpose
Name four people who spoke God's message about Jesus' coming.

Materials
Bibles
copies of page 25 cut apart
pencils

▼ Bible Story ▲

This "P" will help us remember the word *promise* in our story. When I hold up this letter during the story, say the word *promise*.

"God Makes a Promise"

Every morning and every night someone must put new incense on the incense table in the temple. It is a special job for a priest like me. Not every priest gets to do this. But I got to! I got to smell the sweet aroma rising upward in worship to God. Then what a scare I got. I saw an angel! Me! Zechariah! I knew God had sent His angels to visit people in the past. But why would God send an angel to visit me?

Well, the story started many, many years ago. When people first chose to sin, God made a promise to send someone to get rid of sin. The prophet Isaiah told people part of this promise. Isaiah said, "God will give a Son to us." Another prophet named Micah spoke another part of the promise. He said God's promise would come from Bethlehem. The story of God's promise continued on the day I took in the incense.

I walked through the courtyard, into the holy place, and over to the incense table. There on the right side of the table, the angel of the Lord stood before me.

Purpose
Name one thing each person told about Jesus' coming.

Materials
a large "P" printed on a paper or a stuffed "P" pillow

My eyes got big. My mouth fell open. The angel must have known I was scared. "Do not be afraid," he said. But my legs were still quivering when he made a promise to me. The angel said, "Your wife, Elizabeth, will give birth to a son. You will name him John. " That's impossible, I thought. I added, "How can I know that what you say is true?"

I knew the promises Isaiah and Micah made were true. But the promise from the angel was harder to believe. My wife Elizabeth couldn't have children, and now we were very old. Up till now, I had done everything God commanded. I obeyed the law. Even though we prayed for children, I still had trouble believing what the angel said.

But it was true. Friends and relatives filled our house the week after John was born. Everyone jabbered about how good God had been to us. Even me! God's spirit moved me to praise the Lord. "Let us thank the Lord God of Israel. God has come to help his people…Now you, child, will be called a prophet of the Most High. You will…prepare the people for his coming." Now I was sure God's promise to Isaiah and Micah was about to come true. And, I also knew that my son John would tell people to get ready for the Savior, the promise from God.

Say each of the following riddles and ask, "Who said it?"
- **I will send someone to get rid of sin.** (God)
- **How can I know this is true?** (Zechariah)
- **Do not be afraid; Elizabeth will have a son**. (angel)
- **God will give a Son to us.** (Isaiah)
- **God's promise will come from Bethlehem**. (Micah)
- **Get ready for the Savior.** (John)

(For a harder review, ask what each character said.)

Summary questions: **What two prophets spoke God's message about Jesus' coming?** (Isaiah, Micah) **What promises of God did the prophets make?** (God will give a Son to us; He will be from Bethlehem.) **Who was the angel who spoke God's message?** (Gabriel) **What message did Gabriel tell?** (Zechariah would have a son, John. John would tell people to get ready for the Savior, the promise from God.)

▼ Bible Verse ▲

Purpose
Begin to memorize Isaiah 25:1.

Materials
Bibles
copies of page 26
pencils

Isaiah was God's prophet. He spoke for God many times. Since God always keeps His promises, Isaiah knew God would keep His promise to send Jesus. That's one reason Isaiah wrote our Bible verse. Isaiah worshiped God with the words in Isaiah 25:1.

Each child will find Isaiah 25:1 in a Bible. As the teacher reads the verse aloud from page 26, children can fill in the word *you* every time the teacher pauses. Continue to read and fill in the blanks. While reading the verse the second time, children can point and/or look up each time they say *you*. This helps set a pattern for addressing personal worship directly to God. Then say the verse in rhythm and ask the children to join in the second time. (See the verse rhythm on unit page 12.)

Who wrote this verse? (The prophet Isaiah) **To whom is Isaiah talking in this verse?** (God) **What three things does Isaiah say God has done?** (Amazing things, what He said, what He planned)

▼ Bible and Me ▲

We worship God because He always keeps His promises. Some of the children on this page are worshiping God by telling God He is special. Which ones are worshiping? Which ones are not worshiping?

The children will select which song, prayer, poem, and picture worships God. Guide children to cross out the pictures that are not worship. Then use the questions below to help them tell you that "worship is using different ways to tell God how special we know He is."

Which song worships God? How can you tell? Which prayer? Which poem? Which picture? How do you know they worship God? So, what does it mean to worship God? (Tell Him how special He is.)

Purpose
Tell what it means to worship God.

Materials
copies of page 27
pencils or crayons

▼ Bible Project ▲

Before class, make a tentative decision about what will be included in the worship time. Then you will be able to give children choices and direct their decisions. Meet with church leaders to schedule time for the children to share their worship project.

We are learning many ways to worship God. We can sing worship songs, pray worship prayers, write worship poems, and draw worship pictures. Let's plan together a worship time that we can lead. We will be helping other people worship God because He keeps His promises.

Each child will choose one activity in which to participate. As you explain what could be included in the worship time, print the worship activities on a long piece of shelf paper (verse, song, choral speaking, and so on). Each child will sign her name under the activity she chooses. Next week, students will begin working on their activities. Allow students to switch activities next week if necessary.

Purpose
Worship God because He kept His promise.

Materials
shelf paper
markers

▼ Bible Sharing ▲

While we eat our snack, let's pretend we have just heard John the Baptist tell about Jesus. (The Bible says John ate locusts and wild honey.) John said, "Get ready! Jesus is coming!" Maybe the people said, "This is wonderful! Let's worship God for giving us this special promise." Maybe someone remembered what Isaiah wrote.

Distribute completed Bible Verse pages. Slowly read the Bible verse together. Then ask children to listen as you prayerfully read the verse again. Close with a prayer that thanks God for sending people to tell His promise to send Jesus. Worship God for keeping His promise.

Purpose
Share how Jesus' birth helps you worship.

Materials
crackers and honey for a snack
napkins
completed Bible Verse page
   (page 26)

God Sends a Message to Mary

Luke 1:26-56

Goals
- Name three things the angel told Mary.
- Tell how Mary responded to the angel's message.
- Memorize Isaiah 25:1.
- Tell why we worship God.
- Worship God because He kept His promise.

▼ **Bible Search** ▲

The angel Gabriel appeared to Mary with a very important message from God. Let's look in our Bibles to find out what Gabriel told Mary.

Children will work in pairs to complete the Bible Search page. (If you have beginning readers, complete the page together.) Distribute a copy of page 28 to each pair. Guide the children to find the book of Luke in the table of contents of their Bibles. Locate the page the book begins on, then the big 1 for the chapter and the small 31 for the verse. Encourage the children to do as much as possible by themselves. Read the verse and help children fill in the blanks using the word bank. Then help children find verse 35 and complete the page.

Who appeared to Mary? (an angel, Gabriel) **What three things did the angel tell Mary?** (Mary will have a Son; name Him Jesus; He will be called the Son of God.)

Purpose
Name three things the angel told Mary.

Materials
Bibles
copies of page 28
pencils

▼ **Bible Story** ▲

Display baby items when appropriate during the story.
Parents do many things to get ready for a new baby. Listen for what Mary did when she learned she would have a baby.

"God Sends a Message to Mary"
Mary and Joseph were going to be married. How happy they would be together. Soon they would have their own home and their own family. But Mary's plans were interrupted one day when the angel Gabriel came to Nazareth to see her. "Greetings," the angel said.

Mary gasped in fear. Was this really an angel? Why was he here? Mary probably stopped what she was doing so she could hear exactly what the angel said. The angel continued, "Don't be afraid. God is pleased with you. You will have a baby boy. Name him Jesus." Mary was probably glad to hear that she didn't need to be afraid. But the part about a baby boy seemed a little unusual. She and Joseph were not even married yet. Then the angel told Mary what her son would be like: "He will be great. He will be the Son of the Most High God."

Mary wondered aloud, "How will this be?" The angel carefully answered her question, "The baby will not be a son of Joseph. He will be the Son of God. God's Holy Spirit will make it happen. Your relative Elizabeth is going to have a son even though she is very old. That shows God can do anything."

What the angel said was true. In just three more months, Elizabeth's baby would be born. That was a miracle. If God could do it for Elizabeth, He could do

Purpose
Tell how Mary responded to the angel's message.

Materials
a baby blanket, baby bottle or small baby toy
one index card for each child

it for Mary, too. Maybe Mary was beginning to see that she would be part of God's promise to bring a Savior to the world. Mary had always tried to please God. Again this time, Mary showed she wanted to do whatever God asked. She said, "I am the Lord's servant."

After the angel left, Mary just had to talk to someone. Ah, Elizabeth would understand. Mary wasted no time. She hurried off to Elizabeth's home in Judea. Both Elizabeth and Mary may have jumped for joy in that little house in Judea. Praising the Lord came easy for Mary, and she burst into song: "My soul praises the Lord; my heart is happy because God…has done what he promised."

Mary stayed with Elizabeth for three months. When Mary traveled back to Nazareth, she was ready to do the hard job God had given her. As she walked she may have praised God again for letting her be the mother of Jesus. She was going to help God's promise come true.

Give each child an index card with a smiling face on the front and a frowning face on the back. They can show smiling faces for true statements and frowning faces for false statements. Let them correct the false statements.
- **An angel came to visit Mary.**
- **The angel's name was Michael.** (Gabriel)
- **Gabriel said Mary would have a baby.**
- **The baby's name was to be John.** (Jesus)
- **Mary went to visit Joseph.** (Elizabeth)
- **Mary didn't believe what the angel said.** (did)
- **Elizabeth was too tired to see Mary.** (excited)
- **Mary sang to God because she was happy.**

Summary questions: **What did the angel tell Mary?** (You will have a baby boy. Name Him Jesus. He will be the Son of God.) **What did Mary do?** (She said, "I am the Lord's servant"; she praised God.)

▼ Bible Verse ▲

God's prophet Isaiah knew God would keep His promise to send Jesus. That's one reason Isaiah wrote our Bible verse. Isaiah worshiped God with the words in Isaiah 25:1.

The children will put the verse strips from page 29 in order. Each time they read (or recite) the verse, they can remove one strip. Children should have much of the verse memorized by the time all strips are removed.

Who wrote this verse? To whom is Isaiah talking in this verse? What three things does Isaiah say God has done? (amazing things, what He said, what He planned) **What are Isaiah's three worship statements?**

Purpose
Memorize Isaiah 25:1.

Materials
Bibles
copies of page 29
an envelope for each child

Purpose
Tell why we worship God.

Materials
CD or cassette of worship
  songs to God
CD or cassette player

▼ Bible and Me ▲

We worship God because He is so special. He always kept His promises in the Bible. Let's sing a worship song about how special God is.

Sing a worship song to God. If possible, use a recording of a song that is familiar to the children. If you are introducing a new worship song, play the song through once for the children. Then ask the children to join as much as they can. When the song begins to be familiar, stop to ask the questions below each time you sing the song.

What is special about God? Why do we worship God? What verse can we say to worship God? (Isaiah 25:1.) **What are some amazing things God has done? What promises did God make to Mary? to the prophets Isaiah and Micah? to Zechariah? How did God keep His promises?**

Purpose
Worship God because He kept His promise.

Materials
items to create worship
  pictures, prayer, poems, or
  learn worship songs:
paper (drawing, shelf, lined,
  construction)
pencils, markers, crayons,
  colored pencils
music (CD or cassettes and CD
  or cassette player or music
  to sing or play)

▼ Bible Project ▲

Just like Mary, we want to worship God. Let's work together to create a worship time that will help other people worship God.

Children will begin working on the activities they chose last week. Display the shelf paper with listed worship activities and children's names. Assign each group a place to work and provide needed materials. It is important to plan with each group how they will accomplish their part of the worship project. Specific suggestions are included on the unit page.

▼ Bible Sharing ▲

Pretend you are Mary. The angel Gabriel has just appeared to you. What three things did Gabriel tell you? (You will have a son; you will name Him Jesus; He will be God's Son.) **Gabriel has gone. How do you feel?** (excited, eager to worship God) **Let's worship God for keeping His promise to send Jesus.**

Give each child an opportunity to suggest a worship song and say a worship prayer (perhaps the activities begun in the Bible Project section). Begin by sharing your own prayer or song suggestion.

Close by singing a worship song to God.

Purpose
Share how Jesus' birth helps you worship.

Materials
napkins
angel-shaped cookies

God Keeps His Promise

LESSON 3

Luke 2:1-7

Goals

- Name two parts of the promise God kept in Luke 2:1-7.
- Tell who foretold each part of the promise.
- Recite and explain Isaiah 25:1.
- Demonstrate ways to worship God because He keeps His promises.
- Worship God because He kept His promise.

Memory Block
"Lord, you are my God. I honor you and praise you. You have done amazing things. You have always done what you said you would. You have done what you planned long ago" (Isaiah 25:1).

▼ Bible Search ▲

The prophet Micah said that Jesus would be born in Bethlehem. The prophet Isaiah said that God would send a Son. Let's find in our Bibles when those promises of God were kept.

Children will work in pairs to complete the Bible Search page. Distribute a copy of page 31 to each child. Read the instructions for each section before beginning. Guide the children to find the book of Luke in the table of contents of their Bibles. Locate the page the book begins on, then the big 2 for the chapter and the small 6 for the verse. Then they can find and read verse 7. Children should circle the picture of Mary holding Jesus and the picture of Mary putting Jesus in a manger.

What two promises of God did Isaiah and Micah tell about? (Micah said Jesus would be born in Bethlehem; Isaiah said God would send a Son.) **What part of the promise did God keep in Luke 2:6?** (Jesus was born in Bethlehem.) **What part of the promise did God keep in Luke 2:7?** (Mary had a baby boy.)

Purpose
Name two parts of the promise God kept in Luke 2:1-7.

Materials
Bibles
copies of page 31
pencils

▼ Bible Story ▲

Where do you like to travel and stay overnight? Listen to see where Mary and Joseph stayed overnight when they were traveling.

"God Keeps His Promise"

"What will I need?" Mary wondered as she packed her traveling bag. She folded soft clean cloths and some clothes, a blanket for a bed and some food. She and Joseph were almost ready to leave on a long trip to Bethlehem. Mary didn't feel much like traveling, but the king wanted to know how many people were in his kingdom. He had ordered everyone to be counted in the place where their family had come from.

Mary's roundness made it difficult to move very fast. Sometimes she could feel the baby move inside. Soon, He would be born. Mary remembered how the angel had told her it would be a boy. And the angel had even given the name for the baby—Jesus. The most amazing thing, though, was that the angel said this baby would be God's Son. But now, it was time to go. It was going to be a long, hard trip.

When Joseph and Mary saw Bethlehem in the distance, they could hardly wait to find a place to sleep. Mary was so tired she could hardly go another step. A fresh bed would feel so good. But all the rooms in Bethlehem were full. So they made their bed near where the animals slept.

Purpose
Tell who foretold each part of the promise.

Materials
a small travel bag,
items to pack in the bag (cloths or towels, a blanket, some bread or other food)
a soft cloth to toss to each child

That night, God's most special promise came true. Jesus was born. Mary's soft clean cloths were just right for wrapping up her new baby boy. There was no baby cradle for Him to sleep in, so Joseph cleaned out the wooden box that was used for feeding the animals. Joseph may have padded the box with clean fresh straw. There, Mary could lay the baby Jesus down to sleep, safe and warm.

The prophets Isaiah and Micah and God's angel Gabriel had told about God's promise. This was the night when God kept His promise, just as He said He would.

Toss a soft cloth to each child to decide who will say the next sentence to retell the story. Start by saying, **"Mary was getting ready to go on a trip."** Let each child add to the story until it is finished.

Sing a short worship chorus to God between each of the following summary questions: **What promise made by Isaiah came true?** (God sent His Son.) **What promise made by Micah came true?** (Jesus was born in Bethlehem.) **What promise made by the angel came true?** (Mary had a baby boy.)

▼ Bible Verse ▲

Purpose
Recite and explain Isaiah 25:1.

Materials
a set of verse phrases (page 29) and a set of pictures (page 30) for each child
Plasti-Tak® reusable adhesive

God's prophet Isaiah knew God would keep His promise to send Jesus. That's one reason Isaiah wrote our Bible verse. Isaiah worshiped God with the words in Isaiah 25:1.

Use a set of verse phrases (page 29) and a set of pictures (page 30) to recite and explain Isaiah 25:1. First, let the children put the verse phrases in order on a wall or table. Then next to each phrase, the children can put one picture that helps explain the phrase. The children will have fun doing this matching activity with partners.

Why is the child in the picture raising his hands? Why are the two children singing? What might they be singing? Why is a picture of creation included? Why is a picture of Noah and the ark on dry ground included? Why is a picture of Jesus in a manger included? Who can say the whole verse by memory? Who can tell (in his own words) what the verse talks about?

▼ Bible and Me ▲

Purpose
Demonstrate ways to worship God because He keeps His promise.

Materials
cards from page 32 (one set for each group of three children)
paper
pencils
markers

Just like Isaiah, we can worship God for keeping His promise. Children will choose one of the cards from page 32 to read and follow directions. If they have time, they may choose other cards to complete. Help the children keep their focus on worshiping God for sending Jesus.

What does it mean to worship God? Which is your favorite way to worship? Keep the children's completed worship activities and cards to use next week.

Option: Set up five areas in your room. Put a card from page 32 at each area and the supplies needed to complete the instructions on the card. At your signal, children move from area to area. When they are finished, allow them to choose one of their ways of worship to share with the group during Bible Sharing.

▼ Bible Project ▲

Worshiping God means telling God how special He is. In what way are you planning to worship God? Give each child an opportunity to report his part of the worship project. Children will need to complete the worship project activities in order to rehearse next week.

Before children work in their small groups, share any information you have about when and where children will lead their worship plan. Your enthusiasm and eagerness to worship God and lead others in worship will be contagious.

Guide children to complete the worship activities.

Purpose
Worship God because He kept His promise.

Materials
materials to help children complete the worship activities (see Lesson 2)

▼ Bible Sharing ▲

Mary and Joseph were the first people to know that God had kept His promise to send Jesus. They were probably so excited that they could not stop worshiping God. What do you think Mary said? What do you think Joseph said? What can you say to worship God right now?

Give each child a turn to worship God. Children may worship using the task cards from page 32 used in the Bible and Me section, or they may hold the traveling items used during Bible Story and make a worship statement. Begin the worship time by singing a worship song to God. Share a way you can worship. Then invite children to share their worship.

Purpose
Share how Jesus' birth helps you worship.

Materials
napkins
a snack of animal-shaped cookies (farm animals would be appropriate)
blankets for children to sit on
traveling items from the Bible Story section
CD or cassette of a worship song
CD or cassette player

Luke 2:8-20

Goals

- Name two groups who worshiped God.
- Tell how the angels and shepherds worshiped.
- Recite and explain Isaiah 25:1.
- Demonstrate ways to worship God because of Jesus' birth.
- Worship God because He kept His promise.

Purpose
Name two groups who worshiped God.

Materials
Bibles
copies of page 33
pencils

Bible Search

Two different groups worshiped God because of Jesus' birth. The Bible says they praised God. Let's look in our Bibles to find out who they were.

Children will work together to complete the Bible Search page. Distribute a copy of page 33 to each pair. Read the instructions as children follow along. Guide the children to find the book of Luke in the table of contents of their Bibles. Locate the page the book begins on, then the big 2 for the chapter and the small 13 for the verse. Encourage children to do as much as possible by themselves. Read the verse. Then children can find Luke 2:20 in their Bibles. Read the verse and help children complete the page.

Who worshiped God? (angels, shepherds) **How did they worship?** (praised God, thanked God) **Why did the angels and shepherds worship God?** (Jesus was born.)

Purpose
Tell how the angels and shepherds worshiped.

Materials
sticks of wood to make a pretend campfire
an index card for each child with the word *angel* or *shepherd* printed on each card

Bible Story

Gather children around a pretend campfire. **Have you ever camped out at night? Listen to what happened to some shepherds who were camping out.**

"The Shepherds See Jesus"

Close your eyes. Imagine you are a shepherd…sitting on a grassy hillside. It's dark except for a small fire. The sheep are baaing softly as they quiet down to sleep near you. Other shepherds are taking their turns to guard the sheep. You shiver and scoot a little closer to the fire as you begin to drift off to sleep. Suddenly you OPEN your eyes to see what is shining so brightly all around you. *(Children can open eyes.)*

The light was so bright that it scared all the shepherds. But it wasn't meant to scare them. The light was the glory of the Lord, and it showed that the angel in front of them was bringing a message from God.

(Read Luke 2:10-13.) The angel said, "Don't be afraid, because I am bringing you some good news. It will be a joy to all the people. Today your Savior was born in David's town. He is Christ, the Lord. This is how you will know him: You will find a baby wrapped in cloths and lying in a feeding box."

Suddenly, a great number of angels were there. Together they praised God with their words. *(Read Luke 2:14.)* "Give glory to God in heaven, and on earth let there be peace to the people who please God."

Just as quickly as the angels came they were gone. The shepherds probably looked at each other, amazed at what they had just seen and heard. There was just one thing to do. *(Read Luke 2:15b.)* "Let us go to Bethlehem and see this thing that has happened. We will see this thing the Lord told us about."

The shepherds rushed into town. They didn't stop until they found Mary and Joseph. They must have smiled when they saw the baby snugly wrapped and lying in the animals' feeding box. This was the baby sent from God! They were so excited! They just had to tell what the angels had said about this baby. Everyone was amazed at what the shepherds said to them.

As the shepherds went back to care for their sheep, they couldn't stop praising God. They thanked God for sending angels to tell them that Jesus was born. They thanked God for letting them see this special baby. They praised God because He had done just what He had said He would do.

Give each child a prepared index card. The children can tell who might have said the following statements by holding up the correct answer card.
- **I cared for sheep.** (shepherd)
- **I told some good news.** (angel, shepherd)
- **I praised God with my words.** (angel, shepherd)
- **I praised God all the way home.** (shepherd)
- **I helped people know Jesus was born.** (angel, shepherd)
- **I told what I had seen and heard.** (shepherd)
- **I shone brightly.** (angel)
- **I was afraid.** (shepherd)
- **I said, "Don't be afraid."** (angel)
- **I heard some good news.** (shepherd)

Summary questions: **What promise did God keep? How did the shepherds worship God?** (They thanked and praised God for the angels and baby.) **How did the angels worship God?** (They said, "Give glory to God in heaven.")

Bible Verse

Before class, make one verse game cube from page 34 to use.

Our Bible verse reminds us to worship God because He kept His promise to send Jesus. Let's find the verse in our Bibles.

Guide the children to find the book of Isaiah in the table of contents of their Bibles. Locate the page Isaiah begins on, then find the big 25 for the chapter and the small 1 for the verse. Read the verse from the Bible.

Take turns throwing the game cube. The directions on the cube will guide what the children will do.

What does the verse remind us to do? (Worship God.) **How can you do the verse this week?**

Option: Print the instructions on the game cube on the sides of a medium-sized cardboard box. Let the children take turns rolling the box and following the instructions.

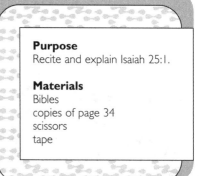

Purpose
Recite and explain Isaiah 25:1.

Materials
Bibles
copies of page 34
scissors
tape

Bible and Me

Just like the shepherds and angels, we can worship God for keeping His promise.

Take turns choosing worship activities the children completed last week and reading or showing them to the children. Children can tell you the way to worship that the activity demonstrates. Then make a large poster or mural of the ways to worship. Children can glue their activities and the activity cards onto the mural paper and design a colorful title for the mural. Save the mural to use during Bible Sharing.

What does it mean to worship God? (Tell God how special He is.) **Why do we worship God?** (He kept His promise to send Jesus.) **How will you worship God?**

Bible Project

Plans for participation in a worship service should be confirmed. If possible, arrange to have children rehearse in the room where they will lead in the worship time. You may want to allow extra time for this section of the lesson. You may wish to make invitations to send to parents and friends.

Just like the shepherds, we can share our joy about Jesus with other people. When we lead in the worship time, we will be showing our praise and thanks to God for keeping His promise.

Children will rehearse each part of the worship they will lead. Guide the children to think about God as they speak or sing. Emphasize the importance of helping the people in the congregation worship with them. Encourage them to speak slowly and clearly.

Why are we worshiping God today? (He kept His promise to send Jesus.) **In what different ways are we worshiping God?** (singing, telling, praying, drawing, writing)

Bible Sharing

Arrange the flashlights upside down on the floor to make a "campfire." Turn the flashlights on and the room lights off as the children gather around the fire.

Let's pretend we are the shepherds. We have just come back from seeing baby Jesus. As we eat a late night snack, let's praise God for keeping His promise of a Savior.

Display the mural the children made during Bible and Me. Choose a worship activity on the mural to use to worship God for Jesus' birth. Let children take turns using the mural to sing, pray, draw, write, or read their worship to Jesus.

Close by singing a worship song to God.

Bible Search

Cut apart the cards. Follow the directions on one card. Find out what one person said about Jesus' coming.

Find Isaiah 9:6 in your Bible. Read what Isaiah said God would do. Circle the right answer below.

Isaiah said, "God will give a _____ to us."

  star

      son

          song

Find Luke 1:19 in your Bible. Who told Zechariah good news? Circle the right answer.

"I am _____. God sent me to talk to you."

  Goliath

      Gabriel

          Gideon

              Gad

Find Micah 5:2 in your Bible. Read what Micah said about Jesus' birth. Circle the right answer below.

Micah said Jesus would be born in the town of _____.

  Bethany

      Bethsaida

          Bethlehem

Find Matthew 3:1 in your Bible. Who preached that Jesus was coming? Circle the right answer.

"_____ the Baptist came and began preaching in the desert."

  James

      Jude

          John

              Joshua

Bible Verse

Find Isaiah 25:1 in your Bible.
Fill in the missing words.

Lord, _____ are my God.

I honor _____ and

praise _____. _____

have done amazing things.

_____ have always done what

_____ said _____ would.

_____ have done what

_____ planned long ago.

Isaiah 25:1

 UNIT 1, LESSON 1

Read what the children are saying to worship God. Choose the song, prayer, poem, and picture that worship God because He keeps His promises.

Bible and Me

Bible Search

1. Find Luke 1:31 in your Bible.
   What did the angel tell Mary?

2. Find Luke 1:35 in your Bible.
   What did the angel say Jesus would be called?

Word Bank

Jesus   God   Son

Cut apart the memory verse phrases. Attach a magnetic strip to the back of each phrase. Put the verse phrases in order on a cookie sheet.

Bible Verse

Lord, you are my God.

I honor you and praise you.

You have done amazing things.

You have always done

what you said you would.

You have done what you

planned long ago.   Isaiah 25:1

Bible Verse

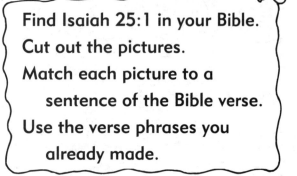

Find Isaiah 25:1 in your Bible.
Cut out the pictures.
Match each picture to a
   sentence of the Bible verse.
Use the verse phrases you
   already made.

Bible Search

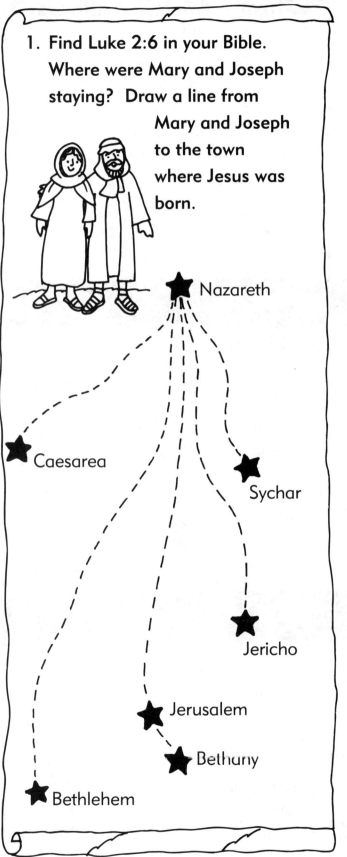

1. Find Luke 2:6 in your Bible. Where were Mary and Joseph staying? Draw a line from Mary and Joseph to the town where Jesus was born.

Nazareth

Caesarea

Sychar

Jericho

Jerusalem

Bethany

Bethlehem

2. Find and read verse 7. What does the Bible say Mary did in Bethlehem? Circle your answers.

What two parts of God's promise did He keep in Luke 2:6, 7?

Bible and Me

Cut apart the cards.
Keep each set of cards in
an envelope.
Use the cards as directed
in Lessons 3 and 4.

cut

Worship God by praying.

Finish this worship prayer.
Then add a sentence of your own.

Dear God,
You are wonderful! Only You always
keep your promises. Thank You for

Worship God by singing.

Write worship words to the tune "Row
Your Boat" or sing these words to the
tune of "London Bridge."

Mary had a baby boy,
baby boy, baby boy.
Mary had a baby boy.
God kept His promise.

Mary thanked God for His Son . . .
God kept His promise.

Worship God by drawing.

Draw a picture of Mary and Joseph
watching baby Jesus.
Write what Mary or Joseph might
have said to worship God.

Worship God with a poem.

Practice reading this poem or write
one of your own.

God keeps His promises.
He always hears our prayers.
He sent His Son, Jesus.
He's the One who cares.

Worship God by writing.

Write a worship sentence.
Start your sentence like this.

Only God can . . .
  Or
God is great because He . . .
  Or
God is special. Only He . . .

 Unit 1, Lesson 3

Bible and Me

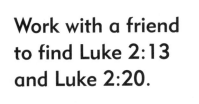

Work with a friend to find Luke 2:13 and Luke 2:20.

1. Who worshiped God? Circle your answers.

2. How did they worship God? Put a ✔ by your answers.

☐ Angels praised God.
☐ Shepherds played their flutes.
☐ Angels drew worship pictures.
☐ Shepherds praised God.
☐ Angels wrote a poem to God.
☐ Shepherds thanked God.

Bible Verse

Recite Isaiah 25:1 together.
Cut out the verse cube and tape it together.
Take turns tossing the cube and following the directions.

Say the verse by yourself.

Show a way to do something in this verse.

Ask a friend to say the verse.

Tell what this verse means.

Show how to find this verse in the Bible.

Ask a friend to say the verse with you.

Jesus Was a Child Just Like Me

Lessons 5–8

Unit Memory Block
"Jesus went with them to Nazareth and obeyed them.... Jesus continued to learn more and more and to grow physically. People liked him, and he pleased God" (Luke 2:51, 52).

Memory Challenge
"The little child began to grow up. He became stronger and wiser, and God's blessings were with him" (Luke 2:40).

5 Baby Jesus in the Temple
Luke 2:22-40
When Jesus was a baby, His parents took Him to the temple in Jerusalem. Simeon and Anna knew that Jesus was the baby God had promised.

6 The Wise Men See Jesus
Matthew 2:1-12
The wise men follow a star to bring gifts to little Jesus. They found Jesus with Mary in a house in Bethlehem.

7 Jesus Is Saved from Danger
Matthew 2:13-23
God warned Joseph to go to Egypt to keep Jesus safe from King Herod. When it was safe to return, Jesus' family lived in Nazareth.

8 Jesus Grows Up
Luke 2:40-52
After the Passover, when Jesus was twelve years old, Jesus stayed in the temple to ask questions and listen to the teachers. His parents worried, but Jesus never disobeyed His parents.

By the end of the unit, the leaders and learners will
KNOW what the Bible tells about Jesus' childhood.
FEEL close to Jesus because He was a child "just like me."
DO Tell about Jesus' childhood.

Unit Value

This unit focuses on what the Bible tells about Jesus when He was a child. When He was a tiny baby, His parents took Him to the temple. He lived in a house, but had to move several times. His parents were very careful to keep Him safe from harm. He liked to learn new things and make right choices. As he got older, He got taller. People liked Jesus. And best of all, God was pleased with how Jesus was growing up: He always obeyed His parents. This unit makes a concrete connection in time between the stories of Jesus' birth and the stories of Jesus' ministry. Learning how Jesus was like children today adds to the realness of Jesus' life.

There is a value in imitating Jesus' behavior as a child. But rather than seek this as a measurable outcome, the unit places emphasis on helping the children experience and speak freely about the facts of Jesus' childhood. The Bible verses to memorize for this unit will help the children remember some of these facts. As the children talk comfortably and easily about Jesus' childhood, they will be more apt to feel close to Jesus. If your classroom is an exciting place to be, they will be excited about what they are learning. Then, in addition to the stated goal of telling about Jesus' childhood, you are likely to see Jesus' behavior showing up in their lives.

▼ Bible Project ▲

A Big Book

The learners will design and create a big picture book about Jesus' childhood to share with other children. The book will enable the children to tell others about Jesus' childhood.

Use the activities and reproducible pages throughout the unit to give the children ideas of what to draw and write and in what order to put the book together. A large piece of poster board will be needed for each page of the book. Provide drawing materials and old Sunday school visuals for the children to use in designing the book.

Week 1: Talk about the picture for each page of the book. Assign each page to a small group or pair of children.

Week 2: Review. Sketch ideas. Discuss captions for the pictures.

Week 3: Finish pictures. Print out the story.

Week 4: Bind the big book. Practice reading the story.

Bible Project Enrichment

Include the following information as you work on the project. Children's Bible dictionaries and handbooks are great sources of Bible times pictures. Pictures and information about living in Bible times will made the storybook project more interesting to make and read.

Bible times house: A typical home when Jesus lived was made of clay. The windows were small and high, just holes in the wall. The dirt floor was packed hard and smooth. As a boy, Jesus slept on a mat on the floor, using his cloak for a blanket. Many families built a small room on the roof of the house. A stairway to the roof was built on the outside wall. All the cooking was done outside the home, as well as many other chores, because the house was very small.

Bible times food: Jesus' family probably ate two main meals a day. Breakfast might have been a snack of bread with butter and honey. At noon, lunch might have included bread, cheese, and fruit—perhaps grapes. In the evening, the meal might consist of bread, olives, figs, and vegetables; sometimes there might be eggs or fish, or a stew with sparrow or mutton with vegetables. Children drank goat's milk.

Bible times travel: When Jesus was growing up, He might have traveled by riding a mule or a donkey. But probably Jesus walked to most places. People who were wealthy could have traveled on horseback, or in a chariot pulled by horses, or on camelback.

Bible times church: Jesus and His family worshiped on the Sabbath. The Sabbath began at sunset the night before. Special blessings were said by His parents, and then they ate the Sabbath meal. The next morning, they went to worship in the synagogue in Nazareth. The synagogue stood on the highest ground in the village. The men and boys always sat together on one side. The women and girls sat on the other side. After the worship time, the family ate the noontime Sabbath meal. The rest of the day was spent visiting friends and family. No work was done on the Sabbath. For special important celebrations, like the Passover, Jesus and His family traveled to Jerusalem to worship in the temple.

Bible times games: Jesus probably enjoyed swimming, rock climbing and exploring, climbing trees, and playing with a favorite animal pet. We don't know a lot about children's games and activities in Bible times, but archaeologists have found dolls and toy furniture, balls and toy tools.

Materials
Provide materials to help the children design and complete a big picture book:
one piece of poster board for each page of the book
drawing materials (crayons, colored pencils, straight edge)
old Sunday school pictures
leftover take-home papers
extra Bible story visuals
metal rings to "bind" the book

Baby Jesus in the Temple

Luke 2:22-40

Lesson Goals
- Report who Anna told about Jesus.
- Report what Anna and Simeon told about Jesus.
- Begin to memorize Luke 2:51, 52
- List three things about Jesus' birth to tell someone.
- Tell about Jesus' childhood.

Memory Block
"Jesus went with them to Nazareth and obeyed them. . . . Jesus continued to learn more and more and to grow physically. People liked him, and he pleased God" (Luke 2:51, 52).

▼ Bible Search ▲

Joseph and Mary took Jesus to the temple when he was still a small baby. Anna was there at the temple. Let's read our Bibles to find out who Anna was and what she did.

Children will find Luke 2:36-38 in their Bibles and work together to complete the Bible Search page. Give a copy of page 49 to each child. Guide the children to find the book of Luke in the table of contents of their Bibles. Locate the page the book begins on, then the big 2 for the chapter and the small 36 for the verse. (Doing the same procedure each time will help children gain skill in finding Bible verses.) Slowly read verses 36-38 as children follow along. Help children complete the page, using their Bibles to check their answers: very old, prayed, thanked God, married 7 years, prophetess, 84 years old, family of Phanuel, worshiped God, talked about Jesus to all.

What was Anna like? (Give a child a turn to tell an answer from the page.)
Who did Anna talk to about Jesus? (everyone)

Purpose
Report who Anna told about Jesus.

Materials
Bibles
copies of page 49
pencils or crayons

▼ Bible Story ▲

Put on the headpiece before you tell the story. Use the masking tape to make a tic-tac-toe grid on the floor. Draw large *Xs* and *Os* on the construction paper. Make Xs for half of the students and Os for the other half.

Who do you tell when you have good news? Listen for whom Anna told.

Purpose
Report what Anna and Simeon told about Jesus.

Materials
Bible times headpiece (towel draped around head, tied on top with a length of cloth or heavy yarn)
masking tape
construction paper
markers

"Baby Jesus in the Temple"

Sleeping on a hard floor is not a comfortable way to rest when you are 84 years old like me. My name is Anna. Sometimes in the morning I have to rub my stiff knees before I can stand up. But even when it hurts, I am happy when I think about what God has done. I stay at the temple because it helps me to spend my time fasting and praying. Night and day, I worship God because He is great, He is good, and He always does what He says.

Many other people come here to worship. Some come to pray. Some bring a sacrifice to give to God. Some people travel from far away to worship God in this beautiful temple. Others, like my old friend Simeon, live right here in Jerusalem. Many of us, like Simeon, were waiting for God to send the one He had promised. God had said Simeon would not die until he had seen Jesus. Whenever parents brought in a small baby, we would wonder, "Is this the one God promised?"

One day, Simeon made a special trip to the temple because God's Spirit had told him to be there. On that same day, a young couple named Mary and Joseph walked through the temple gate. They came to give a sacrifice because of the birth of a firstborn son. I could tell they were poor because they had two pigeons to sacrifice instead of a lamb.

Hugging the baby close, they entered the courtyard. Simeon must have known immediately who they were. He moved to where they were standing and reached for the small bundle in Mary's arms. Mary must have been puzzled, but she allowed Simeon to take the baby. As Simeon held the baby, he thanked God for keeping His promise to send Jesus. The words Simeon spoke were amazing to Mary and Joseph, "Lord, now you can let your servant die in peace. I have seen your salvation with my own eyes."

I knew this was the baby we had been waiting for. "Oh, thank You, God," I said. I was so excited, it didn't matter if my body ached. I had to speak about this baby to everyone who was waiting for Jesus to come. When Mary and Joseph finished their worship, they traveled back home. But in spite of my tired bones and stiff knees, I couldn't stop telling people what God had done. I wanted everyone to know that God had kept His promise just like He said He would.

Give half of the children Xs and half Os. For a right answer, a child stands on any empty square on the grid. Use as many questions as needed to get three Xs or three Os in a row.
- **Who prayed night and day?** (Anna)
- **Who was waiting to see baby Jesus?** (Anna, Simeon)
- **Who got to hold the baby?** (Simeon)
- **What did Simeon say about Jesus?** (He called Him God's salvation.)
- **Why did Joseph and Mary come to the temple?** (Give a sacrifice)
- **Where did Anna see Simeon?** (Temple)
- **Who did Simeon talk to?** (God)
- **What was the baby's name?** (Jesus)
- **Who did Anna tell about Jesus?** (Everyone)

Summary questions: **What did Simeon and Anna do when they saw Jesus?** (praised God) **What did Simeon say about Jesus?** (God kept His promise to send Jesus. He had seen God's salvation with his own eyes.) **Who did Anna tell about Jesus?** (everyone who was waiting for Jesus to come)

▼ Bible Verse ▲

Our Bible verses tell about Jesus when He was a child, just like you!
Help the children find and read the verses aloud from a Bible. Then they will fill in the blanks of the verse activity on page 50. As the teacher says the verse, pause to let the children print the correct word in each blank. The teacher can continue to read the verse with pauses in various places so the children can supply the next word. For variety, let the whole group answer, then groups of two or three can answer in the pauses.

Tell me the next word of the verse when I pause. What does this verse help us know about Jesus?

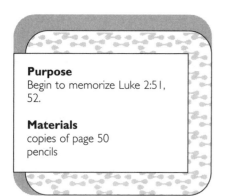

Purpose
Begin to memorize Luke 2:51, 52.

Materials
copies of page 50
pencils

▼ Bible and Me ▲

Jesus was a child just like you. Some things He did were like the things you do. Some things He did were very different. We already know some things that happened to Jesus when He was small. Let's make a list.

Let the children list events from Jesus' life. (These will be used to make a big picture book for the unit project.) First, put down everything they know. Then put the events in the correct order for a book. After the list is made, ask the children to tell one thing about how each event is like or how it is different from what happens to them as children. For example: Jesus was a tiny baby like me. But He slept in a manger and that's not like me!

Optional: Use the pictures of Jesus' early life on page 51. The children number them in order. Then they can tell how each event is like and how it is different from what happens to them.

What kinds of things did Jesus do just like you? What kinds of things did Jesus do that were different from you?

Purpose
List three things about Jesus' birth to tell someone.

Materials
copies of page 51
pencils

▼ Bible Project ▲

Unit page 36 gives an overview of the unit project as well as suggestions for enrichment activities.

We have been learning about how Jesus was like us and how He was different from us. Because He is the Son of God, Jesus is very special and we want to tell everyone about Him. Let's make a big book about Jesus so we can tell about Him just like Anna did.

If you did not already do so in Bible and Me, make a list of events from Jesus' early life. Talk about the scenes to draw. List the scenes on poster board or a planning tablet. Assign or enlist volunteers to design each page of the book.

Explain that each page of the book will be made with one sheet of poster board. Children may begin thinking about how to design their pages: drawing, torn paper, old Bible story pictures, copies of pictures on page 51. If you have time to begin, see additional instructions in Lesson 6.

Purpose
Tell about Jesus' childhood.

Materials
poster board
drawing materials
old Sunday school pictures
leftover take home papers
extra Bible story visuals

▼ Bible Sharing ▲

Gather the children together on the floor. Eat the fruit snack as you talk about what kinds of food Jesus would have eaten growing up in Nazareth. See the unit pages for Bible times customs.

Let's play a game. When you wear the head piece, share with the group one thing you can tell about Jesus. Tell how Jesus was a child just like you or tell how Jesus is different from you. Then give the head piece to someone who hasn't had a turn to share.

Close with a short guided prayer. Help the children thank God for Jesus.

Purpose
Share how Jesus was a child just like you.

Materials
snack of fruit slices (apples, bananas, oranges)
Bible times head piece (from Bible Story)

Memory Block
"Jesus went with them to Nazareth and obeyed them. . . . Jesus continued to learn more and more and to grow physically. People liked him, and he pleased God" (Luke 2:51, 52)

Lesson Goals
- Name the people who wanted to know where Jesus was born.
- Tell what the king and the wise men wanted to do when Jesus was born.
- Memorize Luke 2:51, 52.
- Give a good reason to tell about Jesus.
- Tell about Jesus' childhood.

▼ Bible Search ▲

Purpose
Name the three people who wanted to know where Jesus was born.

Materials
Bibles
copies of page 52
pencils

Two different kinds of people wanted to know where Jesus was born. They wanted to see Jesus for different reasons. Let's find out about these people in our Bibles.

Children will find Matthew 2:1-4 in their Bibles and work together to complete the Bible Search page. Give a copy of page 52 to each child. Guide the children to find the book of Matthew in the table of contents of their Bibles. Locate the page the book begins on, then the big 2 for the chapter and the small 1 for the verse. (Doing the same procedure each time will help children gain skill in finding Bible verses.) Slowly read verses 3 and 4 as children follow along. Help children complete the top half of the page. Then read verses 1 and 2 so children can complete the bottom half of the page.

Who wanted to know where Jesus would be born? (King Herod, wise men) **Why do you think Herod wanted to know about Jesus?** (Let children make suggestions.) **Why did the wise men want to know about Jesus?** (They wanted to worship Him.)

▼ Bible Story ▲

Purpose
Tell what the king and wise men wanted to do when Jesus was born.

Materials
copy of page 53
strips of paper
pen
scissors
tape

Display the map from the top of page 53, enlarged if possible. Print the review questions at the end of this activity on strips of paper and tape them to the map for the Bible story review. Cut out the figures at the bottom of page 53 and fold them to make stand-up figures. Make one set of figures for every 3-4 children. Save the figures to use during review.

This map shows where some wise men lived and where they went. The Bible doesn't say how they traveled, but you can listen to see how they knew where to go.

"The Wise Men See Jesus"
"The star! The new star," I exclaimed. There it was, twinkling hello in the night sky. The other wise men and I had waited and waited for it to appear. As I jumped up with joy, I could see it was rising in the east. It could mean only one thing. The king of the Jews had been born. Hurriedly, we packed supplies for our trip and three gifts for this tiny new king. As we began our long journey west, our only map was the new star. Always it went before us, leading us toward the new king.

My friends and I traveled up hills and down dusty roads for days and days. Finally, we saw the city of Jerusalem ahead. Inside the city gates, we stopped to inquire, "Where is the one who has been born king of the Jews? We saw his star in the east and have come to worship him." People shook their heads and looked away. They seemed worried. Perhaps the people didn't like kings, even tiny ones!

King Herod must have heard about our questions. He was even more disturbed than the people of Jerusalem. He was worried enough to do his own investigation. Frantically he called in the chief priests and teachers in Jerusalem. Then Herod demanded to know where the Christ would be born. They told him. They knew the prophet Micah said it would happen in Bethlehem.

Herod invited us to a special secret meeting. Maybe he didn't want people to know he was worried. First, Herod asked when this unusual star had appeared. We told him exactly when it had risen in the sky. Then Herod told us we would find the child in Bethlehem, only a few miles from Jerusalem. It wouldn't take long to get there. He added a strange request, "When you go to Bethlehem, find the child and then come back to see me." He appeared to be sincere, but now I think he was plotting to get rid of this new king.

As we left the palace, we pointed and shouted, "There's our star, again!" We trembled with excitement as we lumbered toward Bethlehem. We had almost found the new king! The star moved on ahead of us until it stopped right over the house where we found Mary and Jesus. We fell down before the new king, opening our gifts of gold, frankincense, and myrrh. God warned us in a dream not to go back to Herod. So we sneaked out of Judea to go back home a different way. Herod was probably angry with us, but we certainly were happy. We had seen and worshiped the new little king.

Ask volunteers to choose a question taped to the map (page 53). For each question, point to the place on the map that goes with that question. Example: the wise men question and "the East."

Who lived in the East? (wise men)

Who lived in a palace in Jerusalem? (Herod)

Who lived in a house in Bethlehem? (Jesus, Mary, and Joseph)

Why did the wise men travel so far? (They followed the star. They wanted to see the king of the Jews.)

Why did Herod want to know where Jesus was? (He wanted to get rid of the new king.)

What special things happened at Jesus' house in Bethlehem? (Wise men gave Jesus gifts and worshiped Him.)

Summary questions: **Who wanted to know where Jesus was born?** (wise men, Herod) **Why did Herod want to know where Jesus was born?** (He was worried about a new king. He wanted to get rid of Jesus.) **Why did the wise men want to know where Jesus was born?** (They wanted to worship Jesus and give Him gifts.)

If you have time, allow the children to use the stand-up figures of Mary and Jesus, King Herod, and the wise men to retell the story.

▼ Bible Verse ▲

Fill in the missing words in the verse poster on page 50 and display it for the children. Print the following words on the index cards: **Nazareth, obeyed, learn, grow, people, God.** Put the cards in a sack.

Our Bible verses tell about Jesus when He was a child, just like you! Let the children find and read Luke 2:51, 52 aloud from a Bible. Then they can take turns choosing a verse card from a sack and saying the phrase that goes with that card. (Use the poster when needed.) Place the cards in order on the wall (or have children stand in a circle and hold them in order). Let the children use the cards as clues for which phrase comes next as they recite the verse.

What does this verse help us know about Jesus? Let's have the boys say

Purpose
Memorize Luke 2:51, 52.

Materials
Copy of verse poster on page 50
six index cards
marker
sack

the whole verse. Let's have the girls say the whole verse. Let's have groups of two or three say the whole verse.

▼ Bible and Me ▲

Purpose
Give a good reason to tell about Jesus.

We tell about Jesus because Jesus is so special. In some ways He was just like me. But, because He was the Son of God, He was different from me. He is special because He is both like me and different from me!

The teacher names ways that Jesus was like or different from us: was a tiny baby, obeyed parents, grew bigger every year, did miracles when He was a man, came back alive after He died, went to live in Heaven with God. If the teacher names a way Jesus is like us, children should stand up. If the teacher names a way Jesus is different from us, the children should sit down.

Do you think it's more special for Jesus to be like you or different from you? Which of these things do you think is the most special thing about Jesus? Why do we tell what we know about Jesus? (because He is special; He is like me and He is like God—the Son of God)

▼ Bible Project ▲

Purpose
Tell about Jesus' childhood.

Materials
materials listed in lesson 5

Every week we will learn more about Jesus and have more to tell others about Jesus' childhood. Let's continue to work on our picture book about Jesus.

Review the unit project with the children. Display the pictures of Bible times houses, food, games, clothing, and customs. A few items are pictured on unit page 36. Then assist children as they begin drawing in pencil or putting together old Sunday school pictures. Talk about the captions for the pictures. Suggest they include how Jesus was a child like them and how He was different. Example: "Just like me, Jesus was born. But Jesus was born in a stable, in a manger where food for animals is kept."

▼ Bible Sharing ▲

Purpose
Share how Jesus was a child just like you.

Materials
a drawing tablet
black marker
a snack of rice cakes spread
    with peanut butter

Gather children together on the floor. Eat the rice snack as you talk about the wise men's visit to Jesus.

Let's play a picture game to share what is special about Jesus. I'll start by drawing a simple picture. You guess what I drew, and I'll tell you something about Jesus.

Give each child a turn to draw a picture, let the group guess, and tell something about Jesus. You may need to encourage the children to draw some of the following items: star (wise men followed it to Jesus' house), house (Jesus lived with Mary and Joseph in a house), gold (a gift given to Jesus), perfume bottle (myrrh, a gift to Jesus), three wise men (visited Jesus from a far away country), Mary (Jesus' mother who took care of Him), young boy (Jesus was a toddler), angel (warned the wise men).

Jesus Is Saved from Danger

LESSON 7

Matthew 2:13-23

Lesson Goals

- Tell the messages the angel gave Joseph.
- Tell how God cared for little Jesus.
- Recite and explain Luke 2:51, 52.
- Demonstrate ways to tell how God cared for little Jesus.
- Tell about Jesus' childhood.

▼ Bible Search ▲

Someone gave Joseph a very important message. Let's find in our Bibles who talked to Joseph and what the message was.

Children will find Matthew 2:13 in their Bibles and work together to complete the Bible Search page. Give a copy of page 56 to each child. Guide the children to find the book of Matthew in the table of contents of their Bibles. Locate the page the book begins on, then the big 2 for the chapter and the small 13 for the verse. Slowly read the verse as children follow along or prepare a good reader to read. Help the children complete the page, using their Bibles to check circled answers (Mary and Jesus, Egypt, Herod wanted to kill the child, Stay until I tell you).

What was the message the angel gave? (Take Jesus and Mary and go to Egypt. Stay until I tell you to return.) **How did God plan to care for little Jesus?** (He told Joseph to take Jesus to Egypt to save Him from Herod.)

Purpose
Tell one message the angel gave Joseph.

Materials
Bibles
copies of page 56
pencils or crayons

▼ Bible Story ▲

Display the envelope, newspaper, and telephone. **These are ways to receive news. Listen to see how Joseph received some bad and good news.**

"Jesus Saved from Danger"

Joseph woke me in the middle of the night. "Get up, get up," he said. "The angel of the Lord told me to take you and Jesus and escape to Egypt." Joseph continued with the worst possible news. The angel had said Herod was going to look for our Jesus. Herod wanted to kill our Jesus.

Joseph insisted we leave immediately. Perhaps Herod's soldiers were on the road to Bethlehem right now. My thoughts raced through my head. We could carry few things with us. We would need clothes and food. We must take the gifts Jesus had received—gold, frankincense, and myrrh. Trying to be calm, we picked up our little sleeping Jesus. Quickly, quietly we stepped outside. There was no one in the street. There was no one to say good-bye. There was no one to tell where we were going. Soon the dark streets of Bethlehem were behind us.

Once we were on the road, there was more time to think about what was happening. We were going to Egypt! It would be hard to live far away in another country. But it would be better than living in fear of King Herod.

Later we learned our escape was just in time. Herod had waited and waited for the wise men to return to Jerusalem. When they didn't come, his fury grew and grew until he exploded with rage. He ordered his soldiers to kill all the boys in

Purpose
Tell how God cared for little Jesus.

Materials
copies of page 54
an addressed envelope
newspaper
toy telephone

Bethlehem under two years old. His desperate plan showed how wicked he really was.

In Egypt, life was different for us. We had to find a new place to live, learn a new language, and meet new friends. But one thing was the same: God always cared for us. And God had promised He would tell us when it was safe to go back. We were grateful for God's care, but we longed for the day when we could return to Israel.

One day Joseph brought good news from the angel of the Lord. The angel said Herod had died. It was time to get up and go back to Israel. Getting ready for the trip this time was much more enjoyable. We knew it would be a long trip, but Jesus was a little older and we knew God would be with us. Eagerly we made our way down the road toward home.

Back in Israel, Herod's son was the new king. After another warning in a dream, Joseph took us back to Galilee to the town of Nazareth. That's where we lived before Jesus was born. It was good to be back among friends. In Nazareth, Jesus could grow up safe from wicked rulers. Someday we would tell Him how God saved Him from danger when He was just a small child.

Begin the review by asking two questions. **Who helped to keep Jesus safe?** (Joseph, Mary, angel) **Who would have harmed Jesus?** (Herod, soldiers)

Let the children take turns charading as one of these people. For each one, first guess if it is someone safe or harmful. Then guess the person's name.

Option: Review using the crossword puzzle on page 54. Children can work in pairs to complete the puzzle. Children should fill in the <u>down</u> place names and then fill in the <u>across</u> people names.

Summary questions: **What messages did the angel give Joseph? What did God do to care for little Jesus?**

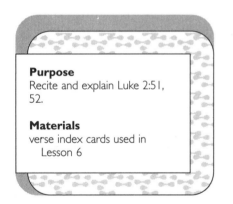

Purpose
Recite and explain Luke 2:51, 52.

Materials
verse index cards used in Lesson 6

▼ Bible Verse ▲

Our Bible verses tell about Jesus when He was a child, just like you!

Let the children find and read Luke 2:51, 52 aloud from the Bible. Then they can work together to put the verse cards in order. (Use the verse poster from page 50 on the wall if needed.) As the children recite the verses, pause for each card and think of an action or motion to help explain the word on the verse card. The whole group can then recite or say the verses in rhythm and use the motions to explain what the verses say. If possible, do the verses in small groups.

Suggested motions: Nazareth (tent fingers like the roof of a house); obeyed (nod head up and down); learn (hold hands open like a book); grow (hold hand out, palm down, indicating how high someone has grown); people (point to others around you); God (point upward).

What do these verses help us know about Jesus? Let's have the boys say the verses with the motions. Let's have the girls say the verses with the motions. Let's have groups of two say the verses with the motions.

▼ Bible and Me ▲

We tell about Jesus because Jesus is so special. There are lots of ways to tell about Jesus on this page. Distribute page 55.

Each child or pair of children can choose from the page one way to tell and act it out for the rest of the class. Each demonstration can tell how God cared for little Jesus in the story today. Pictured ways to tell: book, Bible verse, puppet, letter, song, mural.

What way will you use to tell about Jesus? What other ways to tell about Jesus are pictured on this page? Which way is the easiest? hardest? most fun?

Purpose
Demonstrate ways to tell how God cared for little Jesus.

Materials
copies of page 55

▼ Bible Project ▲

Today we have learned another part of Jesus' growing up story. Let's put the finishing touches on our picture book about Jesus.

Review the unit project for visitors and newcomers. Help the children complete the artwork for each page and then print the story. A way to write the story captions was suggested in Lesson 6. You may wish to print the story as the children dictate sentences, or allow plenty of time for children to print the story themselves.

Today's story about Jesus' family going to Egypt provides a good opportunity to talk about traveling in Bible times. See the information printed on unit page 36.

Purpose
Tell about Jesus' childhood.

Materials
materials listed in Lesson 5

▼ Bible Sharing ▲

Gather the children together in a circle. Eat the finger food as you share about Jesus.

Let's play a game to share what we know about Jesus. Display the telephone. **Is this how Joseph received his message to take Mary and Jesus to Egypt? No, the message the angel brought from God was too important. But let's play a telephone game while we snack on food Joseph and Mary might have packed for the trip to Egypt.**

Begin by whispering a sentence about Jesus to the child on your right; then that child will whisper the message to the next child, and so on. The game is probably familiar to most, but stress the importance of telling about Jesus. Correct any wrong information reported at the end of each turn. Give each child an opportunity to tell something. (Suggestions: Just like me, Jesus was born and lived with His family. Just like me, Jesus was a child. Just like me, Jesus liked to learn new things and make right choices. Just like me, Jesus learned to obey His parents. Just like me, Jesus learned to please God. Just like Jesus, I want to please God.) Sing favorite unit songs to close the session.

Purpose
Share how Jesus was a child like you.

Materials
the telephone used at the beginning of the Bible story
a snack of cheese cubes and grapes (fast finger food for traveling)

Jesus Grows Up

Luke 2:40-52

Memory Block
"Jesus went with them to Nazareth and obeyed them. . . . Jesus continued to learn more and more and to grow physically. People liked him, and he pleased God" (Luke 2:51, 52).

Lesson Goals
- Tell why Jesus was in the temple.
- Name five things we know about Jesus when He was growing up in Nazareth.
- Recite and explain Luke 2:51, 52.
- Demonstrate ways to tell about Jesus when He was a boy.
- Tell about Jesus' childhood.

▼ Bible Search ▲

Purpose
Tell why Jesus was in the temple.

Materials
Bibles
marker board and markers or chalkboard and chalk

Print Luke 2:46 on the marker board or chalkboard. "Jesus was sitting in the Temple with the religious teachers, listening to them and asking them questions."

Jesus was special, but He also grew from a baby to a child to an adult—just like you. Let's find some verses in our Bibles that tell about Him growing up.

Guide the children to find Luke 2:46 in their Bibles. Slowly read the verse. Show the verse you have printed on the board.

Where does the verse say Jesus was? Ask a volunteer to come forward and put a circle around where the verse says Jesus was (the temple).

Who was with Jesus? Ask a volunteer to put a box around the answer (religious teachers).

Why was Jesus there? Ask a volunteer to put a line under the answer (listening and asking questions).

How do you think this helped Jesus grow up?

Option: Print the words to Luke 2:46 on a piece of paper and make a copy for each student. They may circle, box, and underline the answers on their papers.

▼ Bible Story ▲

Purpose
Name five things we know about Jesus when He was growing up in Nazareth.

Materials
a birthday cake with twelve candles
twelve slips of paper
marker

Print the twelve underlined words in the story on the slips of paper and keep them to use for review. Display the birthday cake with the candles.

How old would you be if these candles were on your birthday cake? Listen to see what happened to Jesus after His twelfth birthday.

"Jesus Grows Up"

Every spring, Jesus' family and friends traveled together from Nazareth to Jerusalem for the Passover celebration. After waiting twelve years, Jesus was finally old enough to go along. It was a long trip. If they had been birds, they would have flown at least seventy miles across the hills. But traveling up and down dirt roads, over hills, and through the valleys made it even farther. Jesus was growing stronger, so He could make the trip. And traveling together with friends helped. They could sing and talk and laugh as they went. But by evening their heavy feet would plod along and their aching legs would beg to stop for rest. Everyone was grateful to arrive at the gates of Jerusalem.

At the end of the Passover celebration, Jesus' family and friends began their long trip back to Nazareth. Joseph and Mary didn't realize Jesus was not with them. He was old enough to walk with His friends. But Jesus was still in Jerusalem. He was eager to listen and talk to the teachers in the temple. He wanted to be in His Father God's house.

After traveling a day, Joseph and Mary began to <u>look</u> for Jesus. They looked among their relatives. He wasn't there. They looked among their friends. He wasn't there. As Mary realized He was not in their group, she probably felt tears in her eyes. She didn't know where Jesus was. Was He safe? Did He have food? Would He keep warm?

Joseph and Mary started back towards Jerusalem. They had already traveled a day toward Nazareth. Now they had to travel the same distance again, back to Jerusalem. They were worried. Where was Jesus? Was He okay?

Back in Jerusalem, they decided to look in the <u>temple</u>. It had been <u>three</u> days since they had seen Jesus. As they neared the temple, they probably wondered what they would do if Jesus wasn't there. Where would they look next?

But Jesus was there. As He <u>listened</u> to the teachers and <u>answered</u> questions, the people around Him were amazed. When His parents saw Him, they had a different feeling. Mary said, "Son, why have you done this to us? Your father and I were very <u>worried</u> about you. We have been looking for you." Jesus explained that He wanted to be in His Father God's house. Jesus wanted to learn more about what God wanted Him to do. But Jesus also wanted to go home with Joseph and Mary.

Jesus was with His parents as they passed through the Jerusalem gates one more time. Mary wondered many times about what had just happened. She and Joseph didn't understand what Jesus had explained to them in the temple. But Joseph and Mary were pleased with how Jesus was growing up. He <u>obeyed</u> everything His parents asked Him to do. He kept learning and growing taller. Other <u>people</u> liked Jesus. Most important of all, <u>God</u> was pleased with how Jesus was growing up.

Let each child choose a slip of paper and use the word on the paper to make a sentence about the story. For each correct sentence, remove a candle from the cake. The children can give their sentences again, in order, for more review. Eat the cake at Bible Sharing time.

Summary questions: **Why was Jesus in the temple?** (to listen and ask questions) **We have been memorizing Bible verses about when Jesus grew up in Nazareth. What five things do we know from those verses about Jesus growing up in Nazareth?** (If children need help, they can find Luke 2:51, 52 in their Bibles. Jesus obeyed His parents; He learned; He grew; people liked Him; He pleased God.)

▼ Bible Verse ▲

Give each pair of children a copy of page 57 and ask them to cut apart the pictures.

Our Bible verses tell about Jesus when He was a child, just like you! Let the children find and read Luke 2:51, 52 aloud from a Bible. Volunteers can recite the verses from memory (in groups or as individuals). Take turns telling which phrase of the verses could go with the six pictures on page 57. (The first picture is a synagogue or the temple.) Take turns 1) reciting the verses and 2) using the information from page 57 to explain the verses to each other.

How did Jesus learn? What kinds of things happened when Jesus grew? What did Luke mean when he said, "People liked him"? What did Luke mean when he said Jesus "pleased God"? What else do the verses help us know about Jesus? Let's take turns saying the verses and explaining parts of the verses.

Purpose
Recite and explain Luke 2:51, 52.

Materials
Bibles
copies of page 57
scissors

▼ Bible and Me ▲

We tell about Jesus because Jesus is so special. We don't know everything about Jesus when He was a child, but we do know He always obeyed.

Distribute page 58 and pencils. Complete the page together by matching ways children obey today with ways Jesus might have obeyed at home.

Ask the children to name ways to tell about Jesus. (See page 55 used in Lesson 7 for ideas of ways to tell about Jesus.) Then let each child or small group of children tell about ways Jesus might have obeyed His parents when He was a boy. Help them focus only on Jesus' childhood.

What are some ways we can tell about Jesus? What can we tell about how Jesus obeyed when He was a child? Which way can you use to tell about Jesus when He was a child? Would you rather be a child today or when Jesus was a boy? Why?

Option: Have children act out ways Jesus obeyed and ways we obey from page 58. Other children can guess whether they are acting out a way we obey or a way Jesus obeyed.

Purpose
Demonstrate ways to tell about Jesus when He was a boy.

Materials
copies of page 58
pencils

▼ Bible Project ▲

Before class, prepare suggestions of groups to which the children can present and read their project story book (Sunday school classes, homebound individuals, children's home, nursing home, library, after school clubs, worship time).

Today we have learned another part of Jesus' growing up story. To finish our project, we need to practice reading our story to each other, practice holding the book pages while different readers read, and practice being good listeners. Then together we will plan how to share our story of Jesus with other children and adults.

Review the unit project for visitors and newcomers. Help the children practice reading, holding, and listening with respect.

Today's story about Jesus' family going to the temple in Jerusalem provides a good opportunity to talk about worship in Bible times. See unit page 36.

Purpose
Tell about Jesus' childhood.

Materials
project materials completed during Lessons 5-7

▼ Bible Sharing ▲

Put the twelve candles back on the cake and be prepared to light them. Gather the children together around a table (or several tables pushed together).

Let's celebrate Jesus' twelfth birthday. As each person shares something special about Jesus, I will light a candle on the cake. You may share how Jesus is special and different, or special and just like you.

Give each child an opportunity to share. Light the candles, blow them out, sing "Happy Birthday" if you want, and have fun eating together. Pretend the milk is goat's milk, something Jesus might have had with His birthday celebration. Sing the following words to the tune "Three Blind Mice."

Purpose
Share how Jesus was a child just like you.

Materials
birthday cake and candles from the Bible Story time
matches or a lighter
paper plates
napkins
forks
milk to drink

Just like me, just like me.
Jesus grew, just like me.
He read God's Word and did obey.
He had jobs to do and games to play.
He worshiped God and bowed to pray,
Just like me, just like me.

Just like me, just like me.
Jesus grew, just like me.
He listened to God and sang good songs.
He pleased God in all things and did no wrong.
He learned more and more and grew tall and strong,
Just like me, just like me.

Bible Search

Find Luke 2:36-38 in your Bible.
Circle the words that tell about Anna.

young girl

thanked God

prophetess

family of
Phanuel

34 years old

married
7 years

prayed

very old

kept
quiet

never
married

84 years old

talked about
Jesus to all

worshiped
God

Anna

Who did Anna tell about Jesus?

  49

Bible Verse

Find Luke 2:51, 52 in your Bible.
Read the verse with your teacher.
Fill in the blanks using the words
in the word bank.

Jesus went with them to _____

and _____ them. . . . Jesus continued

to _____ more and more and to

_____ physically. _____

liked him, and he pleased _____.

Luke 2:51, 52

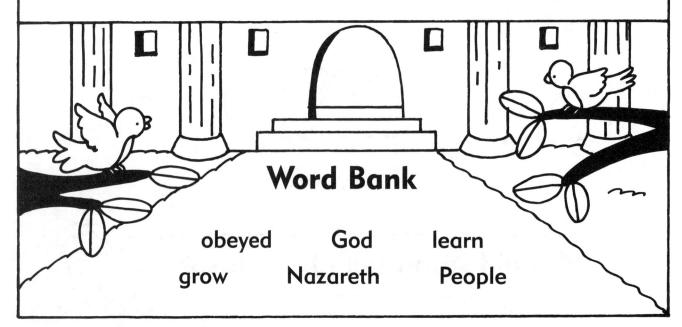

Word Bank

obeyed	God	learn
grow	Nazareth	People

 UNIT 2, LESSON 5

Bible and Me

Look at the pictures.
Tell about each time in Jesus' life.
Number the pictures in order.

What kinds of things did Jesus do just like you?
What kinds of things did Jesus do that were different than what we do?

Bible Search

Find Matthew 2:3, 4 in your Bible.

This man heard about Jesus' birth.
This man was worried.
Who is this man?

___ ___ ___ ___   ___ ___ ___ ___

What did this man want to know?

Find Matthew 2:1, 2 in your Bible.

These men heard about Jesus' birth.
These men saw His star.
These men wanted to worship Jesus.
Who are these men?

___ ___ ___ ___ ___

What did these men want to know?

UNIT 2, LESSON 6

Bible Story

Use the map to review the story.
Use the stand-up figures to tell the
Bible story.

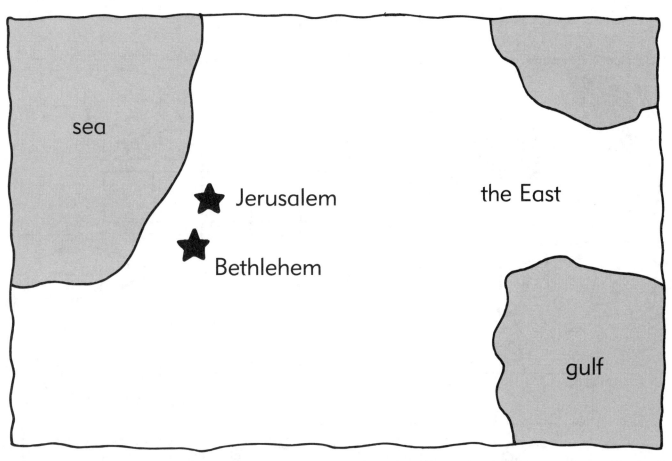

sea

⭐ Jerusalem

⭐ Bethlehem

the East

gulf

King Herod

wise men

Mary and Jesus

Bible Story

Tell how God cared for little Jesus.
Use the words to fill in the puzzle.

People names go
<u>across</u>:
- Jesus
- angel
- Herod
- Joseph

Place names go
<u>down</u>:
- Nazareth
- Egypt
- Bethlehem

We tell about Jesus because Jesus is so special. There are lots of ways to tell about Jesus on this page.

Luke 2:52 says, "Jesus continued to learn more. . . . People liked him, and he pleased God."

A Big Book About Jesus

Dear Joe, Jesus is our Savior! Do you...

What ways will you use to tell about Jesus?

Bible Search

Find Matthew 2:13 in your Bible.
What did the angel tell Joseph?
Circle the answer to each question.

1. Who was Joseph to take with him?

donkey   Mary and Jesus   wise men

2. Where were they going?

the river   the East   Egypt

3. Why did they have to go?

They wanted to   Herod wanted to   They needed a vacation.
visit friends.   kill the child.

4. How long did they need to stay?

Stay until I tell you.   Stay until you are rested.   Stay for three weeks.

Cut apart the pictures.
Use the pictures to explain Luke 2:51, 52.

Bible Verse

cut

Bible and Me

Read each sentence about a job you might do.

Look at the pictures of how Jesus might have helped at home.

Match each sentence about you to a picture of Jesus.

I can get water in the glasses for supper.

I can help my mother vacuum the carpet.

I can make the heat turn on when it is cold.

UNIT 3

Jesus Wants Me to Follow Him

Lessons 9–13

Unit Memory Block
Twelve apostles: Peter, Andrew, James, John, Philip, Bartholomew, Matthew, Thomas, Thaddaeus, Simon, James, Judas

Memory Challenge
Ephesians 6:1; Philippians 2:14; Ephesians 4:25; Hebrews 13:16; Luke 10:36, 37; Matthew 6:9

9 Jesus Is Baptized
Matthew 3:1-17
When John preached, people repented and were baptized. But Jesus did no wrong. John baptized Him because it was the right thing to do.

10 Jesus Is Tempted
Matthew 4:1-11
Each time Satan wanted Jesus to do wrong, Jesus remembered a Bible verse that helped Him to do right. We follow Jesus when we remember Bible verses that help us do right.

11 Jesus Invites Fishermen to Follow Him
Matthew 4:18-22; Mark 1:16-20; Luke 5:1-11
Peter, Andrew, James, and John left everything to follow Jesus. We follow Jesus when we do what He did and do what He said.

12 Jesus Chooses Twelve Apostles
John 1:43-49; Luke 6:12-16; Mark 2:13, 14; 3:13-19
Jesus chose the twelve apostles to help Him tell God's message to people. We follow Jesus when we help tell God's message to people we know.

13 Jesus and God's House
John 2:13-16
Jesus helped people use the temple for worship and praying to God. We follow Jesus when we worship with our church family.

By the end of the unit, the leaders and learners will
KNOW Bible people who followed Jesus.
FEEL a desire to do what Jesus did and said.
DO Use Bible verses to remember ways to follow Jesus.

Unit Value

This unit helps children know some Bible people who followed Jesus and some specific ways we can follow Jesus. Throughout the unit the children can work to learn the names of the twelve apostles and some information about each of them. Following Jesus means doing what Jesus asks us to do or behaving in the way Jesus would behave. Stories 10-13 provide some concrete ways children can follow Jesus: 1) use Bible verses to help them know what is right; 2) feel a desire to follow Jesus; 3) help tell God's message to people they know; and 4) worship with their church family. Throughout the unit, the children will have repeated opportunities to learn what it means to follow Jesus, why we follow Jesus, and how to tell when they are or are not following Jesus.

The unit has an additional strength in its suggestions for helping children go beyond knowing ways to follow Jesus. Lessons 10-13 have options for helping the children follow Jesus' example of using Bible verses to remember what is right. For children who are learning about Jesus for the first time, this unit will be a great introduction to what it means to follow Him. For children who have grown up knowing who Jesus is, this unit provides the challenge of using Scripture to know what is right, just like Jesus did.

▼ Bible Project ▲

Mini-Dramas

The learners will choose and participate in a mini-drama that illustrates a way to follow Jesus. Each mini-drama should incorporate a Bible verse the children can use to help them follow Jesus. Assign an adult leader to guide each group of 4-6 children. (Use the memory challenge verses listed on page 59.) The adult leader will direct conversation and write rough and finished dramas so the children can concentrate on creating the situation and dramatizing it.

Use the activities and reproducible pages throughout the unit to give the children ideas of what to dramatize. Provide materials for props.

Week 1: Talk about situations in which children must make decisions to do what Jesus said. Choose a Bible verse to use and make a rough draft of the mini-drama.

If the children need suggestions, provide a simple description of what they could act out.

Ephesians 6:1—A child is drawing with sidewalk chalk; Dad asks her to pick up the sticks in the yard.

Philippians 2:14—Teacher asks a child to help the new student fill in his paper. Child welcomes new student.

Ephesians 4:25—Child and sister run in house from outside and child tracks mud before taking off shoes. Mom asks who tracked in mud, and child tells her.

Hebrews 13:16—Child has new computer game and lets brother (or friend) take turns playing.

Luke 10:36, 37—Dad gets home from grocery store and child goes out without being asked to help carry in groceries.

Matthew 6:9—A child is very hungry and sits down to eat lunch, but stops to pray first.

Week 2: Review. Write finished drama. Discuss needed props.

Week 3: Make props. Practice.

Week 4: Memorize the Bible verse. Practice.

Week 5: Rehearse all mini-dramas for each other as a dress rehearsal before the scheduled presentation.

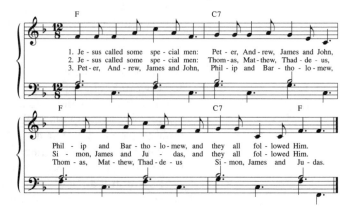

Jesus' Followers
Traditional "Mulberry Bush"

1. Je - sus called some spe - cial men: Pet - er, And - rew, James and John,
2. Je - sus called some spe - cial men: Thom - as, Mat - thew, Thad - de - us,
3. Pet - er, And - rew, James and John, Phil - ip and Bar - tho - lo - mew,

Phil - ip and Bar - tho - lo - mew, and they all fol - lowed Him.
Si - mon, James and Ju - das, and they all fol - lowed Him.
Thom - as, Mat - thew, Thad - de - us Si - mon, James and Ju - das.

Materials
Provide materials to help the children create and dramatize "following" situations.
Print on a large piece of poster board the memory challenge verses.
Provide materials for props children suggest.

Bible Times Bread
Use this recipe in Lessons 13 and 25.

- 1 cup flour
- 1/2 teaspoon salt
- 1/4 cup vegetable oil
- 3 tablespoons milk

Make the dough. Pat or roll the dough into flat cakes. If children help you prepare the bread, divide the dough among the children. Direct them to pat the dough or roll it with small rolling pins or olive jars. Prick the flat cakes with forks. Bake in an oven at 475° for six minutes or until brown around the edges.

Jesus Is Baptized

Matthew 3:1-17

Lesson Goals

- Tell what message John the Baptist preached.
- Tell why Jesus said He should be baptized.
- Begin to memorize the names of Jesus' twelve apostles.
- Tell what it means to follow Jesus.
- Demonstrate times and ways to follow Jesus.

Memory Block
Twelve apostles: Peter, Andrew, James, John, Philip, Bartholo-mew, Matthew, Thomas, Thaddaeus, Simon, James, Judas

▼ Bible Search ▲

John gave people an important message to help them get ready to follow Jesus. Let's find John's message in the Bible.

Children will find Matthew 3:2 in their Bibles and work together to complete the Bible Search page. Give a copy of page 77 to each child. Guide the children to find the book of Matthew in the table of contents of their Bibles. Locate the page the book begins on, then the big 3 for the chapter and the small 2 for the verse. Slowly read the verse as children follow along. Help the children follow the directions on the page to complete the puzzle and write John's message on the bottom of the page.

Who helped people get ready to follow Jesus? What message did he give the people? What does *repent* mean? (tell God you're sorry for wrong things you've done and promise to change and do right things)

Purpose
Tell what message John the Baptist preached.

Materials
Bibles
copies of page 77
pencils

▼ Bible Story ▲

Before class, bend the wire into a stick figure. In the loaf pan of water, show how people in Bible times were typically baptized by bending their knees and going forward under the water. Show how we typically do it today. If you have a video of someone being baptized, show it to the children.

Whether you are baptized forward or backward isn't important. But your reason for being baptized is important. Listen to see why Jesus was baptized.

Purpose
Tell why Jesus said He should be baptized.

Materials
a chenille wire
a loaf pan of water
a video of someone being baptized (optional)

"Jesus Is Baptized"

The desert is a lonely, wilderness place. Usually no people are there. But a man named John wanted to be in the desert. John wore unusual clothes made of camel's hair. He fastened a leather belt around his waist and he wore sandals on his feet. Out in the desert, John ate unusual food: locusts and wild honey. And, out in the desert John had an unusual job. He spoke God's message: "Repent."

When John preached, the desert wasn't lonely anymore. Crowds of people came out of Judea, Jerusalem, and the area around the Jordan River. They came and went. They listened and thought about what John said. He told them, "You must change." People who decided to change said, "We have done wrong. We are sorry." Then John baptized them in the Jordan River. They walked down the river bank right into the water. John helped them go down under the water and come safely back up. Dripping wet, they may have felt like singing to God right there in that wilderness place.

In the crowd of people coming and going, Pharisees and Sadducees also came to see what was happening. Their flowing robes and somber faces made them look important to the people in the crowd. But John wasn't fooled. God helped John see that these men were only pretending to do what was right. John gave them a very stern message.

"You are snakes. You talk about doing right, but you never change. Show you want to do right by the things you do. Someone more important than me is coming. He will know you are only pretending to do right."

John was talking about Jesus. Jesus had been living in Galilee. Jesus came all the way to the Jordan River for John to baptize Him. But Jesus had never done anything wrong. John had done wrong things, so John said, "I need to be baptized by you." Jesus still wanted John to baptize Him because it was the right thing to do. So John agreed.

When Jesus came up from the water, God showed He was pleased. Heaven opened and God sent His Spirit, in the shape of a dove, down onto Jesus. A voice from Heaven spoke, "This is my Son and I love Him. I am very pleased with Him." Jesus was not like the Pharisees and Sadducees. He didn't just talk about doing right. Jesus did what was right.

Seat the children in four groups to represent the people in the story: John, crowd, Pharisees and Sadducees, Jesus. The group(s) whose name answers a question should stand and give the answer. Add more questions if time allows.

- **Who preached, "Repent!"?** (John)
- **Who did not change?** (Pharisees and Sadducees)
- **Who always did right and still was baptized?** (Jesus)
- **Who did John baptize?** (Jesus, crowd)
- **Who changed and was baptized?** (crowd)
- **Who came to the desert?** (crowd, Pharisees and Sadducees, Jesus)

Summary questions: **What message did John preach?** (You must change. Be sorry for the wrong things you have done. Start doing right.) **Why did John not want to baptize Jesus?** (Jesus had never done anything wrong.) **Why did Jesus want John to baptize Him?** (It was the right thing to do.)

▼ Bible Verse ▲

Purpose
Begin to memorize the names of Jesus' twelve apostles.

Materials
copies of pages 78 and 79 for each child
scissors
crayons or colored pencils
clear tape
twelve short cardboard tubes for each child
fabric scraps and yarn (optional)
copy of "Jesus' Followers" song from page 60

Before the session, learn the "Jesus' Followers" song from page 60. If possible, record the song onto an audio cassette or CD to play for the children.

Jesus chose twelve followers (called apostles) to work for God with Him.

Guide the children to cut out the twelve figures from pages 78 and 79. Tape each figure to a cardboard tube. As the children listen to the song "Jesus' Followers," they can line up the figures in the order they are named. Then give the children time to practice pronouncing their names.

If you have time, children may color the clothes or add cloth tunics (a rectangular piece of cloth with a slit cut for the head); tie the waist with yarn.

How many men did Jesus choose to be His apostles? Let's say their names. (Teacher says one, children repeat it.) **Let's take turns naming the apostles.** (As a child names one, turn the figure around. Continue until all names have been said. Repeat.)

Option: Instead of using cardboard tubes, provide 12 index cards for each child. Children will color the figures from pages 78 and 79 and glue them to the index cards.

▼ Bible and Me ▲

Following Jesus means doing what He said or doing what He did. Bible verses can help us know what Jesus said to do. Let's make up a cheer that helps us remember ways to follow Jesus.

Help the children come up with a cheer about following Jesus and make up hand motions. An example follows:

"F (pump one fist in air), O (pump other fist in air)

L (pump both fists in air), L (pump one fist out beside body)

O (pump other fist out), W (pump both fists out).

Fol- (cross one arm on chest) low (cross other arm on chest)

Je- (put on fist up in air) sus (put other fist up in air)."

Name a way to follow Jesus each time the cheer is done. The children can use the pictures on page 76 to give them ideas and Scriptures.

What does it mean to follow Jesus? Let's do a cheer about what it means. What is one way to do what Jesus said? What is one way to do what Jesus did? How can we know what Jesus said or did? (Learn Bible verses.)

Purpose
Tell what it means to follow Jesus.

Materials
copies of page 76

▼ Bible Project ▲

Print the following verses on large pieces of poster board: Ephesians 6:1; Philippians 2:14; Ephesians 4:25; Hebrews 13:16; Luke 10:36, 37; Matthew 6:9. You will need one verse for every 4-6 children. Adjust the number of verses to the number of children in your class. You may repeat verses if necessary.

John's message helped people get ready to follow Jesus. In the next few weeks we will learn about some Bible people who followed Jesus and some ways we can follow Jesus. Following Jesus means doing what Jesus asks us to do or behaving in the way Jesus would behave. We are going to create mini-dramas to show how Bible verses help us remember what Jesus says is right.

Assign an adult leader to guide each group of 4-6 children. Give each group a poster board with a Scripture verse on it and paper and pencils. Over the next four lessons, each group will create and present a mini-drama that illustrates that way to follow Jesus. Suggested emphasis of each verse: Ephesians 6:1—obey parents; Philippians 2:14—use kind words; Ephesians 4:25—tell the truth; Hebrews 13:16—share; Luke 10:36, 37—help; Matthew 6:9—pray.

This week, each group should find and read the verse in their Bibles and decide a situation to act out that demonstrates following Jesus as the verse says. If you wish, use the suggestions for the mini-dramas on page 60. Provide needed props.

Purpose
Demonstrate times and ways to follow Jesus.

Materials
materials to help the children create and dramatize "following" situations (toys to share, trash bag to help take out trash, dishes to set on table, and so on)
paper and pencils
large pieces of poster board
markers

▼ Bible Sharing ▲

Consider having your snack in a different room or part of the building so the children can play a game on the way.

Following Jesus means doing what Jesus said or doing what He did. Think of one way you can follow Jesus. Then think of an action to go with it. For example, helping my mother is a way to follow Jesus, and I can help like this (pretend to rake.) **We're going to play "Follow the Leader."**

Whoever is the leader does a "following" action and everyone else follows. Allow the children to take the game on the road (throughout the building, if possible) to the room where the snack is prepared. Close with a prayer about following Jesus.

Purpose
Share how Jesus wants you to follow Him.

Materials
a snack of crackers and honey

Jesus Is Tempted

Matthew 4:1-11

Memory Block
Twelve apostles: Peter, Andrew, James, John, Philip, Bartholomew, Matthew, Thomas, Thaddaeus, Simon, James, Judas

Lesson Goals
- Tell what helped Jesus do right.
- Name times Jesus did what was wrong.
- Memorize the names of Jesus' twelve apostles.
- Tell the difference between examples of following and not following Jesus.
- Demonstrate times and ways to follow Jesus.

▼ Bible Search ▲

Knowing Bible verses helped Jesus do right. Let's practice finding the verses Jesus used.

Give a copy of page 81 to each child. Guide the children to find Matthew 4:4. Slowly read the verse as children follow along. Then read from page 81 what the verse means. Repeat this procedure for the next two verses. Match the verse to the picture that shows what the verse means.

What helped Jesus do right? (knowing Bible verses) **Make a guess of how many times Jesus did right.** (Children can guess a number. Jesus did right every time. Jesus never did wrong.)

Purpose
Tell what helped Jesus to do right.

Materials
copies of page 81
Bibles
pencils

▼ Bible Story ▲

Before class, print the underlined sentences in the story on index cards. Keep the cards to use during the review.

Hold a Bible in your hand as you tell the story. Each time in the story Jesus says a Bible verse, hold a Bible near your head.

What are some Bible verses you have learned? Let children share verses they have memorized. **When Jesus needed to know what the Bible said, He didn't have to look in His Bible. He had learned many verses, so His Bible was in His head. Listen to see how that helped Jesus.**

Purpose
Name times Jesus did what was wrong.

Materials
Bible
six index cards
marker

"Jesus Is Tempted"

Forty days and forty nights is a long time to be hungry. That's how long Jesus was out in the desert without any food. The desert is a wilderness place. The Spirit of God had led Jesus out to the desert so the devil could try to get Jesus to do wrong. And now, forty days later, Jesus' body was weak and very hungry.

The devil knew Jesus needed food. So that's what the devil used to try to get Jesus to do wrong. The devil said, "If you are the Son of God, tell these rocks to become bread." The devil wanted Jesus to use God's power to make life easy instead of using God's power to do God's work. Jesus was weak. Jesus was tired. Jesus was alone. It would have been easy to do wrong. But Jesus also knew God would help Him remember Bible verses He had learned. One verse from Deuteronomy helped Him do right. Jesus told the devil this verse.

"A person does not live only by eating food." That verse meant doing what God says is the best way to live, even if it means not having everything you want. Saying that verse aloud must have given Jesus a surge of strength to keep defeating the devil.

The devil didn't give up easily. He took Jesus to Jerusalem, the holy city. Up on a high place of the temple, the devil asked Jesus to jump off. <u>The devil wanted Jesus to see if God's angels would catch Jesus.</u> Jesus knew about angels. Wouldn't it be fun to try it just once? Jesus also knew what God said in Deuteronomy in the Bible. "<u>Don't test God.</u>" That meant we should not demand that God show His power for selfish reasons. This verse helped Jesus choose right again.

The devil tried a third time. He took Jesus up to a high mountain. He showed Jesus all the countries of the world and the great things in them. The devil said, "<u>I'll give all this to you if you will bow down and show that you think I'm better than God.</u>" How would it feel if everything great in the world could belong to you? It sounded exciting, but Jesus knew it was one of the devil's tricks.

"Go away," Jesus commanded. Then Jesus spoke another verse He knew. The verse helped Jesus to do right again. "<u>It is written in the Scriptures, 'You must worship the Lord your God. Serve only Him!</u>'"

Three times the devil tried to get Jesus to do wrong. Each time the devil failed because Jesus remembered a Bible verse that helped Him choose right. God had helped Jesus remember these verses. Then, after the devil left, God's angels came to help and care for Jesus.

Use the six cards on which you have printed the underlined sentences from the story. Ask the children to put the six cards in order. Then the children can read the cards as they dramatize the story. Different pairs of children can dramatize each temptation.

Summary questions: **What helped Jesus to do right? How many times did Jesus do wrong?**

▼ Bible Verse ▲

Jesus chose twelve apostles to work for God with Him. These men wanted to learn what Jesus would teach them. They wanted to do what Jesus did and obey what Jesus told them to do.

In a random group, set up the twelve apostles figures made in Lesson 9. As the children listen to (or sing) the song "Jesus' Followers," they can arrange the figures in order, into the four groups the song suggests.
  1—Peter, Andrew, James, John
  2—Philip and Bartholomew
  3—Matthew, Thomas, Thaddaeus
  4—Simon, James and Judas
Continue to sing the song (or do it as a spoken rhythm). Each time, remove one of the figures. When the large group begins to memorize the twelve names, take turns doing the song (or spoken rhythm) in small groups for more review.

Purpose
Memorize the names of Jesus' twelve apostles

Materials
audio CD or cassette recording of the song "Jesus' Followers" from page 60
CD or cassette player
a set of Jesus' apostles made in Lesson 9 (pages 78 and 79)

▼ Bible and Me ▲

Following Jesus means doing what He said or doing what He did. Let's see which of the pictures on our page show children who are following Jesus.

The three situations (on page 80) each have two possible endings. Guide the children to choose which ending shows a child following Jesus and tell how they know that child is following Jesus. Check the Bible verse to see what Jesus would do. Use the following questions with each situation.

What is happening in the first situation? What does the first answer show? What does the second answer show? Which picture shows the child following Jesus? How can you tell? (The child did what Jesus said to do.) **What is the difference between following Jesus and not following Jesus in that situation?** (One picture shows the child doing what the Bible/Jesus says; one picture does not.) **What can help you do right?** (knowing Bible verses)

Option: Children can work in three groups to act out the situations on page 80, showing the child following and not following Jesus. The group can decide which situation showed the child following Jesus.

Purpose
Tell the difference between examples of following and not following Jesus.

Materials
copies of page 80
crayons

▼ Bible Project ▲

Jesus used Bible verses to help Him do right. Our mini-dramas with Bible verses will help us remember what Jesus says is right.

Each group should have an idea for a mini-drama that emphasizes one of the following verses: Ephesians 6:1—obey parents; Philippians 2:14—use kind words; Ephesians 4:25—tell the truth; Hebrews 13:16—share; Luke 10:36, 37—help; Matthew 6:9—pray.

This week, students should complete a rough draft of their drama and come up with a final list of needed props.

Purpose
Demonstrate times and ways to follow Jesus.

Materials
materials to help the children create and dramatize "following" situations (see Lesson 9)
printed verses on poster board from Lesson 9

▼ Bible Sharing ▲

Serve the snack of hard rolls to remind children of Jesus' first temptation (to turn the stones to bread).

After the snack, use the Bible to help the children recite Bible verses they have memorized. (For children who are learning about Jesus for the first time, prepare slips of paper with one verse from the Bible Project section printed on each. Put these slips in the Bible.)

Display the Bible. **You can put this Bible on your head, in your hand, under your arm, and carry it with you all the time. But knowing what the Bible says, keeping the Bible in your mind, is the best!** Hold the Bible and recite a verse that helps us do right. Then give the Bible to a child. Encourage each child to recite a verse or part of a verse he has learned; or let him pull a slip of paper out of the Bible and read a verse about following.

Purpose
Share how Jesus wants you to follow Him.

Materials
a Bible that can be handled by the children
small individual hard rolls (with margarine or jelly)

Jesus Invites Fishermen to Follow Him | LESSON 11

Matthew 4:18-22; Mark 1:16-20; Luke 5:1-11

Lesson Goals

- Name four men who were fisherman.
- Tell what Jesus invited the fisherman to do.
- Recite the names of Jesus' twelve apostles.
- Tell why we follow Jesus.
- Demonstrate times and ways to follow Jesus.

> **Memory Block**
> Twelve apostles: Peter, Andrew, James, John, Philip, Bartholomew, Matthew, Thomas, Thaddaeus, Simon, James, Judas

▼ Bible Search ▲

There were many ways to earn a living in Bible times. One way was to be a fisherman. Let's read about fishing in the Bible times and find the names of four men who were fishermen.

Distribute page 83. Read the descriptions of each picture as the children follow along. Then guide the children to find the names of the fishermen in Matthew 4:18, 21. Guide the children to find the book of Matthew in the table of contents of their Bibles. Locate the page the book begins on, then the big 4 for the chapter and the small 18 for the first verse. Children can write the names of the fishermen on the bottom of page 83.

Guide the children to use the information on the page and the net you brought to demonstrate Bible times fishing (pretend to be the four fishermen).

Who were the four fishermen? (Simon, Andrew, James, and John) **Show us how they earned money to buy food and clothes.**

> **Purpose**
> Name four men who were fishermen.
>
> **Materials**
> Bibles
> copies of page 83
> pencils
> props for Bible times fishing (badminton or volleyball net, construction-paper fish)

▼ Bible Story ▲

Print the review questions at the end of the story on the paper fish and put them in a net.

Display the fishing pole and allow children to practice casting with the pole or display the picture of someone fishing. **People in the Bible caught fish, but not like this. What did they do?** Ask the children to report what they learned from the Bible Search activity. **Listen for something else the four fishermen did.**

> **Purpose**
> Tell what Jesus invited the fishermen to do.
>
> **Materials**
> a fishing pole or a picture of someone fishing, a net (net used in Bible Search, or nylon netting or plastic fruit bag)
> paper fish
> a marker

"Jesus Invites Fishermen to Follow Him"

Lake Galilee is a great place for fishing. My name is Andrew. My brother Simon and I, and our partners James and John, were experts at fishing. All four of us were fishermen until the day Jesus came and used our boat. He didn't take our boat away. I'll tell you what He did.

We had fished all night with our nets and boats. What a waste! When the sun came up, our nets were empty but our job was not done. Weeds, sticks and other things get caught in your net when you drag it through water. If you don't keep your net clean, it will break. Keeping the nets clean was not fun, but we still had to do it.

That day, there was someone to listen to while we worked. Jesus was speaking God's message near us on the shore. So many people wanted to hear Him that they were pushing and pressing to get closer and closer. He would have backed right into the water if He hadn't climbed into Simon's boat. In the boat Jesus could sit down, the people could see Him, and He continued to speak.

When Jesus was done, He said to Simon, "Take your boat into deep water. If you will put your nets in the water, you will catch some fish." Well, how could Jesus know where the fish were? He wasn't a fisherman. Simon explained to Jesus how hard we worked fishing all night long. But Simon also wanted to do what Jesus had told him. So we rowed to the deep water with Jesus.

We hoisted the net over the side of the boat. The ropes and net slipped quietly into the water, then, in a moment, the net started to pull away from me. It was getting heavier and heavier. It was getting away. "Help!" we called to James and John. "Come quick!" James and John arrived not a moment too soon. We struggled to haul the net in, but there were too many fish for our boat. In fact, there were too many fish for both boats. Our boats were so full of fish we were almost sinking.

What had happened? This was not a normal catch of fish. It had something to do with Jesus and we were scared. Simon spoke what he felt, "Go away from me Lord. I am a sinful man!" All of us were in awe of what Jesus had done.

But Jesus told us, "Don't be afraid." He wanted us to go with Him. He said we would fish for men. Straining at the oars, we started back to shore. We thought about what Jesus said, and all four of us decided to follow Jesus. We left our nets. We left our boats so we could follow Him. We wanted to go where Jesus went, do what Jesus did, and obey what Jesus asked. We didn't wait for a second invitation. We followed Jesus.

From a net, let the children pull out paper fish with questions about the story.
- **Name two fishermen.** (Simon, Andrew, James, or John)
- **Why did Simon call for help?** (The net was too full of fish. Their boats were almost sinking.)
- **What was Jesus doing on shore?** (teaching the people; speaking God's message)
- **What did Jesus invite the men to do?** (Follow Him; fish for men.)
- **What did Jesus tell Simon to do?** (Take his boat into the deep water to fish. Follow Him.)

Summary question: **What did the fishermen decide to do?** (They left their fish and their nets and followed Jesus.)

▼ Bible Verse ▲

Jesus chose twelve apostles to work for God with Him. These men wanted to learn what Jesus would teach them. They wanted to do what Jesus did and obey what Jesus told them to do.

Display the apostles from pages 78 and 79. Speak in rhythm (or sing) the song "Jesus' Followers" (from page 60) to review their names. Then give each child a copy of page 82. As you read the phrases, have the children match each word card to the picture of the apostle.

Who can say the names of the twelve apostles? Which apostle used to be a tax collector? (Matthew) Continue asking questions about each apostle, using the information on page 82.

Purpose
Recite the names of Jesus' twelve apostles.

Materials
copies of page 82
set of apostles from pages 78 and 79
pencils

▼ Bible and Me ▲

Following Jesus means doing what He said or doing what He did. Sometimes it's easy. Sometimes it's hard. Even when it's hard, we still want to follow Jesus. Let's learn why we follow Jesus.

The children will take turns reading a situation on page 84 and spinning the paper clip (as shown) to learn some ways and reasons for why we follow Jesus. When the paper clip stops on section 3, the child will give her own reason why we should follow Jesus. On sections 1 and 2, the child reads the answer given.

What does it mean to follow Jesus? How can you know what to do to follow Jesus? (Bible verses.) **What are some ways to follow Jesus?** (Children can name the situations on page 84 and name similar ways they follow Jesus.) **What might make it hard to follow Jesus? Why do we follow Jesus?**

Purpose
Tell why we follow Jesus.

Materials
Bibles
copies of page 84
pencils
paper clips

▼ Bible Project ▲

Jesus invited four fishermen to follow Him. We can follow Him, too. Our mini-dramas with Bible verses will help us remember to do what Jesus said or did.

Each group should have a rough idea/draft for their drama. For this session, work on making props, choosing parts, and making a final draft of the mini-dramas.

Note: Investigate possible groups for whom the children can present their mini-dramas. Encourage the children to work hard so they can demonstrate for others these ways and times to follow Jesus.

Purpose
Demonstrate times and ways to follow Jesus.

Materials
materials to help the children create and dramatize "following" situations
the printed verses prepared for Lesson 9

▼ Bible Sharing ▲

Before class, print one of the six Bible verse references on each fish (Ephesians 6:1; Philippians 2:14; Ephesians 4:25; Hebrews 13:16; Luke 10:36, 37; Matthew 6:9). Put the fish in a net.

Gather the children together on the floor and let them snack while you introduce the activity.

Following Jesus means doing what He said or doing what He did. Sometimes it's easy. Sometimes it's hard. Even when it's hard, we still want to follow Jesus. That's why we want to learn Bible verses that will remind us to do right.

Distribute paper fish and ask children to look at the verse reference. At a signal, children should get up and find others who have their same verse. Once in the verse group, children can work together to learn the verse and say (or read) it with motions. Give groups three minutes to work; then ask everyone to share the verses.

Purpose
Share how Jesus wants you to follow Him.

Materials
fish crackers for a snack
a construction-paper fish for each child
net (used in Bible Search and Bible Story)

Memory Block
Twelve apostles: Peter, Andrew, James, John, Philip, Bartholomew, Matthew, Thomas, Thaddaeus, Simon, James, Judas

Lesson Goals
- Tell what Jesus did before choosing twelve apostles.
- Tell what Jesus' apostles did.
- Recite the names of Jesus' twelve apostles.
- Tell what makes it hard to follow Jesus.
- Demonstrate times and ways to follow Jesus.

Purpose
Tell what Jesus did before choosing twelve apostles.

Materials
Bibles
copies of page 85
colored pencils or crayons
clear tape

▼ Bible Search ▲

Jesus knew it was important to pray. He prayed about making right choices. One time He prayed all night before He chose His twelve apostles.

Guide children to find the book of Luke in the table of contents of their Bibles. Locate the page the book begins on, then the big 6 for the chapter and the small 12 for the verse. Read the verse while the children follow along. Then distribute copies of page 85 and clear tape. Have the children write their prayer, then cut, fold, and tape together the prayer reminder. If they have time, the children can color their prayer reminders.

What did Jesus do before He chose His twelve apostles? (He prayed all night.) **What is one reason it is so important to pray?** (Ask God to help you make right choices.)

Purpose
Tell what Jesus' apostles did.

Materials
a watch or clock with movable hands
copies of page 87
pencils

▼ Bible Story ▲

Display the watch or clock. **What is the longest time you know of someone praying to God? How long did Jesus pray before He chose His twelve apostles?** Ask children to report what they found in Bible Search—Jesus prayed all night. Let children count with you as you move the hands of the clock to show how long Jesus' prayer might have been. Begin at 9 or 10 at night and move the hands to 6 or 7 in the morning.

"Jesus Chooses Twelve Apostles"

Where do you like to be in the spring when the leaves begin to turn green? One spring, I was under a fig tree and that's where Jesus saw me. My name is Nathanael, and Jesus saw me even before I saw Him. That spring, Jesus was traveling up and down the Jordan River to begin His work for God. Wherever he stopped, people listened. Some decided to follow along with Jesus so they could learn more.

My friend Philip and I were up in Bethsaida when Jesus found us. When Jesus invited Philip to follow Him, Philip couldn't wait to tell me. There I was, under that fig tree, when Philip came flying up to me. His words spilled out of his mouth, "Remember what Moses wrote in the law about a man who was coming, and the prophets also wrote about him. We have found him. He is Jesus, the son of Joseph. He is from Nazareth."

Well, yes, I did remember what Moses and the prophets had written. But the part about Nazareth sounded like a joke. I told Philip, "Nazareth! Can anything good come from Nazareth?" But Philip didn't give up. He persuaded me to come and see. Soon I could see I was wrong about Nazareth. When I talked to Jesus, I knew that this great teacher was the Son of God.

On another day, Jesus was teaching down by the lake. Walking along the sandy shore, He saw a tax collector's shelter ahead. Most people stayed away from tax collectors, but not Jesus. He walked straight up to that man. Levi was his name. Levi must have known who Jesus was. When Jesus invited Levi to follow Him, Levi stood up, left everything, and went with Jesus. Wherever Jesus went, people decided to follow Him. Jesus decided this was the time to choose some men to help Him do His work for God. These men would be His apostles. Choosing these men was so important that Jesus talked to God about it first. He picked His way up a mountain to find a quiet place to pray, alone. Then He prayed, all night.

As the sun lit the early morning sky, Jesus was ready. He called all of us who were following Him and explained He was going to choose some apostles. The apostles would travel with Jesus and preach in other places. They would have power to heal sick people and force demons to come out of people. From all of the followers, Jesus chose twelve of us (together, sing or say the names): Peter, Andrew, James, John, Philip, Bartholomew, Matthew (Levi), Thomas, Thaddaeus, Simon, James and Judas. Together, the twelve of us helped Jesus bring God's message to everyone who would listen.

Give each child a copy of page 87. Together complete the page by filling in the names of the twelve apostles.

Summary questions: **What did Jesus do before choosing the twelve apostles?** (He prayed all night.) **What job did Jesus give to the twelve apostles?** (They helped bring God's message to anyone who would listen.)

▼ Bible Verse ▲

Jesus chose twelve apostles to work for God with Him. These men wanted to learn what Jesus would teach them. They wanted to do what Jesus did and obey what Jesus told them to do.

Speak in rhythm or sing the song "Jesus' Followers" (page 60) to review the names of the apostles. Give each child a set of apostle pictures from pages 78 and 79. As you read the description cards from page 83, children hold up the picture and/or name of the apostle that matches.

For more review, play Tic-Tac-Follow. With masking tape, mark a tic-tac-toe playing surface on the floor or table. Set one apostle figure (made from pages 78 and 79) in each of the nine squares. Give each team Xs and Os. If a team can name the apostle and tell one thing about him, they can put their X or O in that spot. Three Xs or three Os in a row wins a round.

What did Jesus' apostles do? Who can sing (or speak) the names of the twelve apostles? Which apostle… (for each time, fill in with information from page 82).

Purpose
Recite the names of Jesus' twelve apostles.

Materials
copies of pages 78, 79, and 83 (used in Lesson 11)
materials to play Tic-Tac-Follow (optional): masking tape, apostles figures from pages 78 and 79, Xs and Os

▼ Bible and Me ▲

Following Jesus means doing what He said or doing what He did. Sometimes it's easy. Sometimes it's hard. Even when it's hard, we still want to follow Jesus. Remembering Bible verses and praying about what we do will help us follow Jesus.

Distribute page 86. Give each child a turn to choose a situation on the page and demonstrate what a follower of Jesus would do.

What is happening? What could you do to follow Jesus? What would make it hard to follow Jesus? What did Jesus do in hard situations? Let's pretend you are the person in the situation. What could you say to God to let Him hear what you are thinking and feeling?

Option: To make the activity more challenging, print the following Bible verses on index cards. Children can find the verses in their Bibles and decide which verses will help them do right in each situation on page 86. Verses: Ephesians 6:1—obey parents; Philippians 2:14—use kind words; Ephesians 4:25—tell the truth; Hebrews 13:16—share; Luke 10:36, 37—help; Matthew 6:9—pray.

Purpose
Tell what makes it hard to follow Jesus.

Materials
copies of page 86

▼ Bible Project ▲

Jesus chose twelve apostles to work for God with Him. These men wanted to do what Jesus did and obey what Jesus told them to do. We can follow Him, too. Our mini-dramas with Bible verses will help us remember to do what Jesus said and did.

Each group should have a finished copy of their mini-drama and needed props. Work on memorizing the Bible verse central to the mini-drama and practicing mini-dramas as much as possible. Next week is dress rehearsal for all groups.

Note: If you have not already done so, plan a time for the children to present their mini-dramas. Encourage the children to work hard so they can demonstrate for others ways and times to follow Jesus.

Purpose
Demonstrate times and ways to follow Jesus.

Materials
props for mini-dramas
the printed verses prepared for Lesson 9

▼ Bible Sharing ▲

Gather the children together on the floor and eat fig snacks. Ask the children to tell which follower of Jesus was sitting under the fig tree. (Nathanael) Choose one or more of the songs to listen to as the children eat. Or do the "Follow" cheer from Lesson 9, Bible and Me. Between times of listening to the songs or doing the cheer, ask the children to tell something about one of Jesus' apostles or share a way to follow Jesus. Set the timer and share as many as possible in one minute between songs or cheers.

Close the session with prayer. If possible, allow the children to choose a spot in the room to be "alone" (like Jesus on the mountain). Guide the prayer time with simple sentences about following Jesus. "Jesus, I want to follow You because . . ." "Jesus, I will follow what You did by . . ." "Jesus, I will follow what You said by . . ."

Purpose
Share how Jesus wants you to follow Him.

Materials
a snack of dried figs or raisins, or cookies with fig filling
a kitchen timer
audio CD or cassette with songs about following Jesus
CD or cassette player (optional)

Jesus and God's House

John 2:13-16

Lesson Goals
- Tell what Jesus did when He came to the temple.
- Tell why Jesus forced the men and animals out of the temple.
- Recite the names of Jesus' twelve apostles.
- Report times and ways they have followed Jesus.
- Demonstrate times and ways to follow Jesus.

Memory Block
Twelve apostles: Peter, Andrew, James, John, Philip, Bartholomew, Matthew, Thomas, Thaddaeus, Simon, James, Judas

▼ Bible Search ▲

One day in the temple, Jesus showed He was angry because the people in the temple were doing wrong. They were not worshiping God.

Guide the children to find the book of John in the table of contents of their Bibles. Locate the page the book begins on, then the big 2 for the chapter and the small 14 for the first verse. Slowly read verses 14-16 while the children follow along. Distribute page 88. Guide the children to read the sentences with you, cross out the wrong sentences, and number the rest of the sentences in story order. Solve the puzzle to tell why Jesus was angry.

What did Jesus do? (He made men who were selling animals and making money leave the temple.) **Why did Jesus make the men leave the temple?** (The temple was a place to worship God, not to make money. The men were not worshiping God.)

Purpose
Tell what Jesus did when He came to the temple.

Materials
Bibles
copies of page 88
pencils

▼ Bible Story ▲

Before class, make a "whip" from 12-15 pieces of 24-inch-long yarn. Knot the yarn at one end and again in the middle, so it looks like a whip. Prepare index cards with review questions.

What things do we use to do spring cleaning? Display the dust cloth or furniture polish. Allow children to suggest other products; then display the "whip." **Listen to see what kind of spring cleaning Jesus did in the temple with one of these.**

"Jesus and God's House"

From far away places, people traveled to Jerusalem for the Passover celebration. Jesus went, too. Maybe He thought about the Passover when He was twelve years old. That year He had stayed in the temple to listen and ask questions. Even then, He knew that God was His Father and that He must do His Father's work. Now, as Jesus brought God's message to people, people listened to Him and asked Him their questions.

At the end of their trip to Jerusalem, people got ready for special things they did at a Passover. They sacrificed a lamb and ate a special meal. For a whole week they ate bread made without yeast and did not work. Children asked, "Why are we doing these things?" And fathers explained how each part of the Passover helped them remember what God had done to bring His people out of Egypt.

But when Jesus entered the temple, He didn't hear people talking about what

Purpose
Tell why Jesus forced the men and animals out of the temple.

Materials
dust cloth or can of furniture polish
12-15 pieces of 24-inch-long yarn
index cards
marker
tape

God had done. Instead, the sounds of flapping wings, lowing cattle, and bleating sheep roared in His ears. Coins clanked as people crowded around the money tables in the courtyard. The temple was not built for buying and selling. It was built for worshiping God. People were not thinking about God. They were thinking about making money by selling animals right in the middle of the temple court. Jesus knew these selfish people were not interested in how the Passover could help them remember God.

Without a word, Jesus took cords and made them into a whip. (*Demonstrate whip.*) Moving across the temple court, He flung the whip back and forth to drive those dirty, noisy animals out. The animals bumped into each other as they crowded to get away from the whip. Oh, the noise! The owners of the animals must have been angry. But Jesus was angry, too. He turned over the tables of the people who were exchanging money, and coins rolled everywhere. You can imagine greedy people trying to grab some coins to stuff into their money bags. Then Jesus turned to those who were selling doves and spoke clearly, "Get these out of here. How dare you make my Father's house a place for buying and selling!" No one argued with Jesus.

Jesus loved His Father, and He loved being in the temple to worship His Father. Jesus did not allow people to use the temple for doing what was wrong. Instead, He helped clean out the temple so people could celebrate the Passover and remember how great God is.

Tape prepared index cards to pieces of yarn in the whip. Print one of the following questions on each card. As you shake the whip, the children can take turns pulling off a question to answer.

- **Why was Jesus going to Jerusalem?** (for the Passover celebration)
- **Had Jesus been to a Passover before?** (He went when He was twelve years old.)
- **What did people do at a Passover?** (sacrificed a lamb; ate a special meal; ate bread made without yeast)
- **What did people remember at a Passover?** (remembered how God brought His people out of Egypt)
- **What did Jesus see in the temple?** (people making money by buying and selling animals)
- **What did Jesus do in the temple?** (used a whip to drive out the animals and the people selling them; turned over the tables of the money changers)

Summary question: **Why did Jesus force the men and animals out of the temple?** (They were more interested in making money than in worshiping God.)

▼ Bible Verse ▲

Jesus chose twelve apostles to work for God with Him. These men listened and learned what Jesus taught them. They learned to do what Jesus did, and they worked hard to obey what Jesus told them to do.

Speak in rhythm or sing the song "Jesus' Followers" (page 60) to review the names of the apostles. If children need more review, play Tic-Tac-Follow. With masking tape, mark a tic-tac-toe playing surface on the floor or table. Set one of the apostle figures (pages 78 and 79) in each of the nine squares. Give each team their Xs and Os. If a team can name an apostle and tell one thing about him, they can put their X or O in his spot.

What did Jesus' apostles do? Who can sing (or say in rhythm) by themselves the names of the twelve apostles? Which apostle... (for each man, fill in with information from page 82)?

Purpose
Recite the name of Jesus' twelve apostles.

Materials
apostle figures from pages 78 and 79
Xs and Os
masking tape

▼ Bible and Me ▲

Make a game using the poster board. Divide the poster board in six sections. In each section, print a way to follow Jesus and a Scripture telling about that way to follow. Obey (Ephesians 6:1); Be kind (Philippians 2:14); Share (Hebrews 13:16); Help (Luke 10:36, 37); Tell the truth (Ephesians 4:25); Pray (Matthew 6:9).

Following Jesus means doing what He said or doing what He did. Sometimes it's easy. Sometimes it's hard. Even when it's hard, we still want to follow Jesus. Remembering Bible verses and praying about what we will do can help.

Play a game to help the children report times and ways they have followed Jesus. Lay the poster board you prepared on the floor and give each child a turn to close his eyes and drop a piece of popcorn onto the board. For each section, the children will report a real way or a real time they did (or could) follow Jesus. Each time someone reports how she followed Jesus, she can autograph that section. Try to continue until every section has at least two autographs.

What does it mean to follow Jesus? Why do we follow Jesus? How do you know if you are following Jesus or not? Each time a child drops popcorn on the circle, ask: **What is a way you followed by... (obeying, praying, telling the truth, helping, sharing, being kind)?**

Purpose
Report times and ways they have followed Jesus.

Materials
poster board
markers
popped popcorn

▼ Bible Project ▲

Jesus knew that God's house was a place for worshiping God. Perhaps He knew that because of the Bible verses He had learned. (In Isaiah 56:7, God's house is called a house of prayer.) **We can follow Jesus by learning Bible verses that help us do right. Our mini-dramas will show others how to do what Jesus said and did.**

Each group should be ready for dress rehearsal. List the order of the mini-dramas on a chalkboard or tablet. (If you only have one group, invite parents to come to the dress rehearsal.) Allow time to assemble props. As the dramas are presented, encourage the audience to listen with respect and applaud each performance.

Announce arrangements you have made for the children to present their drama; distribute prepared permission forms if necessary.

Purpose
Demonstrate times and ways to follow Jesus.

Materials
props for the mini-dramas
verses from Lesson 9
chalkboard and chalk or tablet and marker

▼ Bible Sharing ▲

Display the whip used in the Bible Story. Gather the children together on the floor. Give them the matzos bread to eat while you introduce the activity.

The Passover celebration was very special. The bread you are eating is made without yeast, just like the bread Jesus ate the week of Passover. But the most important part of the story today is the fact that Jesus was right. We can follow Jesus by doing what He said or what He did. As we begin to share ways to follow Jesus, I will untie the whip. For each example you give of following Jesus, we will throw one cord away.

Allow children to share as you untie the cords of the whip. Close the session by worshiping God. Sing and pray together.

Purpose
Share how Jesus wants you to follow Him.

Materials
matzos bread (or unleavened bread, recipe on page 60)
whip used in Bible Story

Bible and Me

Look at the pictures.
Name a way to follow Jesus.

Bible Search

- John the Baptist preached.
  He helped people get ready to listen to
  Jesus.

- Find Matthew 3:2 in your Bible.
  Read what John told the people to do.

- Finish the puzzle below.
  Write the letter that comes next in ABC order.

R	S	N	O

C	N	H	M	F

V	Q	N	M	F

R	S	■	Q	S
		A		

C	N	H	M	F

Q	H	F	G	S

- Write the words on the lines.
  This is what John wanted the people to do.

___ ___ ___ ___   ___ ___ ___ ___

___ ___ ___ ___ ___   .

___ ___ ___ ___ ___ ___   .

Bible Verse

Cut apart the pictures of Jesus' followers.
Tape each one to a cardboard tube.
Sing a song to learn the names of Jesus' followers.

Matthew	**Thomas**	**Thaddaeus**
Simon	**Philip**	**Bartholomew**

 UNIT 3, LESSON 9

Bible Verse

(Simon) Peter

James

John

Andrew

James (the less)

Judas

Bible and Me

Look at the first picture in each row.
Then choose another picture that
shows the child following Jesus.
Cross out the picture not chosen.

UNIT 3, LESSON 10

Bible Search

What verses did Jesus learn to help Him do right?

Match each verse to a picture that shows what the verse means.

1. Find Matthew 4:4 in your Bible. This means: live by doing what God says.
   Find a picture that shows a child doing what God says.

2. Find Matthew 4:7 in your Bible. This means: don't ask God to do wrong.
   Find a picture that shows a child asking God to do right.

3. Find Matthew 4:10 in your Bible. This means: worship only God.
   Find a picture that shows a child worshiping God.

Bible Verse

Cut apart word cards.
Match each word card to the
picture of the apostle.

Simon (Peter)
I was a fisherman.
I followed Jesus.
After Jesus went to
Heaven, I was the first
one to preach the
good news.

Andrew
I am Peter's brother.
I was a fisherman.
When I heard John the
Baptist talk about Jesus,
I hurried to tell Peter.

James
My brother John and I
were fishermen with our
father, Zebedee.
We were called "Sons of
Thunder." We left every-
thing to follow Jesus.

John
With my brother James,
I stopped fishing to
follow Jesus. I wrote
several books in the
Bible. I was a special
friend to Jesus.

Philip
When I met Jesus, I
was eager to tell others.
I told my friend
Nathanael about Jesus.
We both followed Him.

Bartholomew
I'm glad Philip told me
about Jesus. (My other
name is Nathanael.)
Jesus told me He saw
me under a tree. I knew
He was the Son of God.

Matthew
I used to be a tax
collector. No one liked
me. But Jesus told me
to follow Him, and I
did. I wrote a book
about Jesus' life.

Thomas
You may know me as
"Doubting Thomas." I was
gone the first time Jesus
appeared to His followers
when He came back alive.
I believed He was Jesus
when I saw His hands and
side.

Thaddaeus
My other name is
Judas, but not Iscariot.
I followed Jesus and
preached the good
news after He came
back alive.

Simon
I was called "the
Zealot." I didn't like
the Romans who rule
our country.
I followed Jesus and
learned about God's
love for all people.

James (the less)
I am called "the less"
because I am younger
than the other James.
No one knows very
much about me, but I
followed Jesus too.

Judas
I took care of the
money for Jesus and the
rest of the apostles. In
the end, I loved money
more than Jesus.
I stopped following
Jesus for money.

 UNIT 3, LESSON 11

Bible Search

Read about fishing in Bible times.

1 Most fishermen used large nets. These had weights all around the edges, as well as a drawstring.

2 The fishermen threw the net out onto the water. They tried to make the net land flat. The weights pulled the edges down into the water.

3 As the net sank, the fishermen pulled the drawstring, closing the net around the fish inside.

Then they pulled up the net, with the fish inside, into the boat.

4 Sometimes the fishermen used even larger nets and pulled them between two boats.

Find Matthew 4:18 in your Bible. Write the names of two fishermen.

_____   _____

Find Matthew 4:21 in your Bible. Write the names of two more fishermen.

_____   _____

© 2004 Standard Publishing. Permission is granted to reproduce this page for ministry purposes only—not for resale.

Bible and Me

Hold a paper clip on the center of the circle with a sharp pencil. Spin the paper clip.

What are some ways to follow Jesus?
Why do we follow Jesus?

Use kind words when someone speaks to you in a mean voice.
Philippians 2:14

Take time to pray when you are in a hurry to eat.
Matthew 6:9

God says we should obey Jesus.
Matthew 17:5

People who follow Jesus will live in Heaven, just like Jesus.
John 14:2, 3

Tell why you think we should follow Jesus.

Use kind words when you really feel like arguing.
Philippians 2:14

Give away your extra cookie instead of keeping it for yourself.
Hebrews 13:16

Fold the prayer reminder on the dotted lines.
Glue the ends together.

Bible Search

Glue here.

Write your prayer to Jesus here.

Jesus' Twelve Apostles

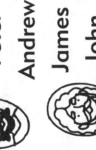
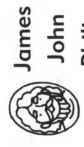
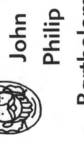

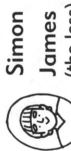

(Simon) Peter
Andrew
James
John
Philip
Bartholomew (Nathanael)
Matthew
Thomas
Thaddaeus
Simon
James (the less)
Judas

Jesus knew it was important to pray.

He prayed about making right choices.

One time He prayed all night before He chose His twelve apostles.

Read about it in Luke 6:12.

Bible and Me

Look at the picture.
What are the children doing?
What could they do to follow Jesus?
What would make it hard to follow Jesus?
What did Jesus do in hard situations?

 Unit 3, Lesson 12

Bible Story

Finish the puzzle about Jesus' apostles.
Use the words in the word bank.

J E S U S
P R A Y E D
T O
G O D

Word Bank

Peter
Andrew
James
John
Philip
Bartholomew
Matthew
Thomas
Thaddaeus
Simon
James
Judas

Bible Search

Find John 2:14-16 in your Bible.
Read the sentences below.
Cross out the wrong sentences.
Number the right sentences
in story order.

Jesus found men selling animals.

Jesus found men praying to God.

Jesus went to the temple.

Jesus went to the palace.

Jesus made the men leave the temple.

Jesus was happy with the men at the temple.

Jesus gave the money to the men.

Jesus turned over the tables with money.

Why did Jesus make the men leave the temple?
Use the first letter of each picture name to finish the puzzle.

Jesus made the men leave the temple because they were not

____ ____ ____ ____   ____ ____ ____ ____   ____ ____

God. They were doing wrong.

Unit Memory Block
"In your lives you must think and act like Christ Jesus. He gave up his place with God and made himself nothing. He was born to be a man and became like a servant" (Philippians 2:5, 7).

Memory Challenge
"Be sure that no one pays back wrong for wrong. But always try to do what is good for each other and for all people" (1 Thessalonians 5:15).

14 Do You Want to Be Great?
Matthew 20:20-28; Mark 10:35-45
James and John wanted to be great. Jesus gave His followers a great idea for how to be great: serve other people.

15 Overcome Evil with Good
Story setting: Matthew 4:25; 5:1, 2, 38-42
If someone bothered Jesus, He did something good to him. Jesus overcame evil with good.

16 Love Your Enemies
Story setting: Matthew 5:43-48
Jesus didn't show love only to people who were nice to Him. If someone acted like an enemy, Jesus showed love and prayed for him.

17 Be a Servant
John 13:1-17; Luke 22:27
Jesus showed His followers how to be great. He washed their feet to show He was willing to be a servant. We have Jesus' attitude when we follow His examples of serving.

By the end of this unit, the leaders and learners will

KNOW Jesus' attitude was "always be a servant."
FEEL Jesus' attitude is best.
DO Follow Jesus by changing their attitudes to be like His.

Unit Value

As children develop, they go through a stage where being the biggest, strongest, or prettiest is what makes them important or great. But that is the opposite of Jesus' attitude. This unit will challenge children to begin to see that Jesus' way of thinking is different. Lesson 1 asks, "Do you want to be great?" If so, you must put on Jesus' attitude of being a servant. Lessons 2 and 3 give the children two ways to be a servant: "Overcome evil with good" and "Love your enemies." The final lesson, "Be a Servant," shows that Jesus did exactly what He taught us to do. When He washed His disciples' feet, He showed that He was a servant of all.

It is difficult to measure if a child's attitude is changing. So after talking about how Jesus would think, the children will work on ways to demonstrate Jesus' attitude. The two ways suggested—overcome evil with good and love your enemies—will be nearly impossible to work on, unless they have begun to look at things the way Jesus would. This gives you a way to evaluate if their attitudes are beginning to become like Jesus' attitude.

The Bible verses to memorize can help the children follow Jesus by having His attitude. Two key phrases from Philippians 2:5, 7—"think and act like Jesus" and "become like a servant"—will help you emphasize the change you are seeking. When the children can suggest ways to think like Jesus would think, you will know you are making progress. That is the value of this unit of lessons: opening children's eyes to how Jesus would think and feel.

▼ Bible Project ▲

Serve Up a Party

Materials

Provide materials to help children create worship pictures, prayers, poems, or learn worship songs:

paper (drawing, shelf, lined, construction)

pencils, markers, crayons, colored pencils

music (CDs or audio cassettes and CD or cassette player or music to sing or play on a keyboard).

The learners will organize a party or meal in which they become the servants for their invited guests. Use your imagination to decide on the kind of party and the theme. Suggestions follow.

Bible Times Party (Bible times food, customs, clothing, activities)

Seasonal Party (Christmas, New Year's, Valentines, Spring, and so on, depending on the time of year you are studying this unit)

Bible Theme Party (based on one Bible story or group of related stories; food and activities are given names that relate to the theme)

Feast (for Thanksgiving, or for recognition/appreciation of parents, church leaders)

Picnic, cookout, swim party (depends on the season and weather)

Don't be afraid to let the children work to prepare for the party. Their hard work will be rewarded and they will have come closer to thinking and acting like Jesus.

Week 1: Decide where and when the party/meal will be given. Decide who to invite (parents, a younger class, grandparents, ministers, and teachers). Discuss every week how to be a servant to the invited guests.

Week 2: Make and send invitations. Enlist the help of parents or sponsors to supply food, plates, napkins, and so on.

Week 3: Plan the menu, activities, games, and decorations.

Week 4: Decide on entertainment. Make games, prepare activities, and make decorations.

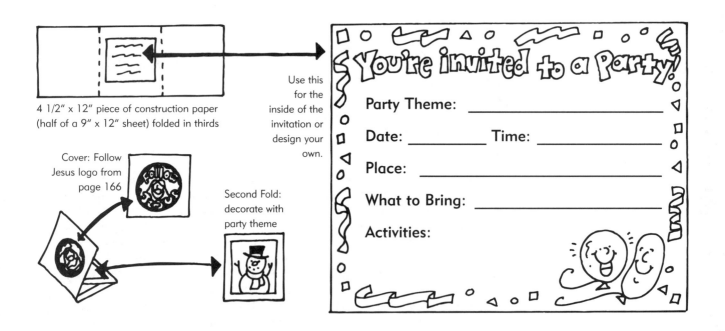

4 1/2" x 12" piece of construction paper (half of a 9" x 12" sheet) folded in thirds

Use this for the inside of the invitation or design your own.

Cover: Follow Jesus logo from page 166

Second Fold: decorate with party theme

You're invited to a Party!

Party Theme: _____

Date: _____ Time: _____

Place: _____

What to Bring: _____

Activities:

Do You Want to Be Great?

Matthew 20:20-28; Mark 10:35-45

Lesson Goals
- Tell what James and John wanted.
- Tell what Jesus said to do if you want to be great.
- Begin to memorize Philippians 2:5, 7.
- Explain what it means to have Jesus' attitude.
- Follow Jesus by having His attitude.

Memory Block
"In your lives you must think and act like Christ Jesus. He gave up his place with God and made himself nothing. He was born to be a man and became like a servant" (Philippians 2:5, 7).

▼ Bible Search ▲

At least two of Jesus' apostles wanted to be great. Let's learn about them.
Distribute copies of page 103. Read the directions and guide the children to find the Scripture verses in their Bibles. Then children will answer the two questions. Let the children report their answers.
Who wanted to be great? What did Jesus say about being great? What do you think it means to serve? What are some ways to serve?

Purpose
Tell what James and John wanted.

Materials
copies of page 103
Bibles
pencils

▼ Bible Story ▲

Display the large question mark. **Have you ever wanted your mom to ask someone an important question for you? Why might it help to take your mom along? Listen for what James and John wanted their mom to ask.**

"Do You Want to Be Great?"

James and John wanted to be great! They wanted to be important—just like Jesus. They wanted to be the best. But how could they get people to say they were important? One of them had an idea. Jesus was always talking about His kingdom. That meant, someday, Jesus would probably have a throne just like other kings. If Jesus had a throne, the most important people would sit next to Him. That was the great idea! They would ask for the most important seats next to Jesus. Then everyone would KNOW they were important!

They couldn't wait to ask Jesus. This was a pretty important question. They got their mother to go along to do the asking. They wanted to be sure that Jesus would say yes. When she came to Jesus, James and John's mother bowed down before Jesus—just like a servant bows to a king. Then came the big moment. Jesus asked, "What do you want?"

She said, "Promise that one of my sons will sit at your right side in your kingdom. And promise that the other son will sit at your left side." She knew Jesus would keep His promises. If He just said yes, then it would be all settled. But Jesus gave an answer they were not expecting.

First Jesus said, "You don't understand what you are asking. Can you suffer the same kinds of terrible things I am going to suffer?" Jesus knew He was going to be beaten and killed on a cross. People who wanted to be important had to be willing to suffer like Jesus.

Suffering didn't sound like fun. But, James and John really did want to be important like Jesus. So they said, "Yes, we can." It was a little disappointing when

Purpose
Tell what Jesus said to do if you want to be great.

Materials
a large question mark on a sheet of paper

Jesus agreed with them that they would suffer like Him. But then Jesus said something even more disappointing.

"I cannot choose who will sit at my right side or my left side. Those places belong to those for whom my Father has prepared them." Their great idea turned out to be not so great. The idea got even less great when the other ten apostles heard about it. They were angry. What made James and John think they were any better than the rest of the apostles?

So Jesus called all the apostles together and told them how to be great. He said being great doesn't mean you are in charge. Being great doesn't mean having the most important place to sit. Being great doesn't even mean being the strongest. People who are great are the ones who serve others. People who are great do what will help other people be happy. Jesus showed how to be great when He served other people.

Read the following sentences. The children can correct the wrong word(s).
James and <u>Jonah</u> wanted to be great. (John)
Their <u>father</u> went with them to talk to Jesus. (mother)
Jesus said people who are great <u>will never have</u> to suffer. (must be willing)
Jesus' <u>mother</u> will choose who sits by Him. (father)
The other apostles were <u>glad</u> that James and John wanted special seats. (angry)
Jesus said the only way to be great is to be a <u>master</u>. (servant)
Summary questions: **What did James and John want?** (special seats next to Jesus, to be great) **Tell what Jesus said to do if you want to be great.** (Be the servant of all.)

▼ Bible Verse ▲

In Philippians, Paul told us how to have Jesus' attitude. He said two important things to remember are 1) think and act like Jesus, and 2) become like a servant.

Children will find and read Philippians 2:5, 7. Find the page number for Philippians in the table of contents. Then find the big number for the chapter and the small numbers for the verses. Together, read the verses aloud from the verse poster on page 104. Ask the children to color behind the two key phrases in shades of red: 1) think and act like Christ Jesus, and 2) became like a servant. They can decorate the rest of the poster however they want. Talk about the verse as they work.

Where did Paul write about how to have Jesus' attitude? What are two important parts of the verse to remember? How much of the verses can we say, together, without reading them?

Purpose
Begin to memorize Philippians 2:5, 7.

Materials
Bibles
copies of page 104
crayons or colored pencils

▼ Bible and Me ▲

What did Jesus say it means to be great? (Serve others.) **What are some ways to serve that aren't much fun?** Make a list on chalkboard or poster board.

Play a game to help students explain what it means to have Jesus' attitude. Students will line up in pairs or triads against the wall. You will stand at the other end of the room and call out instructions to each pair/triad. The goal is to reach the opposite wall. Students may refer to the list you made on the chalkboard or poster board to help them think of ways to serve.

Tell what James and John thought was the way to be important and take 2 baby steps.

Purpose
Explain what it means to have Jesus' attitude.

Materials
chalkboard and chalk or poster board and marker

Tell what Jesus said was the way to be great and take 1 giant step.

Tell a way to serve others and take 3 baby steps.

Tell what it means to have Jesus' attitude and take 1 giant step. (Think and feel as Jesus did.)

Tell what to do if you want to be great and take 4 baby steps.

Tell what a servant is and take 1 giant step.

▼ Bible Project ▲

Before class, make a list of party suggestions. (See the ideas on page 90.)

We want to become more and more like Jesus. We want to be servants and think and feel like Jesus did. So, what are some ways we could "serve up a party"?

Brainstorm party ideas and put them on a chalkboard, or let the children choose from your suggestions. Decide as many details as possible and show your enthusiasm for being a servant. Decide where, when, who, and why today. The "why" should be included each week as you prepare to serve up the party. It is important to help the children understand how hard it is to be a servant like Jesus.

Purpose
Follow Jesus by having His attitude.

Materials
chalkboard and chalk or marker board and marker

▼ Bible Sharing ▲

Before class, decorate two special chairs for snack time. Suggestions: crepe paper, fun confetti, bows, or a sign lettered "honored guest." See if the first children to come to the snack area take the special seats.

Talk about the special seats. **How many of you wanted to sit in the special seats? Why?** (Give children time to respond and encourage honest answers.) **If you want to be great, what do you have to do?** (Be a servant.) **What is a servant? What is a servant of all? What does it mean to have Jesus' attitude?** (Think and feel like Jesus did.)

Sing praise songs to Jesus and close with prayer, asking God to help each one of the students think and feel like Jesus.

Purpose
Share how Jesus teaches you to have His attitude.

Materials
a snack of "great"ed cheese on crackers or another snack of your choice
decorations for two special chairs
CD or cassette of praise songs about Jesus
CD or cassette player

Overcome Evil with Good

Matthew 4:25; 5:1, 2, 38-42

Memory Block
"In your lives you must think and act like Christ Jesus. He gave up his place with God and made himself nothing. He was born to be a man and became like a servant" (Philippians 2:5, 7).

Lesson Goals
- Tell what Jesus would do if someone bothered Him.
- Tell what it means to "overcome evil with good."
- Memorize Philippians 2:5, 7.
- Tell the difference between having and not having Jesus' attitude.
- Follow Jesus by having His attitude.

▼ Bible Search ▲

When Jesus was bothered by someone, He did something good to him. Jesus taught His followers how to have His attitude. Matthew wrote many of the things Jesus said in Matthew 5, 6, and 7. Those chapters are called the Sermon on the Mount.

Using page 105, children will match references and topics. Group children in teams of 2 to 4. Answers: Matthew 5:21, anger; Matthew 5:38, not fighting back; Matthew 5:43, love; Matthew 6:1, giving; Matthew 6:5, prayer; Matthew 7:7, asking God; Matthew 7:15, actions.

Who wrote down these words that Jesus spoke? What kinds of things did Jesus talk about? What do we call the three chapters we have been looking at? What would Jesus do if someone bothered Him?

Purpose
Tell what Jesus would do if someone bothered Him.

Materials
copies of page 105
Bibles
pencils

▼ Bible Story ▲

Before class, print the following words on the index cards: Jesus, overcome, evil, good, serve. Make several cards for each word.

In Matthew 5, 6, and 7, Matthew wrote down things Jesus taught. Our story comes from Matthew 5 and Romans 12:21. Today, pretend I'm a boy a little older than you. Pretend this story happened on the day when Jesus started telling the Sermon on the Mount. (The following is a fictional Bible times story using the setting of the Sermon on the Mount.)

"Overcome Evil with Good"
"Where are all these people coming from?" I wondered. More people than I could count were coming my way. The crowd looked like a field of wild flowers bobbing up and down in the breeze. The great mass of browns, greens, splashes of red and yellow kept moving toward me. It sounded like a swarm of buzzing bees looking for a new hive. These people seemed to be going somewhere particular. So I told my mother I wanted to go along for awhile, too. Something exciting would probably happen in a crowd like that.

Dodging in and out of the crowd, I heard there were people from many different places. A man named Jesus had been healing people of all their sicknesses. And now these people were following Him.

I edged between people so I could see this unusual man. He looked normal to me. But, I thought, if He makes sick people well, He must not be an ordinary man. So I kept walking. I had to see where these people were going.

Purpose
Tell what it means to "overcome evil with good."

Materials
Bibles
index cards
tape or pushpins

After awhile Jesus looked around, climbed up a big hill, and sat down. Was He tired? What would He do next? I wondered if He was surprised to see so many people. They followed right up the hill, so I wiggled in closer until I found a place where I could see His face. I wanted to hear whatever He said.

When Jesus opened His mouth, the rumble of buzzing voices hushed. Everyone listened. I've never heard anyone speak like Jesus. He talked about being angry, about giving, and about so many other things. He talked a long time, but it didn't seem so long.

Jesus seemed to have a different way of thinking and feeling. He had a different attitude about how to treat people. He talked about not fighting back when people bother you. I wondered if He had ever seen my mean neighbor who always trips me—on purpose. Sometimes he tries to take away the toys I make out of wood scraps. Every time, I feel like kicking his shins and telling him how mean he is. But Jesus talked about not fighting back.

Jesus also talked about doing something good to people who bother you. I thought about the time the Roman soldier stopped at our house and made my brother carry his pack a whole mile. What a bother. I thought soldiers should carry their own things. But Jesus said to carry the soldier's pack for two miles instead of just one! Sounded awful to me.

Jesus sure did things differently than I would have done. Jesus' attitude was to serve people, you know, do things to help them. His idea was to overcome evil with good. That means do good things to whoever bothers you or does bad things to you. That would sure surprise people! But how could I ever do something good to my mean neighbor? I had to think some more about Jesus' idea of overcoming evil with good. *(Story is continued in lesson 16.)*

Lay the index cards you prepared before class in random order on the floor. Ask students to follow the instructions you call out.

Put your pinkie finger on a card that tells whose attitude we should have.

Put your toe on a card that tells what we should overcome evil with.

Put your elbow on a card that tells what Jesus said we should do to others.

Put your nose on a card that tells what we should overcome with good.

Put your heel on a card that tells what we should do to evil with good.

Summary questions: **What would Jesus do when someone bothered Him? What does it mean to overcome evil with good?**

▼ Bible Verse ▲

In Philippians, Paul told us how to have Jesus' attitude. We must remember to 1) think and act like Jesus, and 2) become like a servant.

Let the children find and read Philippians 2:5, 7 from a Bible. Then they can read the verses from the wall poster (Lesson 14, page 104). Play "Musical Verse" to help children memorize the words. Play music while groups of up to eight march around their chairs. When the music stops, whoever sits on the chair marked *verse* gets to ask another child to read/say the verses with him.

Where did Paul write about how to have Jesus' attitude? What are two important parts of the verse to remember? How much of the verse can we say, together, without reading it?

Purpose
Memorize Philippians 2:5, 7.

Materials
Bibles
CD or cassette of praise music
CD or cassette player
a small card marked *verse*

▼ Bible and Me ▲

Having Jesus' attitude means thinking and feeling like Jesus did. Thinking and feeling like Jesus means being a servant. When you are serving people, that's when you are great. One way to serve people is to start doing something good, especially when others are doing something wrong. The Bible calls that "overcoming evil with good."

Divide children into groups of 3-4. Assign each group a situation from page 106 to act out. Each group should act out how to have and not to have Jesus' attitude. Use the questions listed at the top of the page to help the children tell you the difference between having and not having Jesus' attitude.

What wrong did someone do? What good did someone do? What does it mean to overcome evil with good? Who had Jesus' attitude? Who did not have Jesus' attitude? How can you tell the difference?

Purpose
Tell the difference between having and not having Jesus' attitude.

Materials
copies of page 106

▼ Bible Project ▲

Are you ready to serve up a party? We want to make invitations and send them to our special guests. Then we will be ready to serve and show Jesus' attitude.

Assign each small group of children a specific task (letter the invitation, decorate it, stuff envelope, address envelope) or let each child choose the person(s) for whom to make an invitation(s). If you have extra time, begin planning the menu, activities, and decorations.

Talk about being a servant. What does it mean to have Jesus' attitude? Which way to serve people would be the hardest?

Purpose
Follow Jesus by having His attitude.

Materials
construction paper or colored printer paper
colored pencils or fine-tipped markers
envelopes
names and addresses printed for the children to copy or pre-printed on the envelopes

▼ Bible Sharing ▲

Choose or ask half of the class to serve the snack to the other half. While eating, give each child a turn to tell who he served or who served him. Then each child can share a time to overcome evil with good. You may want to go first; be sure to thank the person who served you.

Close by singing praise songs to Jesus and encouraging your students to think and feel like Jesus.

Purpose
Share how Jesus teaches you to have His attitude.

Materials
a snack of cookies and milk or juice
CD or cassette of praise songs
CD or cassette player

Love Your Enemies

Matthew 5:43-48

Lesson Goals

- Tell what Jesus would do if someone hurt Him.
- Tell what it means to show love for your enemies.
- Recite and explain Philippians 2:5, 7.
- Tell why it might be hard to have Jesus' attitude.
- Follow Jesus by having His attitude.

Memory Block

"In your lives you must think and act like Christ Jesus. He gave up his place with God and made himself nothing. He was born to be a man and became like a servant" (Philippians 2:5, 7).

▼ Bible Search ▲

In the Sermon on the Mount, Jesus had some ideas that were different from most people's ideas. Let's see what was so different.

Children will work together to complete page 107. Guide them to find Matthew 5:43, 44 in their Bibles. Distribute copies of page 107 and read the instructions with the children. Answers: Draw a line from the people to "Love your neighbor" and "Hate your enemies." Draw a line from Jesus to "Love your enemies" and "Pray for those who hurt you."

What did people think? What did Jesus say? What does it mean to show love to enemies? What do you think Jesus would do if someone hurt Him?

Purpose
Tell what Jesus would do if someone hurt Him.

Materials
Bibles
copies of page 107
pencils

▼ Bible Story ▲

Before class, cut apart the word cards on page 108.

Display Bible. **Where do we find Jesus' Sermon on the Mount?** (Matthew 5, 6, 7.) **Today's story comes from Matthew 5:44. It says, "Love your enemies. Pray for those who hurt you." Last time we pretended that we met a boy who heard Jesus when He gave His Sermon on the Mount. Pretend this story happened to the same boy on his way home.** (The following fictional Bible times story is continued from Lesson 15.)

Purpose
Tell what it means to show love for your enemies.

Materials
Bible
copy of page 108
scissors
tape

"Love Your Enemies"

"It's not much fun to walk by yourself," I thought. My toe bounced little stones to the side of the road. I wondered how far I had walked with the crowd of people following Jesus. Behind me, people were still crowded around Jesus on that low mountain. But I had to go home. My mom was probably worrying about me as she mixed bread for us to eat. Eat! I'd been so busy, I'd forgotten it was time to eat. Scurrying along, I thought about what Jesus said.

After Jesus told us to overcome evil with good, he talked about His enemies. I wanted to know what Jesus would do to an enemy. An enemy is someone who doesn't like you and hurts you. I thought you should protect yourself around an enemy. You know, plan how to hurt him before he hurts you. But Jesus said, "Love your enemies. Pray for those who hurt you.... If you are nice only to your friends, then you are no better than other people." How could Jesus say that! Loving people who hurt you is impossible.

My next thought about made me trip over my own two feet. If Jesus said I should love people who hurt me, then I suppose He meant love my mean neighbor—you know, the one who always trips me on purpose. But he makes me so mad. How could I love and pray for him? That was asking too much.

I shuffled along, kicked more stones and wondered why Jesus wanted me to love my enemies. And why should I do what Jesus said, anyway? Not me. It was too hard. It was too dangerous.

Up ahead, Mom was pulling bread out of the oven. My mouth started watering and my legs started running. I dashed past my mean neighbor's house. Suddenly, out of nowhere, my mean neighbor was right in front of me. I tried to dodge him, but it was too late. We knocked into each other and went sprawling in the dirt. I was still flat on my back trying to catch my breath when the dust settled. My mean neighbor was moaning in pain. As I sat up, I saw blood on his leg. He must have cut it on a rock when he fell.

When I rubbed my aching back and elbow, I realized his leg must have felt even worse. "Serves you right," I started to say. Then I remembered how bad I always felt when he tripped me. I didn't want to be mean like him.

Maybe I could try Jesus' attitude. But what should I do next? I decided to do what Jesus would do. So I helped him sit up. I pressed my hand on his cut to stop the bleeding. We were both surprised that I was helping him. I was surprised because it wasn't as hard as I thought it would be. Silently I prayed. "Dear God, please help his leg heal okay. I'm sorry for not wanting to love him before. And I hope we can learn to be friends now. Amen."

Later, I told Mom everything that happened. I started talking faster and faster when I got to the part about how Jesus' attitude works, "I got rid of my bad feeling by doing something good for him. And I prayed for my 'enemy' so I didn't feel so angry at him. I overcame evil with good! I loved my enemy! I did it! I changed my attitude to be like Jesus!" Mom smiled at me. I looked out the door toward the mountain and smiled too.

Let the children take turns choosing a word to put in one of the blanks on page 108. If a player thinks a word is in the wrong blank, a turn can be used to remove the word. When the players think they are done, let them "pray for those who hurt you" (Matthew 5:44).

Summary questions: **What would Jesus do if someone hurt Him? What does it mean to love your enemies?**

▼ Bible Verse ▲

Purpose
Recite and explain Philippians 2:5, 7.

Materials
Bibles
copy of page 104
CD or cassette of praise music
CD or cassette player
two cards
a marker

Print the number *1* on one card and *2* on the other. Set the chairs in a circle and put the number cards on two of the chairs. Display the verse poster from page 104 for the students.

In Philippians, Paul told us how to have Jesus' attitude. Two things to remember are 1) think and act like Jesus, and 2) become like a servant.

Children will find and read Philippians 2:5, 7. Play a variation of "Musical Verse" (see Lesson 15). When the music stops, the person in the chair marked with a *1* can read or say the verses alone. The person in the chair marked *2* can say the two phrases that explain what we must do. After several rounds, begin covering words on the verse poster so the children say the verses from memory. Talk about the verses with the following questions.

Where did Paul write about how to have Jesus' attitude? What do both verses say? (Volunteers can recite them alone or together.) **What do these verses help us remember?** (Think and act like Jesus; be a servant.)

▼ Bible and Me ▲

Before class, cut out the game cards on page 109. Use one game for every 4-6 students.

When you have Jesus' attitude, you think and feel like Jesus did, and you want to serve people. When you serve people, you are really great. But sometimes it's hard to serve people.

Play a game to talk about how it can be hard to have Jesus' attitude of serving people. Give each group of 4-6 players a game board, cards, and buttons or pennies as game markers. Students may team up in pairs or play individually. For each correct answer, move the number of spaces printed on the card. If necessary, students can talk over the answers to the questions with the other students in their group. They will answer the same questions more than once to get to the end. (Answer for question worth three spaces: overcome evil with good, love your enemy, pray for those who hurt you.)

To summarize, ask the following questions. **What does it mean to have Jesus' attitude? Why might it be hard to have Jesus' attitude?**

Purpose
Tell why it might be hard to have Jesus' attitude.

Materials
buttons (or pennies)
copies of page 109
scissors

▼ Bible Project ▲

Before class, think about menu choices, party activities and games, and appropriate decorations.

We want to show our invited guests that we can be servants like Jesus was. Let's plan some things to help our guests feel special.

List children's ideas on chalkboard or marker board. Plan a simple menu, one that the children can help prepare and serve. Plan games and activities; think about activities the guests will enjoy. Plan the decorations to correlate with the theme of the party. If you have time, begin making the games and decorations. While you work, talk about what it means to be a servant. Repeat questions from the Bible and Me section.

Purpose
Follow Jesus by having His attitude.

Materials
chalkboard and chalk or marker board and marker
materials to make decorations and/or party activities and games

▼ Bible Sharing ▲

As you eat a snack, give each child a turn to share about a time she has shown love to an enemy or a situation in which she could show love this week. Then help the children to summarize this lesson.

What does it mean to have Jesus' attitude? What Bible verses help us remember to think and feel like Jesus?

Close with guided prayer. Pray a sentence; then give the children time to pray silently. "Dear God, Thank You for Jesus. Help us think and feel like Jesus did. Help us love our enemies this week. We want to be Your servants. In Jesus' name, amen."

Sing a favorite unit song you are learning about being a servant.

Purpose
Share how Jesus teaches you to have His attitude.

Materials
a snack of bread and cheese
CD or cassette of favorite praise songs
CD or cassette player

Be a Servant

John 13:1-17; Luke 22:27

Memory Block

"In your lives you must think and act like Christ Jesus. He gave up his place with God and made himself nothing. He was born to be a man and became like a servant" (Philippians 2:5, 7).

Lesson Goals

- Tell what Jesus wanted to show His apostles.
- Tell who Jesus said is the most important.
- Recite and illustrate Philippians 2:5, 7.
- Demonstrate a way to have Jesus' attitude.
- Follow Jesus by having His attitude.

▼ Bible Search ▲

In our story today, people used a bowl of water and a towel for something we don't have today. Let see what it was.

Use copies of page 110 (or a children's Bible dictionary) to read about footwashing in Bible times. Ask questions about the illustrations on the page. If you have time, allow children to practice washing each other's feet, using the bowl, water, and towel.

What would a servant do for guests when they arrived? Why was footwashing important? How do you think a good servant would get the guests' feet clean? Would you want to have the job of washing guests' feet? Why would Jesus be willing to wash people's feet? (to show He was a servant)

▼ Bible Story ▲

For review, print with marker eight numbered words on squares of paper towel: 1—dusty; 2—meal; 3—bowl; 4—towel; 5—Peter; 6—Teacher; 7—Servant; 8—important.

Display the towel and basin. **If you were a Bible-times guest in my house, what would I do with this water?** (Children report and/or demonstrate.) **Listen to see who wanted to wash His friends' feet in the story.**

"Be a Servant"

"These dusty roads are such a nuisance," I muttered to myself. My name is Peter. The other eleven apostles and I were going to eat our evening meal with Jesus. I had been all clean a few minutes ago, but after just a few steps on this dirt road, my feet were already filthy. I would be glad to have someone wash my feet when I got to the meal.

But when I arrived, no servant greeted me with a bowl of cool water and a dry towel. My hot dusty feet stayed hot and dusty. I saw a water jar and a towel in the room, but I didn't want to volunteer to be a servant. If I did, everyone would think I wasn't very important. Actually, none of the other apostles volunteered either. You can imagine how the room smelled.

While we were eating, Jesus stopped and did something very unusual. First Jesus took off His outer tunic and wrapped a towel around His waist. Then He poured water from the jar into a bowl. Kneeling down, He began to wash and dry our dusty feet. We wondered why He was doing the servant's work.

When He finished one, Jesus moved to another. Closer and closer He came.

Purpose

Tell what Jesus wanted to show His apostles.

Materials

Bibles
copies of page 110
a large bowl, water, and towel (optional)

Purpose

Tell who Jesus said is the most important.

Materials

a towel and a large basin with a little water in it
squares of paper towel
marker
bowl

Then it was my turn. I blurted out, "Are you going to wash my feet?" Jesus told me that even though I didn't understand now, later I would understand what He was doing. But it didn't seem right for my leader to be my servant. I blurted out again, "No! You will never wash my feet."

Again, Jesus responded in His careful way, "If I don't wash your feet, then you are not one of my people." I wanted to be one of Jesus' people, so I told Jesus to wash more of me: my feet, my hands, my head. But Jesus said only feet needed washing. I did not understand what He meant.

After washing all of our feet, that water must have been filthy. Our feet felt much better, but we were still confused about what Jesus did. After Jesus put His tunic back on, He sat back down and asked, "Do you understand what I have just done for you?" None of us answered.

Jesus explained that we were right to call Him Teacher and Lord because He was both our Teacher and our Lord. But, He said He was also our Servant. Having important jobs didn't stop Him from doing the servant's job: washing our feet. I guess Jesus wanted to show us how to love and serve people. He told us to serve each other, just like He served us. The important person is the one who serves others. The last thing Jesus said was, "If you know these things, you will be happy for doing them."

Wad up the prepared paper towel squares and put them in an empty bowl. Let each child choose a wad. The child with number 1 goes first and uses the word on the towel to make a sentence about the story. Continue with the rest of the numbers in order.

Summary questions: **Tell what Jesus wanted to do for His twelve apostles.** (show love—that means be a servant, wash feet) **Tell who Jesus said is the most important.** (servant)

▼ Bible Verse ▲

In Philippians, Paul told us how to have Jesus' attitude. Two things to remember are 1) think and act like Jesus, and 2) become like a servant.

Let the children find and read Philippians 2:5, 7 from a Bible. Ask for volunteers to say the verses from memory and tell what two things these verses help them do. If some children are still learning the verses, have them cover words on the poster (from lesson 14) and practice saying them to each other. Children who can say the verses can use page 111 to illustrate the three sentences of the verses. If you have no artists, let them cut apart the three sections and work in pairs to think of a way to act out one of the sentences.

What do these verses help us remember? (think and act like Jesus; serve) **What do these verses say? What do these verses mean?** (Children can explain the illustrations they have drawn or act out situations that illustrate the sentences.)

Purpose
Recite and illustrate Philippians 2:5, 7.

Materials
Bible
copies of page 111
markers or crayons
verse poster from page 104

Purpose
Demonstrate a way to have Jesus' attitude.

Materials
copies of page 112
pencils

▼ Bible and Me ▲

When you have Jesus' attitude, you think and feel like Jesus did, and you want to serve people. When you serve people, you are really great.

Distribute page 112. The children will decode menial ways to serve. Then take turns choosing which one might be the hardest. Tell why it might be hard. Show how to have Jesus' attitude when doing it.

What does it mean to have Jesus' attitude? Which way to serve people would be the hardest? Why might it be hard? Show us how you could have Jesus' attitude when you do it.

Purpose
Follow Jesus by having His attitude.

Materials
a variety of materials to make the decorations planned for the party
games and activities for the party

▼ Bible Project ▲

We want to be like Jesus. We want to have His attitude and show love to all people. While we work on our party preparations, let's also work to be servants to each other.

Distribute materials and help the children make the party decorations (name tags, table favors, wall decorations). Other children can organize the games and activities or make items for games. This is the last week to prepare before the party. Make a list of things yet to be done; assign children or adult sponsors some of the last minute details.

Take time to talk about the children's attitudes at the party. **What does it mean to have Jesus' attitude? Why might it be hard to have Jesus' attitude? At the party, how can you show you are a servant?**

Purpose
Show how Jesus teaches me to have His attitude.

Materials
a snack of vegetables and dip
three index cards
marker
CD or cassette of praise songs
CD or cassette player

▼ Bible Sharing ▲

Before class, print one of the following words on each card: verse, servant, time.

While you eat a snack and listen to praise songs, pass the three cards around the circle. When the music stops, the child with the verse card will stand and say the unit memory verses (or ask another child to say it with him). The child with the servant card will stand and tell what it means to be a servant. The child with the time card will tell or act out (with help of another) a time or way to have Jesus' attitude.

Close with prayer and a reminder about the serving party.

Bible Search

Find Mark 10:35-37 in your Bible.
Listen to your teacher read the verses.
Use your Bible to answer the questions.

Find Mark 10:35. **Who wanted to be great?**

(Circle) your answer.

Judas

Peter

Andrew

James

Thomas

John

Find Mark 10:43. **What did Jesus say about being great?**

Write your answer.

_____

- -

_____

_____

- -

_____

_____

- -

_____

Bible Verse

Find Philippians 2:5, 7 in your Bible.
Color the poster below.
Mount it on construction paper.

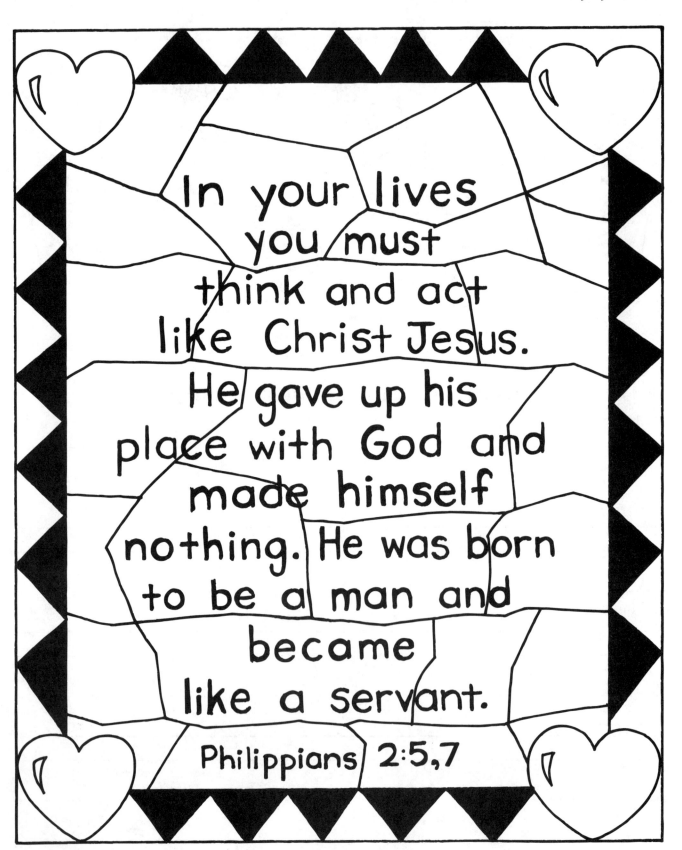

In your lives you must think and act like Christ Jesus. He gave up his place with God and made himself nothing. He was born to be a man and became like a servant.

Philippians 2:5,7

Bible Search

Work with a partner.
Find each Bible verse in the stones.
Match each verse to
something Jesus
taught (in the
clouds).

Jesus teaches about **asking God.**

Jesus teaches about **prayer.**

Jesus teaches about **love.**

Jesus teaches about **anger.**

Jesus teaches about **giving.**

Jesus teaches about **not fighting back.**

Jesus teaches about **our actions.**

Matthew 5:43

Matthew 7:15

Matthew 5:38

Matthew 7:7

Matthew 6:5

Matthew 5:21

Matthew 6:1

Bible and Me

Look at the pictures.
Who has Jesus' attitude?
Who does not have Jesus' attitude?
How can you tell the difference?

 UNIT 4, LESSON 15

Find Matthew 5:43, 44 in your Bible.
Read what Jesus said about love.

Bible Search

1. What does the Bible say people thought?

Read Matthew 5:43.

Draw a line from the people to the speech balloons that tell what people thought.

Cross out the others.

people

Love your neighbor

Don't talk to strangers.

Don't talk to enemies.

Hate your enemies.

Love animals.

2. What did Jesus say?

Read Matthew 5:44.

Draw a line from Jesus to the speech balloons that tell what Jesus said.

Cross out the others.

Jesus

Love your enemies.

Only love your friends.

Pray for those who hurt you.

Hurt your enemies.

Don't pray for your enemies.

3. What does it mean to show love to enemies?

Bible Story

Cut apart the word cards at the bottom.
Choose a word card for each blank.

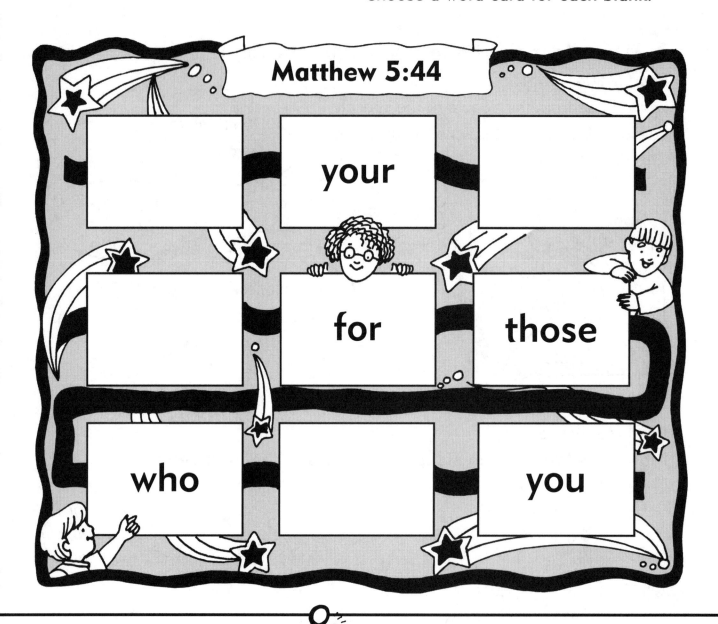

Matthew 5:44

	your	
	for	those
who		you

---

cut

Love	Hate	enemies	friends
Pray	Fight	hurt	help

UNIT 4, LESSON 16

Cut apart the question cards.
Play a game with your friends.
Use buttons for markers.

Bible and Me

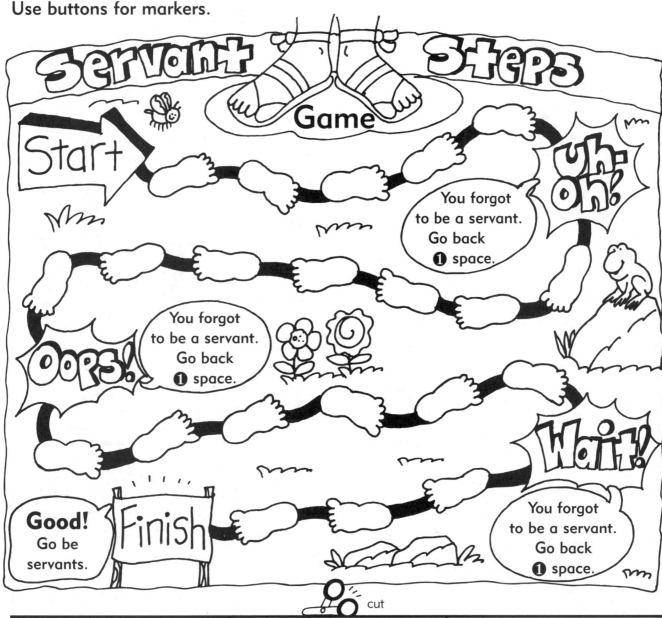

What does a servant do? Move ❷.	What 3 ways have we talked about serving? Move ❸.	What does it mean to love your enemy? Why might that be hard? Move ❹.
What is Jesus' idea about how to be great? Move ❷.	What does it mean to overcome evil with good? Why might that be hard? Move ❹.	What could you say to pray for someone who hurt you? Move ❹.

© 2004 Standard Publishing. Permission is granted to reproduce this page for ministry purposes only—not for resale.

Bible Search

Find John 13:4, 5 in your Bible.
Then read about foot-washing
in Bible times.

foot-washing. In Bible times, people's feet were washed when they entered a house. Washing feet was necessary to keep them clean and comfortable after walking on dusty roads.

Foot-washing also showed the person he was a welcome guest at that house. It was a servant's job to wash the feet of a guest.

 UNIT 4, LESSON 17

Cut apart the sentences of Philippians 2:5, 7.
Draw a picture for each sentence.

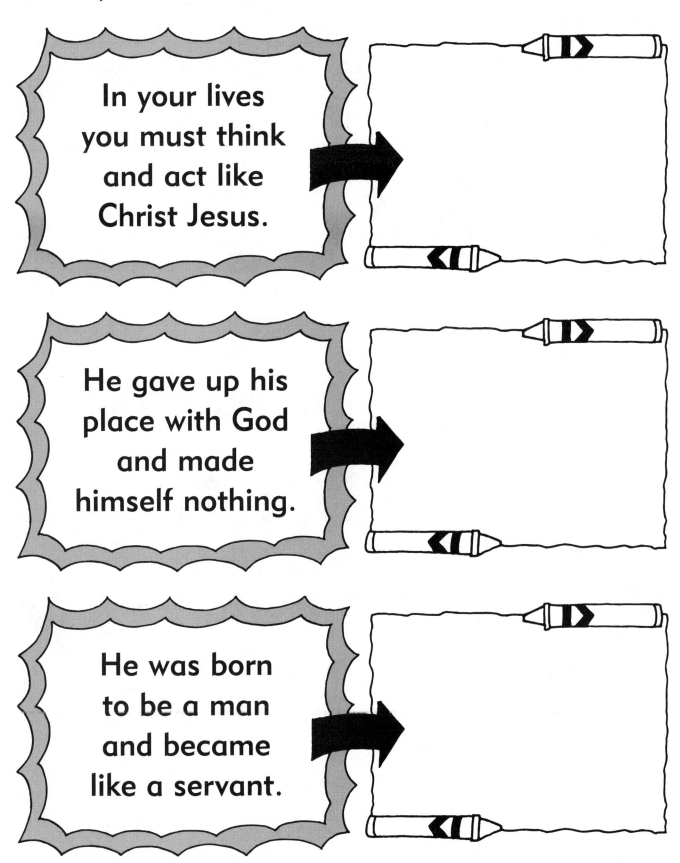

In your lives you must think and act like Christ Jesus.

He gave up his place with God and made himself nothing.

He was born to be a man and became like a servant.

Bible and Me

Decode four ways to serve people. Write the first letter of the picture word in the box below it.

1. Empty

.

2.

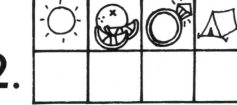

socks.

3.

for parents.

4. Clean

.

❏ What does it mean to have Jesus' attitude?

❏ Which way to serve people would be the hardest?

❏ Why might it be hard?

❏ Show how you could have Jesus' attitude when you do it.

 Unit 4, Lesson 17

Jesus' Stories Help Me Follow Him

Lessons 18–22

Unit Memory Block

"Everyone who hears these things I say and obeys them is like a wise man. The wise man built his house on rock. But the person who hears the things I teach and does not obey them is like a foolish man. The foolish man built his house on the sand" (Matthew 7:24, 26).

Memory Challenge

Matthew 7:24-27

18 The Wise Builder

Matthew 7:24-27; Luke 6:47-49

The wise builder made right choices; the foolish builder made wrong choices. We are wise when we choose to listen to Jesus' stories and then do what Jesus says.

19 The Good Samaritan

Luke 10:25-37

Three men saw a hurt man by the road. Only the Samaritan was a neighbor; he stopped to help. We follow Jesus when we listen to Jesus' stories and then do what Jesus says.

20 The Rich Farmer

Luke 12:15-21

A rich man wanted to store up grain for himself. Jesus said people who loved God want to share. We follow Jesus when we listen to Jesus' stories and then do what Jesus says.

21 The Unforgiving Servant

Matthew 18: 21-34

The servant did not forgive, so the king punished him. Jesus said God will punish us if we do not forgive others. We follow Jesus when we listen to Jesus' stories and then do what Jesus says.

22 The Loving Father

Luke 15:11-24

A father showed love to his son when he stopped doing wrong. He gave him gifts and a big party. God loves us even when we do wrong too. If we stop following Jesus, we can change and start doing what He says.

By the end of this unit, the leaders and learners will

KNOW five Bible stories Jesus told.
FEEL able to do what Jesus taught.
DO Choose to do what Jesus taught in His stories.

Unit Value

This unit helps the children add to what they know about following Jesus. These five stories Jesus told give the children examples of what they can do to follow Jesus. The Wise Builder teaches us to choose to do what Jesus says. The Good Samaritan illustrates helping—even people who may not like us. The story of the Rich Farmer shows it is best to share. The Unforgiving Servant is about forgiving. And the Loving Father helps children see that God wants us to start following Jesus again if we have stopped following Jesus.

Throughout the unit, the Bible verses to memorize come from the story of the Wise Builder. The verses emphasize the importance of not only listening to what Jesus says, but also doing it. In addition to receiving ideas of ways to follow Jesus, the children will also have the opportunity to share times or ways they have been choosing to follow Jesus. They may not remember anything to share the first time you ask. But when you ask again and again, you are demonstrating to them how important you think it is for them to follow Jesus. When they do have reports to share, your enthusiastic response will go far in encouraging them to keep following Jesus.

▼ Bible Project ▲

Wise Builders

The learners will plan mini-projects to help them do what Jesus taught. They will become "wise builders" as they choose to listen to and obey Jesus.

Use the first week to define and plan the Wise Builder projects. Plan four projects that apply the stories Jesus told (helping, sharing, forgiving, loving). Each mini-project should be simple enough to complete during one session (or extend the session, if you choose). Three of the four mini-projects are very concrete. The forgiving project will be harder to accomplish. The story idea below is a demonstration for that project rather than an actual experience.

A project schedule follows with ideas in parentheses.

Week 1: Define and plan projects for the unit.

Week 2: Helping project (wash car windows, shovel snow, sweep sidewalks, pick up litter, sharpen pencils, clean chalkboards)

Week 3: Sharing project (prepare a snack to share; collect and clean toys to share)

Week 4: Forgiving project (write a modern-day story of the unforgiving servant)

Week 5: Loving project (write and send thank-you notes to parents, grandparents, teachers, or leaders; send unused Sunday school papers and a friendly note to children who have missed)

Story Idea for Week 4

The teacher loans Child A a new set of markers to work on a project. Child A loses them and the teacher asks to have them back. The child explains and asks to be forgiven. The teacher forgives the child. Then Child A remembers that Child B borrowed two of his pencils for a writing assignment. Child A demands the pencils be given back. Child B lost them and asks forgiveness. Child A won't forgive and wants to be paid for the pencils. A couple of other children overhear and inform the teacher of the situation. The teacher then asks Child A to come to her desk, explains what she knows, and insists that the child repay her for the markers. (Encourage class creativity: add details, names, dialogue, and feelings to make the story as realistic as possible.)

Materials

After the first week of planning, gather needed supplies for your chosen projects. Keep it simple as possible to help the children feel capable and willing to participate.

The Wise Builder

Matthew 7:24-27; Luke 6:47-49

Lesson Goals
- Describe the difference between the wise and foolish man.
- Tell which man chose right.
- Begin to memorize Matthew 7:24, 26.
- Tell the difference between ways that do and do not follow Jesus.
- Choose to follow Jesus.

▼ Bible Search ▲

Jesus told a story about two men who built houses in two ways. Let's learn what is different about their houses.

Give page 130 to each child. Guide children to find Matthew 7:24 in their Bibles. (Find Matthew in the table of contents. Locate the page the book begins on, then the big 7 for the chapter and the small 24 for the verse.) Circle the right answer. Then find the rest of the verses in Matthew and circle the answers.

Do an experiment about the two houses. Put some sand in the dish pan and pour water over it. **What happened to the sand?** Put the rock in the dish pan and pour water over it. **What happened to the rock?**

What was different about the two houses? (foundations) **Which house was built by a wise builder? a foolish builder? What right choice did the wise builder make?** (built on rock)

▼ Bible Story ▲

Before class, cut apart the sentence strips at the top of page 131 and bury them in the sand.

What happens when water washes against sand? What happens when water washes against rock? (Let children report the experiment from Bible Search.) **Listen to Jesus' story to see if you want to be like Sandy (sand) or Rocky (rock).**

"The Wise Builder"

Black and grey thunderclouds rolled past Sandy's window. Sandy guessed the storm would hit in a few minutes. His beautiful house had never been through a storm. But Sandy was sure it would be just fine. His house wasn't very old.

Sandy loved his house. He built it close to the river where he could see the sun rising on the water. Lapping water sang him to sleep at night. Warm sand oozed between his toes when he walked out his front door. He had ignored warnings about building on sand. He was rather proud of how quickly he had finished this house.

Through soft falling rain, Sandy could see a brand new house across the river. It was built by Rocky, his neighbor. Sandy and Rocky had learned to make houses from the same master builder. But the homes they built were much different.

Rocky took a long time to build his house. First, he had dug down to find a layer of solid rock. After days of hauling away loose sand and dirt, he built a framework

Memory Block
"Everyone who hears these things I say and obeys them is like a wise man. The wise man built his house on rock. But the person who hears the things I teach and does not obey them is like a foolish man. The foolish man built his house on sand" (Matthew 7:24, 26).

Purpose
Describe the difference between the wise and foolish man.

Materials
Bibles
copies of page 130
pencils
large dish pan
pitcher of water
rock to put in dish pan
bowl of sand

Purpose
Tell which man chose right.

Materials
copy of page 131
pan of sand
rock
tape

on that rock. What a waste of time. Sandy had finished his whole house by the time Rocky finished his foundation.

Rocky's house wasn't nearly as neat as his own. He didn't have warm sand in his front yard—just rock. He was so far from the river he couldn't hear the gentle lapping of the water. Rocky just didn't know where to put a house, and he surely didn't know how to do it quickly!

Then, without warning, the wind rose to a steady shriek. The dark sky pelted the roof with bullets of rain. The wind drove the rain through the spaces in the walls and Sandy wished he had filled the cracks more carefully. The river wasn't lapping now. It rushed downstream, ripping off low branches.

Overhead, a roof timber shuddered in the wind and then crashed to the floor with a sickening thud. "That must have been loose," Sandy muttered. Huddled in the corner, Sandy heard a roar. Through a crack he saw a wall of water racing toward him. "Oh, my beautiful house," he moaned. Scrambling to get out, he slipped in the wet sand. Somehow he managed to escape. Miserable and soaked with rain, he stared as the river flushed sand from under his walls. Chunks of wall floated away. Moments later the roof caved in. And everything, everything but the sand, flooded down the river.

Through the rain, Sandy peered across the angry, rushing river. He could barely see the outline of Rocky's house. The same terrible wind and driving rain were beating on his house. But it stood strong on the rock.

Jesus told a story like that to His followers. Jesus said, "People who listen to what I teach and then do what is right are like the wise man who built his house on the rock. But everyone who listens to me and does not do what I say is like the foolish man who built his house on the sand."

Hide the sentences from page 131 in a pan of sand. The children can find each sentence and identify which sentences describe the wise man and which describe the foolish man. Tape the sentences about the wise man to a rock.

Summary questions: **Who did Jesus say is like the foolish man? Who did Jesus say is like the wise man? Which man chose right?**

Purpose
Begin to memorize Matthew 7:24, 26.

Materials
Bibles
copies of page 132
pencils

▼ Bible Verse ▲

Our verses help us remember to listen to Jesus and do what He says.

Let the children find and read Matthew 7:24, 26 aloud from a Bible. Then distribute copies of page 132. After they print the correct words in the blanks on page 132, they can take turns reading the page aloud, pausing at each blank, so the rest can fill in the blanks from memory.

Who does this verse talk about? What kind of person hears and obeys? What kind of person hears and doesn't obey?

▼ Bible and Me ▲

Cut apart the cards at the bottom of page 131. Make enough copies for each child in your class to have a card. Divide the poster board into two columns (or draw two houses). Label one column *Houses on Sand (Children who listen to Jesus but do not want to follow Him)*. Label the other column *Houses on Rock (Children who want to follow Jesus)*.

Following Jesus means doing what He teaches us in His stories. In His story about the wise builder, Jesus teaches us to choose what is right. The most important thing to choose is to want to follow Jesus.

Show children the poster board columns and read the labels. Then ask children to take turns choosing a card from page 131 and deciding where it goes. For each card ask, "What helped you decide if this child wants to follow Jesus?"

What does it mean to follow Jesus? (Do what Jesus teaches in His stories.) **What did Jesus teach us in His story about the builders?** (Listen and do what Jesus says.) **What can we do to be like the foolish man?** (column 1 cards) **What can we do to be like the wise man?** (column 2 cards) **Which man is like the people who follow Jesus?**

Purpose
Tell the difference between ways that do and do not follow Jesus.

Materials
a copy of page 131
scissors
poster board
marker
tape

▼ Bible Project ▲

Print *Wise Builders* at the top of the board. Then list four words to help the children plan: *help, share, forgive, love.*

We want to become wise builders—listening to what Jesus says and then doing it. Our unit project will be four mini-projects to help us do what Jesus taught in His stories. We are going to plan the projects in this session. Let's think of these ways to do what Jesus taught.

Display the list you printed on the board. Ask the children and adult helpers to suggest mini-projects to accomplish the four words listed. Plan simple projects to be done as a group in one session. See unit page 114 for ideas.

Talk about the importance of doing what Jesus taught. **What does it mean to follow Jesus?** (Do what Jesus teaches in His stories.) **What does it mean to be a wise builder?** (Listen and do what Jesus says.) **Jesus wants us to help, share, forgive, and love. What are some ways we can do what Jesus says?**

Purpose
Choose to follow Jesus.

Materials
chalkboard and chalk or marker board and marker

▼ Bible Sharing ▲

Let's think about being wise builders as we eat our snack. Think about ways to choose to do right this week; then raise your hand if you want to share with the whole group. If you brought in a large rock, allow children to take turns standing on it as they tell about ways to follow Jesus.

In between times of sharing, sing songs about following Jesus. If your children know the song "The Wise Man Built His House Upon the Rock," sing that with the group.

Purpose
Share how Jesus' stories help you follow Him.

Materials
snack of rock candy or chocolate cookies that look like rocks
drink
large rock for the children to stand on as they tell about ways to follow Jesus this week (optional)
CD or cassette of praise songs about following Jesus
CD or cassette player

The Good Samaritan

Luke 10:25-37

Memory Block

"Everyone who hears these things I say and obeys them is like a wise man. The wise man built his house on rock. But the person who hears the things I teach and does not obey them is like a foolish man. The foolish man built his house on sand" (Matthew 7:24, 26).

Purpose
Suggest why it was unusual for a Samaritan to help the traveler.

Materials
Bibles
copies of page 133
crayons or colored pencils

Purpose
Describe four ways the Samaritan helped the hurt traveler.

Materials
a box of bandage strips
copies of page 134
pencils

Lesson Goals

- Suggest why it was unusual for a Samaritan to help the traveler.
- Describe four ways the Samaritan helped the hurt traveler.
- Recite Matthew 7:24, 26.
- Tell why it might be hard to do what Jesus taught.
- Choose to follow Jesus.

▼ Bible Search ▲

Jesus told a story about three men who saw a hurt man who was a Jew. Only a man from Samaria stopped to help. Jews hated people from Samaria. Let's learn about the Samaritans.

Guide children to find Luke 10:33 in a Bible. Point out the word *Samaritan*. Distribute copies of page 133. Read the information paragraph at the bottom. Then help the children follow the instructions to mark the map.

What two groups of people didn't like each other? Where did the Jews live? Where did the Samaritans live? Why didn't they like each other?

▼ Bible Story ▲

Display bandage strips. **If you were a mother, what might you do with a box of these? If you were a paramedic, what might you do with a box of these? Listen to see what you might do with these if you were a man from Samaria.**

"The Good Samaritan"

The mountains between Jerusalem and Jericho are a dangerous place to travel. Robbers hide there and wait to attack lonely travelers. As I picked my way down that steep road, my eyes darted from the rocks to the trees. I desperately hoped no robbers would jump out. But I was wrong. They came at me with their fists flailing. They knocked me down. They beat me. They tore off my clothes and took everything I had. I couldn't even move to shake my fist at them as they ran away. I moaned in pain as the blood oozed from cuts all over my body.

Bleeding, aching, I lay in the dirt. What would happen to me? After what seemed like forever, I heard footsteps, faint at first, and then louder. Were the robbers coming back? Oh, please no! Closer and closer the footsteps sounded. I waited half afraid and half hoping that someone would stop.

Finally I could see someone coming. Oh, yes! It was a priest. Of all people, a priest would stop and help me. I watched anxiously as he came closer and closer. Then without even a word, he acted like he didn't even see me. He walked on the other side of the road! I felt like he had kicked me too!

Still lying in the dirt and puddles of blood, I heard more footsteps coming. My hope and fear came back. I watched down the road to see who it was. As he came closer, I saw by his clothes he was a Levite—someone who worked in the temple in Jerusalem. He would help me. Closer and closer he came. And then to my amazement, he too walked by on the other side, as if he hadn't even seen me. After he walked by, I gave up my hope of being rescued.

Sometime later, I thought I heard sounds again. It seemed to be a clip-clop of animal hooves. As the steps came close, I could see he was from Samaria. That meant no help again. Samaritans hated Jews. And we hated them.

Imagine how I felt when the clip-clop came over to my side of the road. Then it stopped. Did he hate Jews so much that he was going to kick me too? I expected insults, but no insults spilled out. He took time to pour medicine into my wounds and then bandage them. (If appropriate, put bandage strips on children sitting near you.) He helped me up onto his own donkey. His donkey bumped me down the road all the way to an inn. It hurt so bad, but if felt so good to have someone care. That night he cared for me and the next day he traveled on. But before he left, he paid the innkeeper two silver coins to care for me until I could travel again. He told the man, "If you spend more money on him, I will pay it back to you when I come again."

Jesus told this story to help people understand who is their neighbor. At the end of the story, Jesus asked, "Which of these three men do you think was a neighbor to the man was attacked by robbers?" A teacher of the law answered, "The one who helped him." Jesus spoke clearly, "Then go and do the same thing he did."

Distribute copies of page 134. Ask the children to number the order of each character's appearance in the story (traveler, robbers, priest, Levite, Samaritan, innkeeper). Then invite them to act out the story. Guide them to use their imaginations to show the different attitudes of the three men who came upon the hurt traveler.

Summary questions: **What four ways did the Samaritan help the hurt traveler? Why was it unusual for a Samaritan to help this hurt traveler?**

▼ Bible Verse ▲

Display the verse poster. **Our verses help us remember to listen to Jesus and do what He says.**

Let the children find and read Matthew 7:24, 26 aloud from a Bible. Invite the whole group to read the verse aloud from the verse poster. Ask the group to form a circle. Lay a rock in the path of the circle. The children will march around the circle, saying the verse. Whoever is standing on the rock at the end gets to choose someone to say the verse by himself.

Talk about the verses with these questions. **Who do these verses talk about? What kind of person hears and obeys? What kind of person hears and doesn't obey? Who can say the verses by himself?**

Purpose
Recite Matthew 7:24, 26.

Materials
Bibles
a large rock or paper cut into a
   shape of a rock
the verse poster from Lesson
   18 (page 132)

▼ Bible and Me ▲

Following Jesus means doing what He teaches us in His stories. In His story about the kind Samaritan man, Jesus teaches us to help people—even those who dislike us. Sometimes it's hard to help people. Who could make these excuses?

Distribute copies of page 135. Children will draw lines from the Samaritan to excuses he could have made, and draw lines from the child to excuses we might make.

What does it mean to follow Jesus? (Do what Jesus teaches in stories.) **What did Jesus teach us in His story about the builders?** (listen and do) **What did Jesus teach us in His story about the Samaritan?** (help) **Why might it be hard to help people? What will you do if you do not follow Jesus?** (give excuses, don't help) **What will you do if you do follow Jesus?** (Children can give an example of helping.)

Purpose
Tell why it might be hard to do what Jesus taught.

Materials
copies of page 135
pencils

▼ Bible Project ▲

Depending on your class schedule, you may want to do the project at the end of the lesson and extend the session if you need more time. Be sure to inform children and parents of any changes.

Briefly introduce the Wise Builder project you planned last week and then do it! **We are going to be wise builders by helping. We listened to what Jesus said and now we are going to do it. Let's go!**

If you have time after the project, talk about the importance of doing what Jesus taught. **What does it mean to follow Jesus?** (Do what Jesus teaches in stories.) **What did Jesus teach us in His story about the builders?** (listen and do) **What did Jesus teach us in His story about the Samaritan?** (help) **What did we just do that is a way to follow Jesus?**

Purpose
Choose to follow Jesus.

Materials
supplies you need to complete a helping project during the session (detergent, rags, towels, brooms, dust rags, and so on)

▼ Bible Sharing ▲

As you serve the snack, have the children pretend to sit down at the "inn."

If you have time to share before or after the mini-project, ask the children to tell how they can follow Jesus by helping this week. Give each child an adhesive bandage to remind him to listen and do what Jesus taught.

Close by singing praise songs to Jesus.

Purpose
Share how Jesus' stories help you follow Him.

Materials
a snack of grape juice and cheese
adhesive bandages
CD or cassette of praise songs and songs about following Jesus
CD or cassette player

The Rich Farmer

Luke 12:15-21

Lesson Goals

- Describe what the farmer did instead of sharing.
- Tell why it was wrong for the farmer to keep what he had for himself.
- Recite and explain Matthew 7:24, 26.
- Report ways they have followed Jesus.
- Choose to continue to follow Jesus.

▼ Bible Search ▲

Before class, cut apart one set of cards from page 136. Place them in a basket. Print the words *same* and *opposite* on two index cards.

Jesus told a story about a rich farmer who "stored up things for himself." Let's play a game to learn about "storing up."

Guide the children to find Luke 12:19 in a Bible. Read the definition of "store up" on page 136. Then play a game with the word cards. Give each child a turn to select a card from the basket, read the word, and tell if the word is the same or the opposite of "store up." Put the words in a same or opposite pile.

What does it mean to "store up" things? What is the opposite of "storing up" things? (sharing) **Which one do you think is the way to follow Jesus? Why?**

▼ Bible Story ▲

What can we make out of grain? Display the items; name others. **We eat grain everyday. Listen to see what the man in the story did with his grain.**

"The Rich Farmer"

The rich man smiled proudly at the fields of ripe grain waving to him in the breeze. What a crop! Soon his workers would be sweating as they cut and thrashed his huge harvest. "Mine, all mine!" he thought to himself. The grain was a perfect golden color. The heads were full of kernels. A loaf of bread from this new grain and a bit of new butter would simply melt in his mouth. He dreamed and planned how this crop would make his life easy.

When the workers began to gather the grain, they reported the good news, "This will be your biggest harvest ever. There is so much grain that it will probably spill out of the windows and doors of your grain barns."

"Not room enough to store the grain? Then what shall I do?" murmured the rich farmer. He began to think about what he could do. He worried about how to keep all the grain for when he would need it. Not once did he think about giving some away. Not once did he think about inviting poor people to come and harvest some for themselves. No. He might need it himself. He must keep it safe. But where?

He thought and counted and planned. Finally he decided what to do. He had several barns, but since these were not big enough, he would tear them down. In their place he would build new, bigger, better grain barns. Ah, yes! It was a

Memory Block

"Everyone who hears these things I say and obeys them is like a wise man. The wise man built his house on rock. But the person who hears the things I teach and does not obey them is like a foolish man. The foolish man built his house on sand" (Matthew 7:24, 26).

Purpose

Describe what the farmer did instead of sharing.

Materials

Bibles
copies of page 136
basket
scissors
index cards
marker

Purpose

Tell why it was wrong for the farmer to keep what he had for himself.

Materials

a slice of bread, pasta, oatmeal, popcorn, cereal
cardboard boxes to stack as blocks or brown construction paper and tape

wonderful plan. Not one kernel would be wasted. He would be able to keep every basketful for himself. He had plenty of other possessions too. With all his possessions and all his grain, he would truly be rich.

What a life he could have now! He wouldn't have to work again. He said to himself, "I have enough good things stored to last for many years. Rest, eat, drink, and enjoy life!" That's just what he planned to do. He could sleep in or take afternoon naps everyday. He could eat plenty of whatever he wanted at every meal and for between-meal snacks. What could possibly go wrong?

But God knew what would happen. God knew the rich man was going to die that very night. God knew his greedy, selfish plan would never come true. God said, "Foolish man! Tonight you will die. So who will get those things you have stored up for yourself?"

Jesus told this story to help people share instead of storing up like the rich farmer. At the end of the story, Jesus said, "This is how it will be for anyone who keeps things for himself and is not rich toward God." People who store up for themselves are not the people who love God. People who love God are willing to share what they have.

Divide the children into two teams and let each team build a "barn" by stacking the boxes or taping the construction paper "blocks" to the wall. Teams take turn answering questions about the story. For every correct answer, they take away a block. For an incorrect answer, they add a block. The team with the smallest "barn" at the end of the game, wins.

Who is this story about?
What problem did the man have?
What did he plan to do to solve his problem?
What was wrong with the man's plan?
What did God tell the man?
Why did Jesus tell this story?
Summary questions: **What did the farmer do instead of sharing? Why was it wrong for the farmer to keep everything for himself?**

▼ Bible Verse ▲

Purpose
Recite and explain Matthew 7:24, 26.

Materials
Bibles
a copy of page 132 displayed on the wall
a plastic bag of sand
a small rock
CD or cassette of praise music
CD or cassette player

Our verses help us remember to listen to Jesus and do what He says.
Let the children find and read Matthew 7:24, 26 aloud from the Bible.

Invite everyone to read the verses aloud from the verse poster on the wall. Then they can sit in a circle and pass the sand and rock while music plays. When you stop the music, the person with sand tells what kind of person built his house on sand. The person with the rock tells what kind of person built his house on the rock. (Optional: The child can recite the verse that goes with the item she is holding.)

At the end, talk about the verse with these questions: **Who does this verse talk about? What kind of person hears and obeys? What kind of person hears and doesn't obey? Who can say the verse by himself?**

▼ Bible and Me ▲

Following Jesus means doing what He teaches us in His stories. In the story about the rich farmer, Jesus teaches us to share. Let's have some fun showing what we can say if we store up things (not follow Jesus) and then what we can say if we share (follow Jesus).

Distribute copies of page 137. For each picture, the children will tell what to say if the child does not follow Jesus. Then they will tell what to say if the child does follow Jesus. The situations pictured on page 137 should prompt the children to think about sharing friends, food, time, toys, markers, and treats.

What does it mean to follow Jesus? (Do what Jesus teaches in His stories.) **What did Jesus teach us in His story about the builders?** (listen and do) **What did Jesus teach us in His story about the rich farmer?** (share) **What will you do if you do not follow Jesus?** (store up, not share) **What will you do if you do follow Jesus?** (Children can give an example of sharing.) **What are some times and ways you have been following Jesus?**

Purpose
Report ways they have followed Jesus.

Materials
copies of page 137

▼ Bible Project ▲

You may want to do the project at the end of the lesson and extend the session if you need more time. Be sure to inform children and parents of any changes.

Briefly introduce the Wise Builder project you planned in Lesson 18, and then do it! **We are going to be wise builders by sharing with others. We listened to what Jesus said and now we are going to do it. Let's go!**

If you have time after the project, talk about the importance of doing what Jesus taught. **What does it mean to follow Jesus?** (Do what Jesus teaches in stories.) **What did Jesus teach us in His story about the rich farmer?** (share) **What did we just do that is a way to follow Jesus?**

Purpose
Choose to continue to follow Jesus.

Materials
supplies needed to complete a sharing project during the session (food snack to prepare and share)

▼ Bible Sharing ▲

If you have time to share before or after the mini-project, ask the children to tell how they can follow Jesus by sharing this week. Encourage the children to be specific about what and when they plan to share. Give each child a kernel of unpopped corn to remind him to listen and do what Jesus taught.

Close with sentence prayers. Begin the prayer time with your sentence prayer and ask the children to repeat the same sentence or put it in their own words: "Dear God, I want to follow Jesus by sharing my things this week."

Purpose
Share how Jesus' stories help you follow Him.

Materials
a snack of grain, such as popcorn (could be the snack you prepare for the Bible Project to share with another group) kernels of unpopped popcorn

LESSON 21 — The Unforgiving Servant

Matthew 18:21-35

Memory Block

"Everyone who hears these things I say and obeys them is like a wise man. The wise man built his house on rock. But the person who hears the things I teach and does not obey them is like a foolish man. The foolish man built his house on sand" (Matthew 7:24, 26).

Purpose
Describe what one servant did instead of forgiving another.

Materials
Bibles
100 pennies
poster board
markers

Purpose
Tell why the master was angry with his servant.

Materials
crown (make from poster board and aluminum foil)

Lesson Goals
- Describe what one servant did instead of forgiving another.
- Tell why the master was angry with his servant.
- Recite and explain Matthew 7:24, 26.
- Report ways they have followed Jesus.
- Choose to continue to follow Jesus.

▼ Bible Search ▲

Divide the poster board into two sections. Label one section *Times Peter wanted to forgive.* Label the other section *Times Jesus said to forgive.*

Jesus told a story about a servant who was punished because he would not forgive. Let's read what Jesus said about forgiving others.

Guide the children to find Matthew 18:21, 22 in their Bibles. Read the verses together.

How many times did Peter want to forgive? (seven times) **How many times did Jesus say to forgive?** (70 times 7)

Show children the poster board. Ask the children to work together to count out enough pennies (or to draw enough Xs) for each side of the poster board.

▼ Bible Story ▲

What are some words that tell what God is like? (Protector, Father, Judge, Creator, Promise-Keeper.) **In today's story, Jesus says God is like a king.** Display the crown. **Listen to see what kind of king God is like.**

"The Unforgiving Servant"

I remember the day when the king asked to see me. I waited to go in and wondered why he had called for me. Maybe the king wanted to thank me for all I had done for him. I did owe him some money, but I thought I was a good servant. Someday I would pay back the money I owed the king. But, right now, I needed all my money for me.

When I was ushered to the king's throne, he asked me about the money I owed. Oh, no! Today was the day he was collecting money from his servants. What could I do? How could I pay? Even if I gave him all I had it wouldn't be enough. Sadly I turned my face to the king and admitted I could not pay.

That's when he ordered for all my possessions to be sold. He would get the money to pay what I owed. My house! My clothes! My animals! Even my wife and children were to be sold. I would never see them again. I couldn't bear it. Frantically, I fell to my knees and begged my master, "Be patient with me. I will pay you everything I owe."

As I waited, my head bowed low, the king must have felt sorry for me. When he finally spoke, he said I did not have to pay. He let me go free! What great news! I thought, "The king must think I'm pretty great to let me go free!" Now, instead of worrying about paying back the king, I could find ways to get more money for me.

Later that day I saw a man who owed me money. I decided to collect my money just like the king collected his. So I walked up beside this man and grabbed him around the neck so he couldn't run off. I said, "Pay me the money you owe me!" It was just a few dollars, and I expected him to pay me right away. He fell to his knees. His sad eyes and frantic voice begged, "Be patient with me. I will pay you everything I owe."

Me? Be patient? No way, I thought to myself. *I'll punish this man so he knows I mean what I say.* If I acted kindly, he might not ever pay me back. So I threw him into prison until he could pay everything he owed. Other servants who were watching must have thought I was a pretty tough guy. They started whispering and ran off.

Later I learned they had told the king what happened. Before long, the king called me in again. I wasn't worried. I thought the king liked me. But something changed. As I marched in, his anger boiled. "You evil servant! You begged me to forgive what you owed. So I told you that you did not have to pay anything. I had mercy on you. You should have had the same mercy on that other servant." Now I am in prison until I pay back the huge debt I owe the king. I wonder why the king changed his mind. I was only trying to get what was mine.

Jesus told this story to help Peter forgive people whenever they did wrong to him. Peter thought that seven times was enough to forgive someone. But Jesus said, "You must forgive someone even if he does wrong to you 77 times." At the end of the story, Jesus said, "This king did what my heavenly Father will do if you do not forgive your brother from your heart."

Crown one child king in the middle of the circle. Whomever the king points to tells what happened next in the story. If someone makes a mistake and the king doesn't correct it, then the king and that child trade places. Story order: King collects money, servant's things to be sold, servant set free, servant demands money, other servant begs, other servant put into prison, other servants tell the king, king puts first servant in prison.

Summary questions: **What did the first servant do instead of forgiving? Why was the king angry with the first servant?**

▼ Bible Verse ▲

Our verses help us remember to listen to Jesus and do what He says.

Let the children find and read Matthew 7:24, 26 aloud from a Bible. Then distribute paper and markers. The children can explain in a picture what the verses mean to them. As they work, go around the group and ask for volunteers to recite the verses from memory. If your children have memorized the verses, let them work on Matthew 7:24-27.

Ask each child to use his picture to explain the verses. Then summarize with the following questions. **Who does this verse talk about? What kind of person hears and obeys? What kind of person hears and doesn't obey? Who can say the verse by himself?**

Purpose
Recite and explain Matthew 7:24, 26.

Materials
Bibles
paper
markers or colored pencils

▼ Bible and Me ▲

Practice the "Forgiveness Rap" before class.
Following Jesus means doing what He teaches us in His stories. In the story about the unforgiving servant, Jesus teaches us to forgive. Let's do a rap to help us remember to forgive.

The rap is printed on page 138. Start the rap and invite the children to join you whenever they can. In between times of saying the rap, answer one or more questions from page 138. Conclude with the following review questions about following Jesus.

What does it mean to follow Jesus? (Do what Jesus teaches in His stories.) **What did Jesus teach us in His story about the builders?** (listen and do) **What did Jesus teach us in His story about the servant?** (forgive) **What will you do if you do not follow Jesus?** (punish people) **What will you do if you do follow Jesus?** (Children can give an example of forgiving.) **What are some times and ways you have been following Jesus?** (Children report.)

Purpose
Report ways they have followed Jesus.

Materials
copies of page 138

▼ Bible Project ▲

Introduce the Wise Builder project planned for today in Lesson 18, and then do it! **We are going to be wise builders by writing a story about forgiveness. Our own version of Jesus' story will help us this week to be forgiving.** See unit page 112 for a simple idea for a modern-day story on forgiveness.

After you write the story, talk about the importance of doing what Jesus taught. **What does it mean to follow Jesus?** (Do what Jesus teaches in stories.) **What did Jesus teach us in His story about the builders?** (listen and do) **What did Jesus teach us in His story about the unforgiving servant?** (forgive) **What did we just write about that is a way to follow Jesus?**

Purpose
Choose to continue to follow Jesus.

Materials
supplies needed to complete a forgiving project during the session (writing tablet and black marker to write a group story)

▼ Bible Sharing ▲

While you eat the royal food, share about times and ways to follow Jesus this week. Pass the crown around the circle and let the child share who wears the crown. The child can share a way to help, share, forgive, or she can recite the unit memory block.

Close by singing some of the children's favorite praise songs.

Purpose
Share how Jesus' stories help you follow Him.

Materials
a snack of the king's royal food ("royal pudding" pops or snacks served on a silver tray)
crown used in the Bible story
CD or cassette of praise songs about following Jesus
CD or cassette player

The Loving Father

Luke 15:11-24

Lesson Goals
- Describe how the father showed love when his son came home.
- Tell why it might seem unusual for the father to give a feast.
- Recite and demonstrate Matthew 7:24, 26.
- Report ways they have followed Jesus.
- Choose to continue to follow Jesus.

▼ Bible Search ▲

Jesus told a story about a father who still loved his son when he came home from doing wrong. Let's find out what the father did to show love to his son.

Guide the children to find and read Luke 15:22, 23. The children can describe in their own words what the father did for his son. Then help the children prepare a "feast" for everyone to eat during Bible Sharing time.

Summarize the activity with these questions: **What did the father do to show love to his son?** (gave him the best clothes; gave him a party; made a feast) **Do you think it was unusual for the father to celebrate? Why or why not?**

▼ Bible Story ▲

Where do you see hats and whistles like these? Display the party hat and whistle. **Listen to see who has a party in this story.**

"The Loving Father"

"It's off to the city I go, . . . I've got lots of money to blow!" *(Sing the words.)* That's probably the kind of song the younger son might have whistled as he left home. His grin probably stretched from ear to ear. He had convinced his father to give him his half of the father's property. The son got everything that he would have received when his father died. He had more money now than he could imagine. His coins jingled in rhythm as he marched down the road to a faraway country.

At home, his older brother worked and worked. He worked as hard as a slave. He never disobeyed. He did everything his father wanted. But in the faraway country the younger brother did everything his father would not have liked. He spent money here, there, and everywhere. He thought his wild living would last and last and last. He didn't think about running out of money. But it happened. Too soon, his pockets were silent; his last coins were gone.

His problem got worse when a famine came over the whole country. Even if he had money, there wasn't any food to buy. The only work he could find was the worst possible job. A man who owned some pigs said the son could go to the field and feed the pigs. Being around those squealy, stinky, muddy pigs made him feel sick. He was so hungry that he thought about eating the pods that the pigs ate. Not once did anyone give him anything to eat.

All he could do was think—of home. Out in the pig field, the son remembered

Memory Block
"Everyone who hears these things I say and obeys them is like a wise man. The wise man built his house on rock. But the person who hears the things I teach and does not obey them is like a foolish man. The foolish man built his house on sand" (Matthew 7:24, 26).

Purpose
Describe how the father showed love when his son came home.

Materials
Bibles
items for children to prepare a "feast" (ice cream and toppings for sundaes)

Purpose
Tell why it might seem unusual for the Father to give a feast.

Materials
a party hat and whistle to display
copies of page 139
a box of Bible story props, such as nice Bible time clothing, ring, sandals (optional)

his own father's fields. He remembered the workers his father fed everyday. Those men had to work hard, but they had plenty to eat. That was better than starving in a field of pigs. Maybe his father would let him be one of the men who worked in the fields. Maybe. He hoped so.

Faint with hunger, he began the long journey home. He thought about what he would say: "Father, I have sinned against God and have done wrong to you. I am not good enough to be called your son. But let me be like one of your servants."

But the father didn't want his son to be a servant. He wanted him to be his son. When the son was still a long way down the road, the father saw him and ran to meet him. His eyes filled with tears when he saw the boy's ragged clothes and starved body. He felt sorry for him in spite of how bad he smelled. The father pulled his son close to him, and he hugged and kissed him.

The son was quick to say, "I have done wrong. I am not good enough to be called your son." Then the father showed love the son did not deserve. The father urged his servants to quickly bring the best new clothes for his son. They put a ring on his finger and sandals on his feet to show that the father still wanted the boy to be his son. Then the father commanded that a fat calf be killed so they could have a feast. The father exclaimed, "My son was lost, but now he is found!" And the celebration began.

Jesus told this story to show how much God loves His children, even when they do wrong. When we do wrong and stop following Jesus, God is waiting for us to change and start obeying Jesus again.

Give copies of page 139 to the children. Help the children solve the riddles to review the Bible story: Father's property or money, faraway land, pig, younger son, father, sandals.

If you have time, allow students to use the Bible story props to act out the story.

Summary questions: **How did the father show love to his son? Why might it seem unusual for the father to give this son a feast?**

▼ Bible Verse ▲

Purpose
Recite and demonstrate Matthew 7:24, 26.

Materials
Bibles, copy of the verse poster from page 132

Display the verse poster. Ask the children to find Matthew 7:24, 26 in their Bibles. Read the verses together. **Our verses help us remember to listen to Jesus and do what He says.**

Ask for volunteers to recite the verses from memory. (Work on verses 24-27 if your children need a challenge.) Then allow small groups to each prepare a brief drama. The children will act out the mini-drama while one child in the group says the verses. Each group needs at least three people: speaker, builder on rock, builder on sand. Other children could be the house on the rock, house on sand, and the storm. Encourage them to use the words of the verses to give them ideas for what to do in their mini-dramas. After the dramas, gather in a group to review.

Who does this verse talk about? What kind of person hears and obeys? What kind of person hears and doesn't obey?

▼ Bible and Me ▲

Following Jesus means doing what He teaches in His stories. In the story about the father who showed love, Jesus teaches us we can start following Him again if we have stopped doing what He taught us.

Ask the children for ideas of times when we do something that does not follow Jesus. For ideas, distribute page 140. The pictures at the top of the page illustrate the four previous lessons: want to follow Jesus; help people, including those who don't like us; share instead of storing up; forgive instead of punish. Then on the lower half of the page, the children can fill in the blanks: wrong, sorry, right.

Conclude with questions to review following Jesus. **What does it mean to follow Jesus?** (Do what Jesus teaches in His stories.) **What did Jesus teach us in His story about the builders?** (listen and do) **What did Jesus teach using His story about the loving father?** (come back) **What are some times and ways you have been following Jesus?**

Purpose
Report ways they have followed Jesus.

Materials
copies of page 140
pencils

▼ Bible Project ▲

Briefly introduce the Wise Builder project you planned for today in Lesson 18, and then do it! **We are going to be wise builders by showing our love to others. We listened to what Jesus said and now we are going to do it!**

After the project, talk about the importance of doing what Jesus taught. **What does it mean to follow Jesus?** (Do what Jesus teaches in stories.) **What did Jesus teach us in His story about the father and son?** (love) **What did we just do that is a way to follow Jesus?**

Purpose
Choose to continue to follow Jesus.

Materials
supplies needed to complete a loving project during the session (paper, pencils, cards, envelopes, Sunday school papers, markers)

▼ Bible Sharing ▲

Serve the "feast" prepared by the children in Bible Search (ice cream sundaes) or provide barbecue sandwiches or hamburgers (like the fatted calf).

While you enjoy the feast, ask the children to tell what way to follow Jesus is in each story Jesus told. Encourage each child to recite the memory verses.

Close with prayer. Hold hands and pray to ask God to help each child follow Jesus. Sing the children's favorite praise songs and songs about following Jesus.

Purpose
Share how Jesus' stories help you follow Him.

Materials
items for the feast prepared during the Bible Search
CD or cassette of praise songs
CD or cassette player

Bible Search

 UNIT 5, LESSON 18

Bible Story

Cut apart the phrases.
Tell who might have said each sentence.

I chose to dig deep to the rock.	The flood did not shake my house.
I built right on the sand.	The wind beat my house down.
I built on a rock foundation.	The wind did not harm my house.
I did not take time for a foundation.	My house was completely destroyed.
I built my house strong.	I listen to and obey Jesus.
The flood washed away my house.	I love to just listen to Jesus' stories.

Cut apart the cards.
Listen as your teacher reads.
Decide if each child wants to follow Jesus.

Jordan saw his little sister fall off her tricycle, but he hurried away, pretending he didn't see her get hurt.	Sally's uncle gave her a bag of candy. She hid it in her bedroom closet when her friends came over to play.	A friend accidentally spilled red punch on Tara's new dress. Tara screamed, "It's ruined. I'll never forgive you."
When Mom got home from the store, Evan stopped playing in the yard and helped Mom carry in all the sacks of groceries.	Elizabeth got two new baby dolls for her birthday. She shared one with a friend who doesn't have a new baby doll.	Justin's little brother broke his Lego® car. His little brother began to cry and said, "I'm sorry." Justin said, "I forgive you. We can fix it. Let's get you a tissue."

Bible Verse

Find and read Matthew 7:24, 26.
Fill in the missing words.

Everyone who _____

these things I say

and _____ them is like

a _____ man.

The _____ man built

his house on rock.

But the person who _____ the things I teach

and does _____

_____ them is like a

_____ man.

The _____ man

built his house on _____.

Matthew 7:24, 26

Bible Search

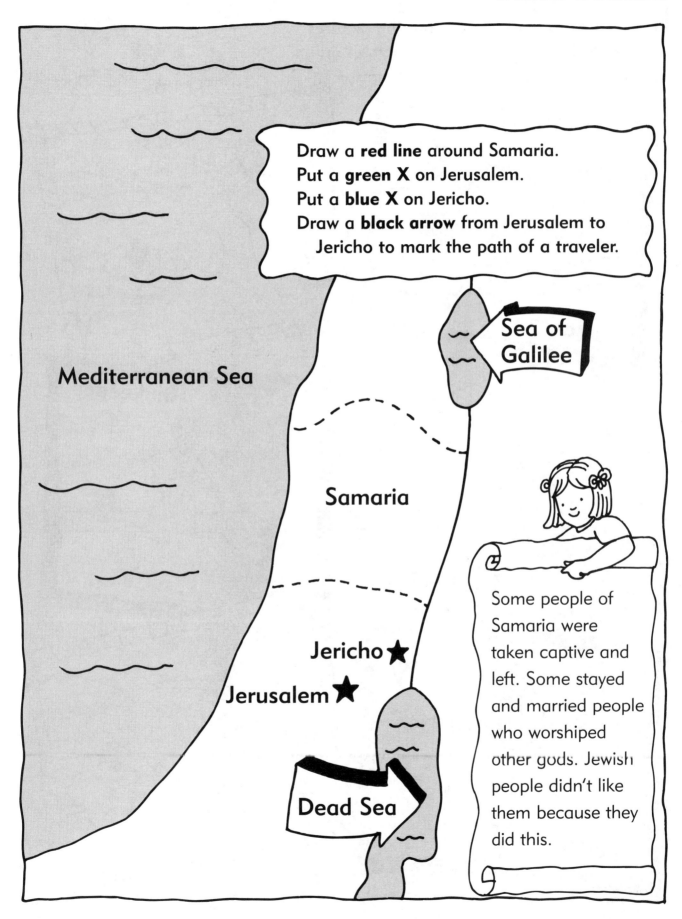

Draw a **red line** around Samaria.
Put a **green X** on Jerusalem.
Put a **blue X** on Jericho.
Draw a **black arrow** from Jerusalem to Jericho to mark the path of a traveler.

Mediterranean Sea

Sea of Galilee

Samaria

Jericho ★

Jerusalem ★

Dead Sea

Some people of Samaria were taken captive and left. Some stayed and married people who worshiped other gods. Jewish people didn't like them because they did this.

© 2004 Standard Publishing. Permission is granted to reproduce this page for ministry purposes only—not for resale.

Bible Story

Krista wants to tell the story, but the pictures
  are out of order. Help her put them in order.

Samaritan

priest

Levite

innkeeper

traveler

robbers

Bible and Me

Sometimes it's hard to help people. Draw lines from the Samaritan to the excuses he could say. Draw lines from the child to the excuses he could say.

He wouldn't help me!

I would have to walk to the inn.

His friends hate me.

He didn't help me last week.

It would cost me money.

My friends would laugh at me.

I'm busy playing now.

It might take too long.

- Why might it be hard to help people?
- What will you do if you do not follow Jesus?
- What will you do if you do follow Jesus?

Bible Search

Find and read Luke 12:19. Then read what it means to *store up* things.

store up (or away)

means to put away something for future use; to lay it up; to put it in a warehouse or other place to keep it safe. The rich man stored up enough crops for many years.

Cut apart the cards. Choose a card. Is the word the same or opposite of *store up*?

greedy	**share**
give away	**selfish**
stingy	**generous**
kind	**self-centered**

 UNIT 5, LESSON 20

Bible and Me

Read the story on each card.
Tell what to say if the child does not follow Jesus.
Tell what to say if the child does follow Jesus.

Elizabeth loves to talk to her best friend, Sally, at recess. They notice the new girl standing by herself on the other side of the playground.

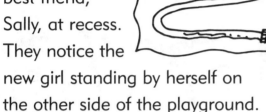

José just heard Justin tell the teacher he can't find his lunch. José walks across the room and looks in his sack. He has ham, his favorite!

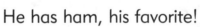

Evan goes every Wednesday after school to play checkers with Grandpa. Since it's such a warm day, it would be fun to run over to the park instead.

Jordan likes his Lego® blocks. When his friend comes to play, he wants to be sure to have enough blocks for the things he builds.

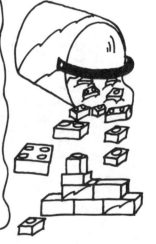

Kyle's grandma just gave him some new bright markers. He doesn't want them to get all used up when his cousins come to visit.

Tara helped Mom make crispy treats for dessert. Mom is in the other room, and she wouldn't see if Tara hid some in her room for later.

Bible and Me

Say the Forgiveness Rap.

F·O·R·G·I·V·E

That is what God does for me!

F·O·R·G·I·V·E

That's the way
I want to be!

Who is like God in the story?

Who is like us in the story?

How did the king treat a servant who did not forgive?

How would the king treat a servant who did forgive?

What can you say when someone treats you wrong?

 Unit 5, Lesson 21

Bible Story

Answer the story riddles.
Use the pictures if you need help.

1. Half of me went to the youngest son.
   Who am I?

2. One son left home to visit me.
   Who am I?

3. I ate pods out in the field.
   Who am I?

father

4. I remembered my father's workers had enough to eat.
   Who am I?

5. I ran to meet the son when he came home.
   Who am I?

son

faraway land

6. Servants put me on the son's feet.
   Who am I?

Bible and Me

Look at the pictures.
The children will remind you of
ways to follow Jesus.

I want to follow Jesus.

I want to help people, even people who don't like me.

I want to forgive.

I want to share instead of storing up things.

When I do something that does not follow Jesus, I can . . .

1. Say, "I was _____ ."

2. Say, "I'm _____ " to Jesus.

3. Do the _____ thing right away.

_____
Name

Word Bank

hurt   right   sorry
bad   wrong   mad

UNIT 5, LESSON 22

Jesus Helps Me Worship

Unit Memory Block
"Praise the Lord, and worship him. Tell everyone what he has done. Tell them how great he is. Sing praise to the Lord, because he has done great things. Let all the world know what he has done" (Isaiah 12:4, 5).

Memory Challenge
"Lord our Master, your name is the most wonderful name in all the earth! It brings you praise in heaven above. You have taught children and babies to sing praises to you" (Psalm 8:1, 2a).

23 Worship by Praying
Matthew 6:15; Luke 11: 1-4
Jesus taught His followers how to act when they pray and what kinds of things to say. Right praying is one way to worship God and tell God how special He is.

24 Worship by Giving
Mark 12:41-44; Luke 21:1-4
Jesus taught His followers what kind of giving pleases God. Right giving is one way to worship God and tell God how special He is.

25 Worship by Remembering
Luke 22:7-20; Acts 20:7
Jesus asked His followers to show He is special by remembering what He had done. Remembering Jesus is one way to worship Him and tell Him how special He is.

26 Worship by Singing
Matthew 21:1-16; Psalm 8:1, 2
Jesus was pleased when He heard crowds of people and even children sing praise to Him. Singing to Jesus is one way to worship Him and tell Him how special He is.

By the end of the unit, the leaders and learners will

KNOW four ways to worship.
FEEL a sense of joy in being able to express worship.
DO Joyfully worship God and Jesus.

Unit Value

Children need two kinds of information to help them learn to worship. One is seeing examples of true worship. The other is hearing what worship is and isn't. If either kind of information is missing, the children's worship will be incomplete. This unit provides both kinds of information. The Bible stories provide examples of worship. The first lesson provides the bad example of the hypocrites and the good example of Jesus' own prayer. Lesson 2 provides the example of the poor widow. The third lesson deals with Jesus' followers remembering Him in the Lord's Supper. And the final lesson focuses on the enthusiastic example of the crowds and the children in the temple.

In addition to seeing Bible examples, children absorb much from the examples of those adults they admire. That means their ability to worship will, in part, reflect your own understanding and enthusiasm for worship. If you feel weak in this area, your worship can grow right along with the children. The Bible verses for this unit will help you know ways to worship. The application activities will help you to identify what it means to worship, examine your reason(s) for worship, plan ways to expand your worship, and actually be involved in worship in each Bible Sharing time. The more enthusiastic you are about your worship, the more enthusiastic the children will be about theirs.

▼ Bible Project ▲

Praise Packet

The learners will make a Praise Packet to help them worship on their level during worship times with family and other adults. The Praise Packet will help children who regularly worship in an adult worship time or who only visit the adult worship time once a month or once a quarter to pray, give, remember Jesus, and sing in a meaningful way.

The Praise Packet is not as much a group project as some projects in the book, but the children can work together and encourage each other to use the packet in worship times.

Week 1: Make the Praise Packet folder. Make the praying hands card.

Week 2: Make the bookmark to help them worship by giving.

Week 3: Make the "Remember Jesus" booklet explained in the Bible and Me section.

Week 4: Make a song list or write a group worship song. Plan a time to use the Praise Packets in worship.

Praying Hands Card

Fold a piece of construction paper in half to make a card. Place your hands on the folded paper with the outside of your hand on the fold. Trace your hand and cut out the shape, leaving the folded edge of the paper uncut.

PRAISE PACKET FOLDER

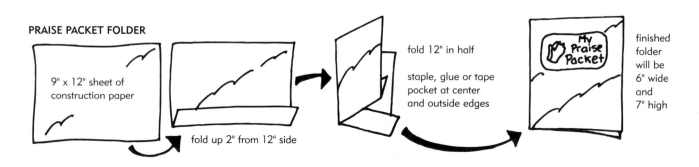

9" x 12" sheet of construction paper

fold up 2" from 12" side

fold 12" in half

staple, glue or tape pocket at center and outside edges

My Praise Packet

finished folder will be 6" wide and 7" high

BOOKMARK
(to be cut out and centered on 2" x 7" piece of construction paper)

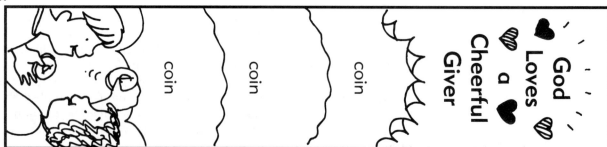

coin

coin

coin

God Loves a Cheerful Giver

Worship by Praying

Matthew 6:5-15; Luke 11:1-4

Lesson Goals
- Tell what Jesus' followers wanted to learn.
- Name three things to remember when you pray.
- Begin to memorize Isaiah 12:4, 5.
- Tell what it means to worship God.
- Joyfully worship God and Jesus.

▼ Bible Search ▲

Jesus' followers wanted to learn how to pray. Let's find three things Jesus told them.

Distribute page 155. Help the children decode the symbols and fill in the blanks. Then guide the children to find and read the verses from Matthew 6. (Find the book of Matthew in the table of contents of a Bible. Locate the page the book begins on, then the big 6 for the chapter and the small 5, 7, or 11 for the verse.) Let the children report their answers.

What did Jesus' followers want to learn? What did Jesus say to do? Not do? Why didn't Jesus say to "fold your hands"? Why do we fold our hands and close our eyes?

▼ Bible Story ▲

Using ten cards, print each sentence of the model prayer and a Primary-level version on index cards. The sentences are listed after the story.

Show a sculpture of praying hands or your own folded hands. **What way to worship does this remind you of? Listen to see if folding your hands is important to do when you pray.**

"Worship by Praying"

People coming to the synagogue could certainly hear someone praying inside. When they walked in, they immediately turned to look at him. Everything he did made people look at him. He prayed loudly so everyone would listen to him. His booming voice droned on and on. Sometimes he said the same things over and over. He thought God would hear him because of the way he prayed.

But people who started following Jesus noticed Jesus' prayers were different. He talked to God instead of talking so everyone around could hear Him. Sometimes He prayed all night, but He didn't just say the same things over and over. One day when Jesus finished praying, one of the disciples said, "John taught his followers how to pray. Lord, please teach us how to pray, too."

Jesus must have been glad to see that the disciples wanted to learn to pray. He told them what not to do and then He told them what they should do. Jesus said it was wrong to pray loudly just so people would listen, like the man in the synagogue. Prayers are for talking to God. Prayers are not a way to talk so people will listen to us. Jesus called the man in the synagogue a hypocrite because he was only pretending to talk to God. Jesus said that God hears us wherever we are. So it

---

Memory Block
"Praise the Lord, and worship him. Tell everyone what he has done. Tell them how great he is. Sing praise to the Lord, because he has done great things. Let all the world know what he has done" (Isaiah 12:4, 5).

Purpose
Tell what Jesus' followers wanted to learn.

Materials
Bibles
copies of page 155
pencils

Purpose
Name three things to remember when you pray.

Materials
index cards
markers
a sculpture or picture of praying hands (optional)

is better to go home and pray in your closet with the door shut than to stand on the street corner so everyone can hear you.

Jesus also said it was wrong to say things over and over and over to get God to listen to you—like the hypocrite. People who pray like that don't really mean anything when they pray. Jesus said God knows what we need even before we ask Him, but He still wants us to ask. And then Jesus did something very helpful. He showed us what we could say when we talk to God.

First, He talked about how special God's name is. Then He prayed for the things God would want to happen. Next He showed us how to ask for things we need, like food for each day. And then He asked God to forgive us for sinning—choosing to do wrong. Finally He asked God to protect us from Satan.

Many times people still pray with the words that Jesus spoke that day. We can pray Jesus' prayer right now. *(Pray Matthew 6:9-13.)*

The followers didn't want to be hypocrites. They wanted to really talk to God—not just say the same words again and again and again every time. They wanted to be like Jesus in both the way He acted when He prayed and in the things He said when He prayed, because the way Jesus prayed is the way to pray that pleases God.

Put the index cards with Jesus' prayer, in order, in a column. Let the children read aloud the other six sentences and match them to Jesus' prayer, in a second column.

Our Father in heaven, may your name always be kept holy. (God, You and Your name are more special than anyone else.)

May your kingdom come and what you want to be done, here on earth as it is in heaven. (We want everyone to do what You want.)

Give us the food we need for each day. (Help us have enough food each day.)

Forgive us for our sins, just as we have forgiven those who have sinned against us. (We forgive people who hurt us; please forgive us for the wrong we do.)

And do not cause us to be tempted, but save us from the Evil one. (Please keep us safe from bad things, especially Satan.)

Summary questions: **What did Jesus' followers want to learn? What are three ways Jesus' followers can pray like Jesus?**

▼ Bible Verse ▲

Purpose
Begin to memorize Isaiah 12:4, 5.

Materials
Bibles
copies of page 156
tape
scissors
strips of construction paper
glue sticks (optional)

Before the session, cut out two sets of verse shapes from page 156.

Our verses help us remember to worship the Lord with our words and our songs. Let's find them in Isaiah 12:4, 5. (Find the book of Isaiah in the table of contents of a Bible. Locate the page the book begins on, then the big 12 for the chapter and the small 4 for the verse.)

Put one set of verse shapes in order on the wall. Scramble the order of the second set and pass them to students or pairs of students. The child with the shape for the first sentence reads it aloud. The rest of the shapes must follow in order. Repeat this several times. If time allows, give each child a set of shapes to glue, in order, on a strip of construction paper.

What do these verses talk about? (worship) **What two ways to worship are in these verses?** (tell, sing) **Where can we find these verses? What is the first sentence of the verses?**

▼ Bible and Me ▲

Worshiping God (or Jesus) means telling Him how special He is. We can do it in a song or in a prayer like it says in our Bible verses.

Distribute copies of page 157. Read the instructions and the definition of worship. In the prayer, children will underline phrases that worship God. In the second section, circle the prayer positions you can use when you worship. In the third section, decode ways to worship God (or Jesus): sing, write, pray.

What does it mean to worship God or Jesus? (Tell Him how special He is.) **What positions are important to use in worship?** (Any way that helps us think about God instead of what is going on around you.) **What are some words that tell God or Jesus He is special? What are some words that don't worship God but still are good words to pray? How can you tell if the words in a prayer are worshiping God?**

Purpose
Tell what it means to worship God.

Materials
copies of page 157
colored pencils

▼ Bible Project ▲

See the instructions for making the praise packet folder and praying hands card on the unit pages. Before class, make a sample folder and card. Print or type the words of Jesus' prayer in Matthew 6 to fit in the praying hands card. Copy the prayer for each child.

Worshiping God (or Jesus) means telling Him how special He is. We are going to make a Praise packet to help us worship God by praying, giving, remembering Jesus, and by singing.

Display the sample folder and explain what things will be made to put in it. Distribute materials and help children make their folders. (See unit page 142.) Children should print Isaiah 12:4, 5 on the fronts of their packets, or print it as they recite what they have learned. Make the praying hands card: trace each child's hand onto folded construction paper, cut out the card without cutting the fold. Glue the words of Jesus' prayer on the inside. If you have time, children can dictate Jesus' prayer in their own words.

Talk about how to use the Praise Packet. Keep the Praise Packets in the classroom. You will add to them in Lessons 24-26.

Purpose
Joyfully worship God and Jesus.

Materials
construction paper
transparent tape
crayons
colored pencils
markers
praying hands pattern
glue sticks
scissors

▼ Bible Sharing ▲

While you eat, ask the children to review the three things Jesus taught about prayer and the kind of words that worship God. Ask for volunteers to tell what they learned.

Lead a time of worship. Sing favorite worship songs or learn new songs. Then close with prayer. Ask the children to use their prayer cards to remind them of some things to say to God. Or read the words of Jesus' prayer together.

Purpose
Share how Jesus helps you worship.

Materials
a snack of something God made—fruit or vegetable plate with dip
CD or cassette of praise songs
CD or cassette player

Worship by Giving

Mark 12:41-44; Luke 21:1-4

Memory Block

"Praise the Lord, and worship him. Tell everyone what he has done. Tell them how great he is. Sing praise to the Lord, because he has done great things. Let all the world know what he has done" (Isaiah 12:4, 5).

Purpose

Describe the woman who worshiped by giving her money.

Materials

Bibles,
copies of page 158
the materials listed on that page

Purpose

Tell what made the woman's worship different form that of other people.

Materials

an offering plate or the money container made in Bible Search
pennies

Lesson Goals

- Describe the woman who worshiped by giving her money.
- Tell what made the woman's worship different form that of other people.
- Memorize Isaiah 12:4, 5.
- Tell why we worship.
- Joyfully worship God and Jesus.

▼ Bible Search ▲

In our story today, Jesus wanted His followers to learn more about giving. One thing they already knew was where to put their money. They didn't put in an offering plate. Let's learn about where they put it.

Guide the children to find and read Mark 12:41, 42 in a Bible. Then distribute copies of page 158. Read about the temple money box. Work together to make a Bible times offering container and coins.

In Mark 12:42, who put two small coins in the offering? How do we usually collect offerings? How did Bible people usually collect offerings? Which way do you like best? Why? Do you think God cares which way we collect offering?

▼ Bible Story ▲

Display the offering plate or container. **What way to worship God does this remind you of? Listen to see if having lots of money to give God is the worship that pleases Him the most.**

"Worship by Giving"

In the right corner outside the temple there were thirteen trumpet-shaped boxes. People put gifts of money for God in those boxes when they came to worship. Jesus sat in the temple one day watching the crowd of people put their coins into the boxes. From where He was sitting, He saw how much money each person brought for God. Some brought a lot. Some brought little.

It was easy to see which people were rich. They had nice clothes. They didn't look hungry, because they had plenty of money to buy food. The rich people liked to come to the temple to bring their gifts to God. As they dropped money into the boxes, the clinking and clanking sound made them feel good.

One woman who came to the temple didn't have nice clothes to wear. She didn't look like she even had enough money to buy food. She was poor because she was a widow; she had no husband to care for her. In her hand she held tightly to all the money she had: two very small copper coins. If she put those coins in the offering, she would have no money left to buy more food. What would she do? Would she walk on past the offering boxes? Would she put in just one coin? If she put them both in, what would she eat?

As Jesus watched that woman, He could tell how much she loved God. He could see how much she wanted to bring her money gift to God. As she quietly made her way to the offering box, she must have been smiling inside. Even though she didn't have much money, she wanted God to have it all. Plink, plink. It dropped softly on top of the other coins.

Jesus called his followers to Him to tell them what He had seen. "I tell you the truth. This poor widow gave only two small coins. But she really gave more than all those rich people. The rich have plenty; they gave only what they did not need. This woman is very poor. But she gave all she had. And she needed that money to help her live."

Jesus spoke His words very strongly. He wanted His followers to learn that giving is a way to show love to God. How much people gave was not the most important thing. The most important thing was how much they wanted to give. Rich people gave much money, but they didn't love God enough to give all they had. They have their extra money. The poor woman loved God so much that she wanted to give to God even what she needed for herself. She gave all she had. The small gift from the poor woman pleased God.

Ask children the following review questions. Give every child a penny each time a review question is answered correctly.

Where was Jesus watching people?
What were the people doing?
How much did the rich people give?
How much did the poor widow give?
Why did the poor widow give all she had?
What did Jesus say to His followers about the woman's gift?
What did Jesus want His followers to learn?

Then help the children talk about how it feels to give all you have. Let them know it is hard to love God so much that you want to give all you have. **If the woman had as many pennies as you are holding, how many do you think she would have put in the box? How would it feel? Why? Would it be easier to be like the rich people or the poor widow? Why? Right now, which person would you like to be like? Why? How many of your pennies would you like to give to God? Why?** Pass on offering plate for those who want to give any pennies to God. This should not be a forced giving time. It's hard!

Summary questions: **Describe the woman in the story. What made the woman's gift different from the gifts of other people?**

▼ Bible Verse ▲

Our verses help us remember to worship the Lord with our words and our songs. Let's find them in Isaiah 12:4, 5.

Guide children to find Isaiah 12:4, 5 in their Bibles. Read the verses together. Distribute the sets of verse shapes. Let teams of 2-3 children put the shapes in order on the table or wall. Then say the verses in a rhythm. Use claps, snaps, and leg slaps. Repeat the verses as a large group until they become familiar. For variation, let pairs or trios of children take turns doing the verses in rhythm.

What do these verses talk about? (worship) **What two ways to worship are in these verses?** (tell, sing) **Where can we find these verses? Who can say the verses?** (Encourage pairs and trios if no one does it alone.)

Purpose
Memorize Isaiah 12:4, 5.

Materials
Bibles and several sets of verse shapes cut from page 156

▼ Bible and Me ▲

We worship God because He is so special. If we give our money to God to show Him how special He is, then our giving is worship, too. Let's think of some of the special reasons we give to God.

Ask children to think of reasons they worship God—Bible stories that tell of special things He has done; promises He has made to us; things He taught us; because we love Him; and so on. Ask them to print or draw their reasons on slips of paper. Pass around the offering container made in Bible Search and have the children put their slips of paper in the container as they tell the reason we give to God.

What does it mean to worship God or Jesus? (Tell Him how special He is.) **Why do we worship God? What are some words to say that tell God or Jesus He is special? What kind of giving worships God?**

Option: Play a guessing game. Have the children act out their reasons to worship, and let the group guess the reason they are acting out.

Purpose
Tell why we worship.

Materials
offering container made in Bible Search
slips of paper, pencils

▼ Bible Project ▲

Before class, make bookmark patterns from page 142. See the description of this project on page 142.

Worshiping God (or Jesus) means telling Him how special He is. We are going to make another item to include in our Praise Packets. The Praise Packet will help us worship God by praying, giving, remembering Jesus, and by singing.

Distribute materials. Cut bookmarks from construction paper using patterns. Decorate them. Print part of the verse from 2 Corinthians 9:7 on the chalkboard: "God loves a cheerful giver." The children can include that verse on their bookmarks. Cover the bookmarks with clear adhesive plastic. With adult help, some children may want to make small slits in their bookmarks to hold one or two coins. Then put the bookmarks in the Praise Packets.

Talk about how to use the bookmark in the Praise Packet (use it during the offering time to remember to give and to thank God; look up 2 Corinthians 9:7 in your Bible; keep money there until offering time).

Purpose
Joyfully worship God and Jesus.

Materials
construction paper
crayons
markers
poster board
scissors
clear adhesive-backed plastic
stickers

▼ Bible Sharing ▲

Serve the coins or fruit snacks. After you eat, play a game. Children sit in a circle and pass a coin around the circle while music plays. When the music stops, the child holding the coin can ask a question about the story or about what it means to worship.

Sing other favorite worship songs.

Purpose
Share how Jesus helps you worship.

Materials
foil covered chocolate coins or rolled-up fruit snacks (in the shape of treasure chests, coins)
a coin
CD or cassette of praise songs
CD or cassette player

Worship by Remembering

Luke 22:7-20; Acts 20:7

Lesson Goals

- Tell what Jesus asked His friends to do.
- Name special things we remember Jesus did.
- Recite and explain Isaiah 12:4, 5.
- Demonstrate ways to worship Jesus by remembering how special He is.
- Joyfully worship God and Jesus.

> **Memory Block**
> "Praise the Lord, and worship him. Tell everyone what he has done. Tell them how great he is. Sing praise to the Lord, because he has done great things. Let all the world know what he has done" (Isaiah 12:4, 5).

▼ Bible Search ▲

Be prepared to answer questions about Passover by reading Exodus 11, 12.
When Jesus ate a Passover meal with His apostles, He talked to them about remembering. Passover was a time for remembering.

Guide the children to find and read Luke 22:8 in a Bible. Then distribute copies of page 159 and read about the Passover. Let the children report.
What did Jesus and His followers remember at the Passover meal? (How God helped their ancestors long ago in Egypt.) **What special foods were eaten at the Passover meal?** (lamb, bitter herbs, bread without yeast) **Why do you think Jesus gave us a special time to remember Him?**

Option: Provide ingredients for Bible times bread. See the recipe and instructions on page 60. A helper may bake the bread for you while you tell the Bible story.

> **Purpose**
> Tell what Jesus asked His friends to do.
>
> **Materials**
> Bibles
> copies of page 159

▼ Bible Story ▲

Before the session, cut apart the letters on page 160.
Display the Bible times bread and let children sample it. **Jesus asked His followers to eat some bread like this to help them remember something important. Listen to see what He wanted them to remember.**

> **Purpose**
> Name special things we remember Jesus did.
>
> **Materials**
> Bible times bread (recipe on page 60)
> copy of page 160
> scissors

"Worship by Remembering"

Peter and I climbed the stairs to a large room. It was the first day of the Passover Feast. My name is John. Peter and I had just asked Jesus where we could fix our Passover meal. Jesus had told us about this room where we could get the meal ready.

Everything had happened just as Jesus said. First we followed a man walking into Jerusalem. He had carried a jar of water to this house. When he stopped here, we knew this was the place. We asked the house owner to show us the room where we could eat our Passover meal. The room was ready just like Jesus said it would be. We worked to get everything ready for the meal. We would have roast lamb, juice, bitter herbs, and bread made without yeast. Peter and I were ready that evening when Jesus and the other apostles arrived. They climbed up the stairs and joined us.

When everyone was ready, we reclined around the low table. As we began to eat, we remembered how God had cared for our people. Passover was a very important time for us because it helped us remember how God saved our ancestors when they were slaves in Egypt. The first time anyone ate a Passover meal was the night before the slaves left Egypt. Each food we ate helped us remember something about the time when God delivered them out of Egypt.

That Passover meal was a special time for Jesus. It was His last Passover. Jesus talked about what was going to happen to Him and how He felt. He said, "I wanted to eat this Passover meal with you before I die. I will never eat another Passover meal until it is given its true meaning in the kingdom of God."

Then Jesus did something that made that Passover very special for us also. He picked up a cup of grape juice, thanked God for it, and gave it to us. He said, "Take this cup and give it to everyone here." Then He took some of the bread made without yeast. After He thanked God for the bread, Jesus broke it into pieces and gave it to us. Then Jesus said some words I still remember, "This bread will help you think of my body that is going to die for you. This juice will help you think of my blood. When you eat this bread and drink this juice, you can remember me."

After Jesus went back to Heaven, all of us who followed Jesus did what Jesus asked. Now, instead of eating the Passover meal, we meet together on Sunday to remember Jesus. The most important thing we do is to break some bread, just like Jesus did. When we eat the bread and drink the grape juice, it is always a special time for remembering all the special things Jesus has done for us.

Play the Remembering Game. Turn the eight letters (cut from page 160) face down. Ask the children the questions for each round. Round 1: a child will turn over a letter for each correct answer. Round 2: for each correct answer, the children will guess what letter comes first, next, and so on, to unscramble an important word from the story.

Round 1, Remember the Story: **Name the special meal. Name who fixed the foods. Name some of the foods. Name who ate this meal. Name where they ate the meal. Name what Jesus gave them to eat. Name what Jesus gave them to drink. Name what Jesus asked them to do.** Round 2, Remember Jesus: **Name someone Jesus made to see. Name someone Jesus made to walk. Name what Jesus did to a storm. Name what Jesus did for 5,000 people. Name someone Jesus made alive. Name Jesus' most special miracle. Name the job Jesus gave us to do. Name what Jesus is preparing for us.**

Summary questions: **What did Jesus ask His followers to do?** (Unscramble "remember.") **What is the most special thing to remember Jesus did?** (He died and came back alive.)

▼ Bible Verse ▲

Purpose
Recite and explain Isaiah 12:4, 5.

Materials
Bibles, several sets of verse shapes from page 156
two index cards
a marker

Before the session, print "Say the verse" on one card and "Tell what the verse means" on the other card.

Our verses help us remember to worship the Lord with our words and our songs. Let's find them in Isaiah 12:4, 5.

Distribute the verse shapes to teams of 2-3 children. Let the teams race to put the verse sentences in order. Then they can take turns saying verses aloud, turning over a shape each time they recite the verses. If the verses are memorized, ask the children to sit in a circle. While saying the verses in rhythm, pass around the two prepared cards. Whoever has the cards when the verse stops can do what the cards say.

What do these verses talk about? (worship) **Who can say these verses?** (Encourage each child to say them by himself.) **What do these verses tell us?** (Children should put them in their own words.)

▼ Bible and Me ▲

Before class, assemble a sample booklet, following instructions on the reproducible pages.

Worshiping Jesus means telling Him how special He is. Remembering Jesus during the Lord's Supper (Communion) is one time to worship Him and tell Him how special He is. Let's work on a way to help us remember Jesus during times when people are having the Lord's Supper.

Help the children make the booklets to keep in the praise packets and use to remember Jesus during the Lord's Supper time. Give each child copies of pages 161-163. The children should cut out the book pages and staple them together to make a twelve-page booklet. The children will fill in the blanks on pages 11 and 12. Then they can color the pictures. Talk about what it means to worship and why we worship.

What does it mean to worship Jesus? (Tell Him how special He is.) **What are some words to say that tell Jesus He is special? Why do we worship Jesus during the Lord's Supper?** (He asked us to remember Him.) **If you are going to worship Jesus during the Lord's Supper, what will you think about?** (Use booklet for ideas.)

Purpose
Demonstrate ways to worship Jesus by remembering how special He is.

Materials
copies of the booklet on pages 161-163
scissors
stapler
colored pencils
crayons

▼ Bible Project ▲

Use the Bible Project time to finish the Remember Jesus booklets. When the children finish the booklets, practice using the booklets to remember Jesus. Talk about how you could use the booklet to remember Jesus and worship Him. Then place the remember booklets in the Praise Packets.

Purpose
Joyfully worship God and Jesus.

Materials
Remember Jesus booklets begun during Bible and Me

▼ Bible Sharing ▲

As you eat, talk about what the Passover foods helped Jesus and His followers remember. Then ask the children to share things they can remember about Jesus.

Lead a worship time to close the session. It would be appropriate to sing a familiar communion song as well as other worship songs you are learning. Let the children close with sentence prayers that worship Jesus. Suggest the following format: "Jesus, You are great! Only You can…" Begin with your worship prayer. Then give each child an opportunity to pray.

Purpose
Share how Jesus helps you worship.

Materials
a snack of passover foods, such as unleavened bread and juice
CD or cassette of praise songs
CD or cassette player

Worship by Singing

Matthew 21:1-16; Psalm 8:1, 2

Lesson Goals
- Tell how the children showed that Jesus is special.
- Sing one of the phrases the children sang to Jesus.
- Recite and demonstrate Isaiah 12:4, 5.
- Demonstrate worship by singing about how special Jesus is.
- Joyfully worship God and Jesus.

▼ Bible Search ▲

Because singing praises to Jesus is an important part of this lesson, carefully choose favorite songs of praise to sing with your children throughout this session.

As people in our story walked to Jerusalem, they shouted and sang praises to Jesus with the word *Hosanna*. *Hosanna* means "O, save!" For hundreds of years, when people went up to Jerusalem for the Passover, they would sing praise to God. This time they sang it to Jesus, too.

Guide the children to find and read Matthew 21:9 in a Bible. Sing a favorite praise song to Jesus and let the children act like the people in the story, praising Jesus, waving their arms, and bowing before Him.

What did the people say to praise Jesus? (Hosanna!) **What way did they worship God and Jesus?** (sing)

Purpose
Tell how the children showed that Jesus is special.

Materials
Bibles
CD or cassette of children's favorite praise songs (especially songs that say "Hosanna!")
CD or cassette player

▼ Bible Story ▲

Display the item you brought. **What way to worship does this remind you of? In our story, listen to see what kind of singing worshiped Jesus.**

"Worship by Singing"

A young donkey's feet clip-clopped down the road out of Jerusalem. The followers were taking the donkey and its mother to where Jesus was waiting at the Mount of Olives. Jesus was going to be the first person to ride this young donkey. The followers placed their coats on the donkey's back before Jesus sat down. Then the donkey began clip-clopping back to Jerusalem. The followers and Jesus joined the large numbers of people going to Jerusalem for the week of the Passover celebration.

Quickly, a great number of people gathered around Jesus. Some people laid their coats on the road in front of Jesus. Others cut tree branches and laid them on the road where Jesus was going to ride. Others waved their branches in the air. You couldn't hear the donkey's clip-clopping feet anymore. But you could hear the praises the people were singing and shouting to Jesus. "God bless the One who comes in the name of the Lord, the One who does what God does. Praise to God in Heaven." As Jesus and the crowd reached Jerusalem, the people of the city got very excited. They asked, "Who is this man?" The crowd praised Jesus again with their answer: "This man is Jesus. He is the prophet from the town of Nazareth in Galilee." Jesus must have been pleased to see and hear the people praise Him with their words and songs.

Purpose
Sing one of the phrases the children sang to Jesus.

Materials
a songbook, CD, or a photograph of people singing

In Jerusalem, when Jesus went to the temple, all the happiness and excitement quickly turned into disappointment and anger. Men were buying, selling, and exchanging money to help people get ready for the Passover. But as they did it, they were also robbing the people. Jesus turned over their tables and scattered the money they had taken wrongfully. In His strong voice, Jesus told the <u>money-changers</u> that the temple was a place for praying and not for cheating people.

As Jesus looked around, He saw more people. Some couldn't see. Some were unable to walk. Jesus wasn't angry with these people. He wanted to help them, and so He healed them. But when the priests and teachers saw what Jesus did, they became very angry. The <u>priests and teachers</u> wanted people to love them— not Jesus. They knew that when Jesus did such wonderful things, people praised Him instead of the leaders. Even the <u>children</u> in the temple sang their praises to Jesus, "Hosanna, to the Son of David." The priests and teachers were so angry they couldn't keep quiet. They asked Jesus, "Do you hear what these children are saying?" They probably wanted Jesus to make the children be quiet. Jesus told them that He had heard them, and that God wanted children and babies to sing to Him. Singing praise to Jesus pleases Jesus very much.

Ask the children to list the people in the story and tell which people praised or sang to Jesus and which did not. (See the underlined words in the story.) Then use the following outline to help the children act out the story. Help them emphasize the difference between people who did praise Jesus and people who did not praise Jesus.
- Jesus rides into the temple.
- Jesus clears the temple.
- Jesus heals the people who can't see or walk.

Summary questions: **How did the children in the temple show that Jesus is special? What is one of the phrases the children sang?** Sing together the praise song sung during Bible Search.

▼ Bible Verse ▲

Our verses help us remember to worship the Lord with our words and our songs. Let's find them in Isaiah 12:4, 5.

Guide children to find the verses in their Bibles. Ask volunteers to recite the verses from memory. Use the verse shapes for review if needed. Then six children can each choose one shape. As another child (or teacher) recites the verses, each child with a shape can do or say something to demonstrate or explain the phrase on his shape. Shuffle the shapes and let the children choose new shapes to demonstrate. Repeat until each child has had a turn doing 2-3 shapes.

What do these verses talk about? (worship) **Who can say the verses?** (Encourage each child to say them.) **What do these verses tell us?** (Encourage children to put the verses in their own words.)

Purpose
Recite and demonstrate Isaiah 12:4, 5.

Materials
Bibles
verse shapes from page 156

▼ Bible and Me ▲

Worshiping Jesus means telling Him how special He is. We have talked about worshiping in prayers, in giving money, and in remembering Jesus. Our Bible verses also talk about worshiping in our songs.

Distribute page 164. Children will choose which children pictured are singing songs that worship Jesus. ("Zacchaeus" and "God is So Good" are good songs, but they do not tell Jesus He is special.) In the empty speech balloon, write in the title of a song that worships Jesus. If your children like to sing, let them sing the songs that worship Jesus in between times of answering the following questions.

What does it mean to worship God or Jesus? (Tell Him how special He is.) **Why do we worship Jesus in songs?** (To tell Him He is special.) **How can you tell if a song worships Jesus?** (It tells something to Jesus or about Him.) **What are some songs to sing that tell Jesus He is special? When you are going to worship Jesus in a song, what song will you choose?**

Purpose
Demonstrate worship by singing about how special Jesus is.

Materials
copies of page 164
pencils

▼ Bible Project ▲

We are going to make the last item to include in our Praise Packets. The Praise Packets will help us worship God.

Choose a familiar tune for which to write a worship song or distribute materials for children to make a song list. If you write a class worship song, suggest the tune and ask the children to give ideas for the words. Make it as simple or complex as you wish. Then help the children copy the song on the 4" x 6" paper. A suggestion is printed on unit page 142. If you choose to make a song list, ask the children to tell their favorite worship songs. Print the titles on the chalkboard for them to copy on the 4" by 6" paper.

Encourage the children to decorate the papers. If you wish, cover the song or list with clear adhesive plastic. Then put them in the Praise Packets. Talk about how to use the song list or worship song in the Praise Packets. Use it during quiet times to think of worship words and what to say to worship God.

Purpose
Joyfully worship God and Jesus.

Materials
a large tablet (or use the chalkboard)
plain paper or light-colored construction paper (4" × 6")
colored pencils
scissors
hymnal
songbooks
stickers (optional)

▼ Bible Sharing ▲

It would be fun to put each child's snack in a large square of material, "travel" to the snack area, and eat as if sitting along the road to Jerusalem.

As you eat, ask volunteers to tell how they plan to use their Praise Packets. Plan when you can worship together as a group and use the packets.

Lead a worship time. Sing the songs on your song list or sing the song you wrote as a class. Let this be a wonderful time to worship God and Jesus!

Purpose
Share how Jesus helps you worship.

Materials
a snack of fruit, cheese, and crackers (travel-to-Jerusalem food)
large squares of material to wrap the snacks (optional)
CD or cassette of praise songs
CD or cassette player

Bible Search

Decode the sentences on the left side of the page.

Match each sentence to a verse in Matthew 6.

Code:

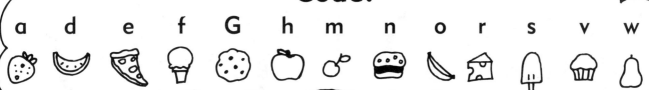

a   d   e   f   G   h   m   n   o   r   s   v   w

1. Don't __ __ __ __

__ __ __ .

Matthew 6:11—
Give us the food we need for each day.

2. Don't say the __ __ __ __

things __ __ __ __

and __ __ __ __ .

Matthew 6:5—
When you pray, don't be like the hypocrites. . . . They want people to see them pray.

3. Ask __ __ __ for
what you __ __ __ __ .

Matthew 6:7—
And when you pray, don't be like those people. . . . They continue saying things that mean nothing.

Bible Verse

Cut out the verse shapes. Use them to put the verse sentences in order.

Praise the Lord, and worship him.

Tell everyone what he has done.

Tell them how great he is.

Let all the world know what he has done.

Sing praise to the Lord, because he has done great things.

Isaiah 12:4, 5.

 UNIT 6, LESSON 23

Bible and Me

What is worship?
Follow the directions on this page
to find out.

Worship is telling
God or Jesus
how special He is.

Dear God,
You are great! Only
You made the world.
Thank You for Jesus.
He can do miracles!
In Jesus' name,
Amen

In this prayer,
draw a line under the
sentences that worship
God or Jesus.

Circle the
pictures that show
prayer positions you
can use when you
worship.

Decode three ways to worship
God. Begin the new word with the
last letter of the scrambled word.

gnis = ___ ___ ___ ___

etirw = ___ ___ ___ ___ ___

yarp = ___ ___ ___ ___

Questions:

What does it mean
to worship God?

What could you say
to worship God?

Bible Search

Read about offerings in Bible times. Then make a Bible times offering container and coins.

In Bible times, people brought a part of their earnings to God. They also brought special offerings and offerings for the poor. In the temple in Jerusalem, there were 13 chests for offerings. Each offering chest had an opening shaped like a trumpet.

Bible Times Offering Container

You will need

- large cardboard box
- construction paper
- aluminum foil
- sharp scissors
- tape
- poster board

You will do (with your teacher)

1. Roll a piece of construction paper into a cone shape. The small end should be a little larger than a large coin. Tape the paper to keep the cone shape.

2. Put the cone on the box. Trace around the small end of the cone. Ask your teacher to cut out the hole. Tape the cone over the opening. Trim the cone if needed.

3. Cut small circles from poster board (size of a large coin). Cover with foil.

UNIT 6, LESSON 24

Bible Search

What is the Passover?
What foods helped Jesus' followers remember the Passover?

The Passover was a time for Jesus and His followers to remember. They remembered how God helped their ancestors when they were slaves in Egypt.

During Passover, a lamb was killed and roasted. It reminded the followers of the lambs killed in Egypt to protect the Israelites from death.

Jesus and His followers ate the lamb with bitter herbs and unleavened bread. The bitter herbs reminded them of the time of slavery in Egypt. The unleavened bread was made without yeast because there was no time in Egypt to let dough rise.

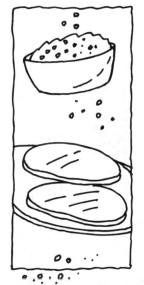

Jesus and His followers reclined at the table. This showed they were no longer slaves. It was a way to celebrate what God had done. They were remembering the night God passed over.

Bible Story

Cut out the eight letters
to use to review the story.

© 2004 Standard Publishing. Permission is granted to reproduce this page for ministry purposes only—not for resale.

Bible and Me

Fold this page on the dotted line and glue the inside. Do the same things to pages 162 and 163. Staple all three folded pages together in the center to make a Remember Booklet.

front cover

glue

glue

page 11

page 2

page 12 (back)

cut

I can sing to remember Jesus.

Jesus said,

"Remember Me."

12

11

2

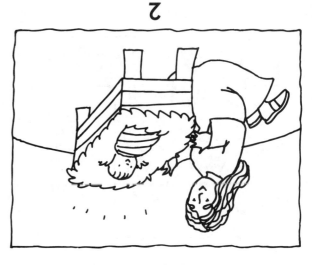

I can talk to Jesus about what He has done.

God kept His promise to send Jesus.

Bible and Me

Fold and glue this page as you did
    page 161.

Put this folded page inside page 161.

Do the same to page 163, and staple
    all three folded pages together in
    the center to make a Remember
    Booklet.

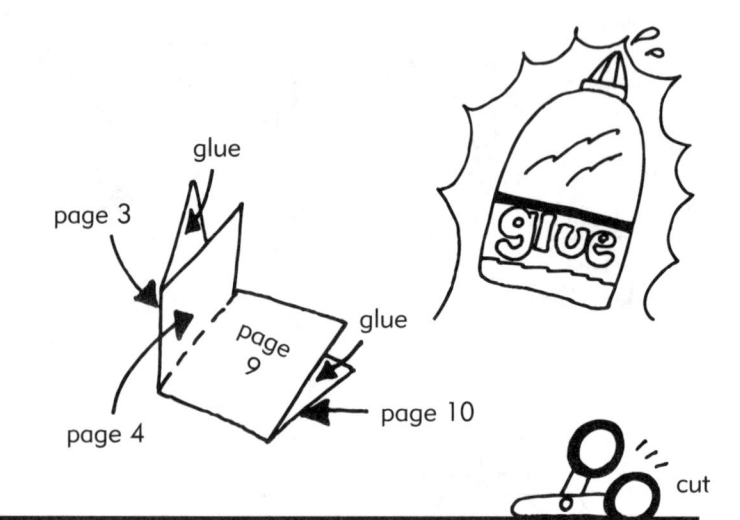

glue

page 3

glue

page 4

page 9

page 10

cut

Jesus was baptized because it was the right thing to do.

4

Jesus came back alive after three days.

9

3

Jesus grew up in Nazareth. He always obeyed.

10

Jesus is in Heaven now, preparing a place for His followers.

UNIT 6, LESSON 25

Bible and Me

Jesus said, "Remember Me" (cover)

cut

Fold and glue this page as you did pages 161 and 162.
Put the three folded, glued pages together as shown.
Make sure the pages are in the right order.
Staple them together in the center to make a Remember Booklet.

Jesus was killed on a cross because of our sins.

8

Jesus never did wrong.

5

7

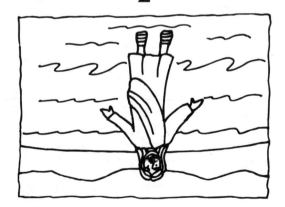

Jesus stopped a storm, walked on water, and fed hungry people.

9

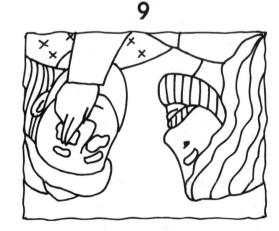

Jesus helped people who were blind, deaf, and unable to walk.

Bible and Me

Jesus Helps Me Be a Friend

Unit Memory Block
"My dear friend, do not follow what is bad; follow what is good. He who does what is good is from God"
(3 John 11).

Memory Challenge
"A person must continue to follow only the teaching of Christ. If he goes beyond Christ's teaching, then he does not have God. But if he continues to follow the teaching of Christ, then he has both the Father and the Son" (2 John 9).

"Follow my example, as I follow the example of Christ" (1 Corinthians 11:1).

27 Jesus Talks to Nicodemus
John 3:1-21
Jesus was a friend to Nicodemus when He talked to him. We can follow Jesus by being a friend—talking to people.

28 Jesus Forgives a Sinful Woman
Luke 7:36-50
Jesus was a friend to a sinful woman when He spoke kindly and forgave her. We can follow Jesus by being a friend—forgiving people who are sorry for doing wrong.

29 Jesus Visits Mary and Martha
Luke 10:38-42
Jesus was a friend to Mary and Martha when He came to visit them. We can follow Jesus by being a friend—visiting people.

30 Jesus Loves the Children
Matthew 19:13-15; Mark 10:13-16; Luke 1:15-17
Jesus was a friend to children and their parents. We can follow Jesus by being a friend—hugging and praying for people.

31 Jesus Eats with Zacchaeus
Luke 19:1-10
Jesus was a friend to Zacchaeus when He spoke kindly, ate with him, and helped him follow Him. We can follow Jesus by being a friend—help others follow Jesus.

By the end of this unit, the leaders and learners will

KNOW times Jesus was a friend.
FEEL eager to be a friend like Jesus.
DO Follow Jesus by being a friend

Unit Value

This unit helps deal with a very real challenge in the children's lives: How do you relate to people around you? Jesus gives us a wonderful example. Be a friend. The five Bible stories in this unit give examples of times and ways Jesus was a friend to Bible people. 1) He talked to Nicodemus and answered questions—even when it was inconvenient. 2) He was kind and forgave a woman who was sorry for doing wrong. 3) He visited people whom He loved—Mary and Martha. 4) He was a friend to children who came to visit Him. He held them and prayed for them. 5) Jesus was kind to a man no one liked—Zacchaeus. Because Jesus was a friend, Zacchaeus stopped doing wrong and started following Jesus.

No one likes to be treated badly; everyone wants to be treated "good." The Bible verse to memorize in this unit helps the children think about the difference between bad and good. It emphasizes that people who do good are from God— just like Jesus. Each lesson helps the children think about specific ways to be a friend like Jesus: 1) talk to people, 2) forgive people, 3) visit people, 4) hug and pray for people, and 5) help people follow Jesus. Special emphasis is given to helping the children tell the difference between being and not being a friend, giving a reason for being a friend, and wrestling with what makes it hard to be a friend.

▼ Bible Project ▲

Making friends

Materials
copies of the *Follow Jesus* logo from this page

The learners will plan a time in which they can be a friend to Jesus. As you help the children plan, be ready with suggestions of people to whom they can be a friend. The best Making Friends project will include times for the children to talk to people and be kind (Lesson 27), help people (Lesson 28), visit with people (Lesson 29), hug and pray for people (Lesson 30), eat with and help people (Lesson 31).

Suggestions: visit a nursing home or children's home; plan a progressive visit to church members who are home bound; plan a welcome visit to people just joining your community or church group. Just "visiting" for first and second graders may be a little awkward, so plan to present a short program (songs you are learning about following Jesus, Bible verses with motions, acting out a story with a cassette recording) or make gifts to give (door decorations, tray favors, place mats, welcome basket, or goodie basket).

Use the *Follow Jesus* logo printed here to decorate your gifts. Include a card that says something like this: "The basket is a gift from the *Follow Jesus* Team, your friends at Your Community Church, Your Town, U.S.A."

Week 1: Decide where and when you're going. (Contact necessary people during the week to finalize plans.)

Week 2: Plan what to give or present, what to say and do to be a friend.

Week 3: Make gifts or prepare presentation.

Week 4: Complete gifts or practice presentation.

Week 5: Role-play the visit. Let an adult play the person being visited and let children practice being a friend.

Jesus Talks to Nicodemus

John 3:1-21

Lesson Goals

- Tell what Nicodemus needed.
- Tell how Jesus was a friend.
- Begin to memorize 3 John 11.
- Tell what it means to be a friend.
- Follow Jesus by being a friend.

Memory Block
"My dear friend, do not follow what is bad; follow what is good. He who does what is good is from God" (3 John 11).

▼ Bible Search ▲

Jesus was a friend to many, many people. Let's find the name of one of these people. He needed some answers. His name and the time he came to Jesus begin with the letter N.

Guide the children to find the book of John in the table of contents of their Bibles. Locate the page the book begins on, then the big 3 for the chapter and the small 1 for the verse. Slowly read the verse as the children follow along. Read the directions on page 182. Help the children find Nicodemus, learn when he went to see Jesus, and then take him through the maze. Read what Jesus told Nicodemus. (Optional: Find the verse in a Bible, John 3:16.)

Who came to see Jesus? (Nicodemus) **When did he come?** (at night) **What did he need?** (answers to questions)

Purpose
Tell what Nicodemus needed.

Materials
Bibles
copies of page 182
crayons

▼ Bible Story ▲

For review, print the following words on index cards: Who? When? Where? What? How?

Darken the room; then light the candle or turn on the small lamp if the room is too dark. **What would you think if someone came sneaking up to your house at night? Listen to see why someone came sneaking up to see Jesus at night.**

Purpose
Tell how Jesus was a friend.

Materials
a candle or small lamp
index cards
marker
Plasti-Tak® reusable adhesive

"Jesus Talks to Nicodemus"

It was dark when Nicodemus left his house. Carefully he tiptoed down the street in Jerusalem. Nicodemus hadn't told anyone where he was going. He didn't want anyone to know. But he wanted to know something. He wanted to know about this man called Jesus.

Nicodemus was a very important leader. He was a Pharisee and he was a member of the Jewish ruling council. He knew many things about God from studying the Scriptures. When people in Jerusalem had important questions, he helped answer those questions. But even an important leader like Nicodemus didn't know all the answers to all the questions. Nicodemus wanted to talk to Jesus about some hard questions he couldn't answer.

Quickly, quietly, Nicodemus walked through the dark streets. As he knocked on the door where Jesus was staying, he must have hoped Jesus would let him come in and talk. He needed answers. He just had to ask Jesus his important questions. Relief spread over him when someone opened the door and let Nicodemus in. He was sure no one had seen him come.

Once he was inside, Nicodemus's words spilled out. "Teacher, we know that you are a teacher sent from God. No one can do the miracles you do unless God is with him." Nicodemus wanted to know if Jesus really was like God. Was Jesus really from God?

Jesus spoke up and said, "Unless one is born again, he cannot be in God's kingdom." Jesus' answer gave Nicodemus more questions. In fact, what Jesus said seemed a little confusing to Nicodemus. Jesus was surprised. Nicodemus was a leader, but he still didn't understand what Jesus was telling him.

But Jesus didn't make fun of Nicodemus. He didn't laugh or call him stupid. Jesus didn't say that his questions were silly. Instead, Jesus was kind. He didn't tell him to come back tomorrow when he wasn't tired. He wanted to help Nicodemus, so He carefully explained what Nicodemus needed to know.

Jesus helped Nicodemus understand how much God loves us. Jesus said, "For God loved the world so much that He gave His only Son. God gave His Son so that whoever believes in him may not be lost, but have eternal life" (John 3:16). Jesus told Nicodemus what God did to show His love. And Jesus helped Nicodemus know how to live forever in Heaven. Jesus was a friend to Nicodemus.

Attach the index cards to a wall with Plasti-tak® reusable adhesive. Each child chooses a question by choosing a card on the wall.

Who wanted to talk to Jesus? (Nicodemus)
When did Nicodemus talk to Jesus? (night)
Why did Nicodemus talk to Jesus? (to get answers to questions)
Where did Nicodemus talk to Jesus? (at the house where Jesus stayed)
What did Jesus tell Nicodemus? (John 3:16)
How did Jesus treat Nicodemus? (as a friend)
Summary questions: **What did Nicodemus need?** (answers) **What did Jesus do to be a friend?** (spoke kindly, gave Nicodemus answers)

Purpose
Begin to memorize 3 John 11.

Materials
Bibles
copies of page 183
colored pencils

▼ Bible Verse ▲

In 3 John 11, one of Jesus' apostles wrote some words to help us follow Jesus. Let's find what John said.

Let the children find and read 3 John 11. (Find the page number for 3 John in the table of contents. Then find a small number 11 for the verse. This is unusual because there is only one chapter in 3 John.) Together, read the verse aloud from the Bible and sing it to the tune of "Three Blind Mice."

Look at page 183 and sing the song again—singing the right word for each blank. After a few times, pause to print words in the blanks. Sing the song again between each question below.

Who wrote this verse about following Jesus? What two instructions does this verse give? Which instruction might be the hardest to obey?

▼ Bible and Me ▲

Following Jesus means doing the kinds of things Jesus did to be a friend. Our verse helps us remember not to follow what is bad, but to follow what is good—Jesus! Let's find some ways to follow Jesus' example of being a friend.

On page 184, use the word search to find and circle answers to the questions. Print each answer in the correct blank.

What did Jesus do to be a friend? (talk, be kind) **What can we do to be a friend like Jesus?** (talk, be kind)

Purpose
Tell what it means to be a friend.

Materials
copies of page 184
pencils

▼ Bible Project ▲

Print each of the following words on index cards: talk, be kind, help, visit, hug, pray, eat. Prepare to help the children suggest ideas for this unit's project, Making Friends. See page 166 for ideas.

We want to be more and more like Jesus. We want to be friends to people just like Jesus was a friend. In our stories we will learn many ways that Jesus was a friend.

Ask volunteers to choose one of the seven cards and read the word for the group. Guide the children to decide what the words have in common (all ways to be a friend to someone; all ways Jesus was a friend to someone). Brainstorm with the children where and when to accomplish the Making Friends project or let them choose from your suggestions. Again, your enthusiasm for being a friend just like Jesus will be a great example for the children. Print on the chalkboard or marker board all details for the project. Keep the plans displayed throughout the unit.

Purpose
Follow Jesus by being a friend.

Materials
index cards
marker
chalkboard and chalk or marker board and marker

▼ Bible Sharing ▲

Talk about being a friend like Jesus. Distribute the seven cards. Play a praise song. When the music stops, each of the children holding the cards can tell about a time she was a friend (using the word on the card). Close by singing favorite praise songs.

Purpose
Share a way Jesus shows you how to be a friend.

Materials
friendship food for a snack—
    heart-shaped finger gelatin or cookies
index cards from the Bible Project section
CD or cassette of praise songs
CD or cassette player

Jesus Forgives a Sinful Woman

Luke 7:36-50

Purpose
Tell what Simon needed to learn.

Materials
Bibles
copies of the top of page 185

Purpose
Tell what Jesus did to be a friend.

Materials
a bottle of perfume

Lesson Goals

- Tell what Simon needed to learn.
- Tell what Jesus did to be a friend.
- Memorize 3 John 11.
- Tell the difference between being and not being a friend.
- Follow Jesus by being a friend.

▼ Bible Search ▲

Jesus told a story to help Simon learn to be a friend who forgives. In Jesus' story, two men needed some coins, but neither one had any. Let's learn how many coins each man needed.

Guide children to find Luke 7:41 in their Bibles. Then distribute the coins on page 185. Help the children count the coins on the page. Decide how many pages equal 500 coins. Tape together a row of 500 coins for one to pay. Keep a row of 50 coins for another man to pay.

Why did Jesus tell a story? How many coins did each man need? (50, 500) **Which row has 50? Which row has 500? If you had to pay someone money, would you rather pay 50 or 500 coins? Why?**

▼ Bible Story ▲

Spray a whiff of perfume into the air. **What do people do with perfume?** (wear it to smell good, cover up bad smells) **Listen to see what someone in the story did with her perfume.**

"Jesus Forgives a Sinful Woman"

Most people hated me. I knew it from the way they pushed me around and insulted me. Even though it hurt, I learned not to cry in front of them. But everything changed when I met Jesus. He was different. He looked at me and He spoke kindly. I couldn't help listening to Him when He talked about being sorry for doing wrong. I had done lots of wrong things; I was a sinner. When I listened to Jesus, I was so sorry for what I had done. I decided to follow Him and be the kind of friend that Jesus was.

One day, I heard Jesus and other important people were going to a dinner at Simon's house. I wasn't invited, but I wanted to show Jesus how much I loved Him. So I took an alabaster jar of perfume to Simon's house. When I found Jesus at the dinner table, I cried. I was so sorry for all the wrong things I had done.

I noticed no one had washed Jesus' feet. My eyes were wet with tears, so I used the tears to wash His feet. I didn't have a towel, so I used my hair to wipe them. After kissing Jesus feet, I opened my alabaster jar of perfume and poured it over His feet. I hoped this showed Jesus how much I loved Him.

Simon noticed me. He seemed a little disgusted because I was there with Jesus. Simon knew about all the bad things I had done. He thought surely Jesus would not want me to even touch Him. Simon wanted Jesus to make me leave.

But Jesus told a story. Two men had to pay back money to a kind man. One had to pay 500 silver coins. The other had to pay 50 coins. But neither man had any money. So the kind man did not make them pay back any money. Jesus asked Simon, "Which man will love the kind man more?" Simon said that it would be the man who was supposed to pay back the most money. That man was like me. I had done more wrong and so now I was showing more love.

Jesus could tell I loved Him more because of the things I did. Simon had not given Jesus water to wash His feet, but I washed His feet with my tears. Simon had not greeted Jesus with a kiss when He came, but I was willing to kiss His feet. Simon had not greeted Jesus with any oil for His head, but I had given Him my perfume—for His feet. Jesus wanted Simon to learn that people who think they've done only a little wrong feel only a little love. But I felt great love because Jesus forgave me for doing many wrong things.

Jesus spoke kindly as He forgave me for all the wrong I had done. Jesus was not like the other people who wanted to punish me. Jesus was truly a friend to me when He forgave me.

Organize the children in a circle to play a game. Start with all the children standing. Count seven children and ask the seventh child the first question. After a child answers, he can sit down. Then ask every seventh child the next question until all the questions are answered.

Who invited Jesus to dinner? (Simon)
What kind of person was Simon? (sinner, had done some wrong)
Who came to the dinner without an invitation? (woman)
What kind of person was the woman? (sinner, had done much wrong)
Who loved Jesus more, the sinful woman or Simon? (woman)
How did Jesus know the woman loved Him more than Simon? (actions)
What did Jesus do for the sinful woman? (was a friend, forgave her)
Summary questions: **What did Simon need to learn? What did the sinful woman do to show she was sorry for doing wrong?** (showed love—washed His feet, wiped them, poured on perfume) **What did Jesus do to be a friend?** (spoke kindly, forgave)

▼ Bible Verse ▲

Put each footprint puzzle in an envelope.

In 3 John 11, one of Jesus' apostles wrote some words to help us follow Jesus. Let's find what John said.

Guide the children to find and read 3 John 11. Ask for volunteer duets or trios to sing the verse as they did in Lesson 27 (see page 183). Then give pairs of children an envelope with a verse puzzle from page 185. Ask them to put their puzzles together. The completed puzzle will look like a footprint. Let the children say the verse, remove a strip from the puzzle, say the verse again, and so on, until they can say it all.

Invite the pairs back into one group to talk about the verse. **Who wrote this verse about following Jesus? What two instructions does this verse give? What is a way to follow what is bad? Why is that bad? What is a way to follow that is good? Why is that good?**

Purpose
Memorize 3 John 11.

Materials
a footprint puzzle (cut apart) from the bottom of page 185 for each pair of children
envelopes

Purpose
Tell the difference between being and not being a friend.

Materials
copies of page 186
pencils

▼ Bible and Me ▲

Following Jesus means doing the kinds of things Jesus did to be a friend. Our verse helps us remember not to follow what is bad, but to follow what is good—Jesus! Let's work to tell the difference between what is bad and good, what Jesus would and what Jesus would not do.

Distribute page 186. The children will cross out the phrases that are "bad"—what Jesus would not do. Circle what Jesus would do and use those words to fill in the puzzle.

After the children complete the puzzle, use the following questions to help the children give examples of the difference between being and not being a friend.

What words are not ways to be a friend? (words crossed out) **What words are ways to be a friend?** (circled words)

Ask the next two questions for each of the six choices.

1. **When might you have to choose between forgiving and punishing?** (when someone hurts you) **praying or insulting?** (when someone makes a mistake) **visiting or staying away?** (when someone new comes to class) **helping or hurting?** (when someone is alone) **answering or ignoring?** (when someone asks you a question) **speaking mean or kind words?** (when you feel angry).

2. **What would Jesus do? Why?**

Purpose
Follow Jesus by being a friend.

Materials
materials needed to complete the ideas the children chose last week (see Lesson 27 and unit page 166)
items needed to make simple gift
cassette recording of one of the unit stories
any props needed to recite the memory block with motions

▼ Bible Project ▲

We want to be more and more like Jesus. We want to be friends to people just like Jesus was a friend. Our Making Friends project will give each of us an opportunity to be a friend just like Jesus.

Using the materials you provided, display sample gifts or demonstrate for the children simple presentations to take to the people they visit. Let the children choose what they want to make or prepare to present. If you have time, begin working on their ideas this week.

▼ Bible Sharing ▲

Ask the children to share a way Jesus helps them be a friend. Each child can use the word *forgiveness, friend,* or *follow* in his sentence. After each child has had a turn to share, sing praise songs about following Jesus and being a friend.

Close with a prayer asking God to help in being friends this week.

Purpose
Share ways Jesus shows you how to be a friend.

Materials
a snack that begins with *f* (forgiveness, friends, follow)— perhaps french fries, fruit rollups, fudge, fig cookies, French toast)
CD or cassette of praise songs
CD or cassette player

Jesus Visits Mary and Martha

Luke 10:38-42

Lesson Goals

- Tell who Jesus visited in Bethany.
- Tell how Jesus was a friend.
- Memorize 3 John 11.
- Tell why we should be a friend.
- Follow Jesus by being a friend.

Memory Block
"My dear friend, do not follow what is bad; follow what is good. He who does what is good is from God" (3 John 11).

▼ Bible Search ▲

Today's story is about people who lived or visited in Bethany. Let's find their names in Luke 10:38, 39.

Guide the children to find and read Luke 10:38, 39 in their Bibles. Help them read the names of the people who lived in or visited the town of Bethany. Children will use the names to complete the puzzle on page 187. Then talk about the people.

Who lived in Bethany? (Mary and Martha) **Who might be visiting them?** (Jesus) **What do you think Jesus might do to be a friend to Mary and Martha?**

Purpose
Tell who Jesus visited in Bethany.

Materials
Bibles
copies of page 187
pencils

▼ Bible Story ▲

Do you think it's more important to do your chores (show broom) **or read your Bible** (show Bible) **and think about it? Listen to see what Jesus said when He visited Mary and Martha.**

"Jesus Visits Mary and Martha"

What should I do next?" I wondered. There was always washing, cooking, baking, cleaning, and more. I sure could have used some help. And then, right in the middle of all my work, someone knocked at the door. It was Jesus and His followers!

They were traveling somewhere when they came through Bethany. We didn't travel with Jesus and His apostles, but we had decided to follow what Jesus did and said. And now, Jesus was a dear friend of ours. So I invited Jesus and the followers to stay for a little while. It was more work to prepare food for them, but we were always happy to have Jesus visit.

After Jesus stopped, all I could think about was getting everything ready for Him: fresh food, a cool drink, a comfortable place to sit. I raced around the house. The more I hurried, the more work it seemed I had to do. All the time I was working, my sister, Mary, was doing absolutely nothing. Well, to me it looked like she was doing nothing. Actually, she was sitting down by Jesus and listening to Him talk. The longer she listened, the angrier I felt.

Finally, I was so upset I couldn't keep quiet a moment longer. I burst into the room and complained, "Jesus, don't You care that Mary has left me alone to do all the housework? Tell her to help me!"

I was sure Jesus would make her get right up and help me. But He didn't. My

Purpose
Tell how Jesus was a friend.

Materials
a Bible
a broom

heart sank when Jesus told me, "Martha, Martha, you are getting worried and upset about too many things. Only one thing is really important. Mary has chosen to do what is important."

Now what did Jesus mean by that? Wasn't it important to get the housework done and prepare for Him? Didn't He want us to help Him have a nice place to stay and good food to eat before He traveled on? Well, yes, Jesus was glad for a nice place to stay and good food to eat. But even more, Jesus wanted people to take time to be with Him. People who spent time with Jesus learned how to follow Him. So, now I know it is good to work hard and do your best to show love to people. But I learned it is even more important to take time to be with Jesus and listen to what He says. My friend Jesus helped me learn to do the most important things first.

Put a broom and a Bible on opposite sides of the room. The children walk to the broom if Martha is the answer; they walk to the Bible if Mary is the answer.

Who invited Jesus to stay in her house?
Who worked hard to fix food for Jesus?
Who hardly worked while Jesus was there?
Who complained while Jesus was there?
Who did the most important thing first?
Who learned to take time to be with Jesus?

Summary question: **What did Jesus do to be a friend?** (stopped to visit, helped Mary and Martha learn about Him)

▼ Bible Verse ▲

Purpose
Memorize 3 John 11.

Materials
Bibles
copies of page 188

In 3 John 11, one of Jesus' apostles wrote some words to help a friend follow Jesus. The friend is whoever reads the verse. Let's find out what it says.

Guide the children to find and read 3 John 11 in their Bibles. Ask for volunteer solos or duets to sing the verse as they did in Lesson 27. (The words and music are printed on page 183.) Then the children can say the verse to connect the correct arrows in a path on page 188.

Who wrote this verse? Who is the friend in this verse? (person reading what John wrote) **What two instructions does this verse give? What is one way not to follow what is bad? What is one way to follow what is good?**

Option: Make this a floor game. Use a footprint pattern and the verse phrases from the footprint puzzle on the bottom of page 185. Glue the phrases to paper footprints. Use page 188 as a guide for placing footprints on the floor. Be excited with each child who follows the path correctly.

▼ Bible and Me ▲

Cut apart, roll up, and tape the question strips from page 189 into little paper rolls. Make at least one set for each child. Drop them into the milk jug or two-liter bottle.

Following Jesus means doing the kinds of things Jesus did to be a friend. Our verse helps us remember not to follow what is bad, but to follow what is good—Jesus! We want to be a friend—because Jesus was a friend.

The children can take turns shaking out a question from the jug or bottle to answer. When the children get the same question twice, you can decide if it is best to put it back or answer it again. Repetition is helpful.

These questions (from the game) will focus the conversation on why we should be a friend. **Why should we be a friend?** (to be like Jesus) **What is a way to be a friend like Jesus? What is a way not to be a friend like Jesus?**

Purpose
Tell why we should be a friend.

Materials
copies of page 189
scissors
tape
a clean gallon milk jug or two-liter bottle

▼ Bible Project ▲

We want to be more and more like Jesus. We want to be friends to people just like Jesus was a friend. While we work on our Making Friends project, think about how Jesus would be a friend to the people we are going to visit.

Encourage the children to work on the projects for their future friends. The gifts or presentations are ways the children can introduce themselves and make new friends. As you work, talk about things friends do, why they like to be together, and how the children can keep new friends they will make.

Purpose
Follow Jesus by being a friend.

Materials
materials for the gifts or presentations you are preparing (see page 166)

▼ Bible Sharing ▲

Seat children in a circle to eat their snack of M&M® candies. Send the broom around the circle one way and the Bible around the circle the other way. Recite or sing the memory block together as the items are passed around. When the children have recited 3 John 11, the person holding the Bible can share a way Jesus was a friend to Mary. The person holding the broom can tell a way to be a friend. Continue the game by singing the verse song again. When you stop the second time, the person holding the broom can tell about a way to be a friend at home and the person holding the Bible can tell about a way to be a friend at church.

Close by singing praise songs about following Jesus or being a friend.

Purpose
Share ways Jesus helps you be a friend.

Materials
a snack of M&M® candies (for Mary and Martha)
the broom and the Bible from the Bible Story time
CD or cassette of praise songs
CD or cassette player

Jesus Loves the Children

Matthew 19:13-15; Mark 10:13-16; Luke 18:15-17

Memory Block

"My dear friend, do not follow what is bad; follow what is good. He who does what is good is from God" (3 John 11).

Purpose

Tell what the people wanted Jesus to do.

Materials

Bibles
copies of page 190
pencils
a doll (optional)

Purpose

Tell how Jesus was a friend.

Materials

a red and a green paper circle, a red balloon and a green balloon for each child

Lesson Goals

- Tell what the people wanted Jesus to do.
- Tell how Jesus was a friend.
- Recite and explain 3 John 11.
- Tell what makes it hard to be a friend.
- Follow Jesus by being a friend.

▼ Bible Search ▲

Today's story is about how Jesus was a friend to children just like you.
Distribute copies of page 190 and guide the children to follow the directions on the page. Find the first verse in Matthew and answer the question. Then find the other verses and answers. Talk about the last two questions together. Then give the children time to report the answers.

What did people want Jesus to do for the children? (Matthew 19:13—put hands on them, pray; Mark 10:13—touch them; Luke 18:15—touch them) **Which words that we use today would be the same as words in the Bible?** (hug, hold, talk to God) **What would doing these things show the children?** (love) **What would you like Jesus to do if you went to visit Him?** If you wish, let children take turns using the doll to demonstrate how Jesus treated the children.

▼ Bible Story ▲

Ask the children to line up next to the wall across from you. When you hold up a green paper circle, they can come on tip-toe towards you; when you hold up a red paper circle, they must go backwards. When all the children reach you, invite them to sit down and listen for who said "go back" and who said "come" in the story.

"Jesus Loves the Children"

I think all of my friends woke up early today, just like me. We were too excited to stay in bed, because today was the day we were going to see Jesus. We had heard our dads and moms talk about how special Jesus was. We knew Jesus could do wonderful things. We could hardly wait to get there. Our faces felt like smiling. Our voices felt like laughing and singing. Our feet felt like hopping and skipping and jumping down the road.

Soon we could see Jesus just up ahead. We could also see other people with Him. But that was alright. We could wait a little longer. It would feel so good just to sit on His lap or hug Him. Our parents wanted Jesus to touch us and pray for us. And soon it would be our turn.

Closer, closer we came to Jesus. When we were almost there, we were surprised to hear a voice say, "Stop, go back home." Jesus' followers told us we couldn't see Jesus. But why? Maybe they thought Jesus was too busy to see children. Maybe they thought Jesus didn't like children. We had been smiling because we were so excited to see Jesus. Now we were frowning because we would have to go back home without seeing or touching Jesus or hearing Him pray. We didn't feel like hopping and skipping and jumping. We felt like dragging our feet in the dust as we walked back home.

But then, we heard another voice, a kind and gentle voice. It was Jesus! He called out, "Let the children come to me. Don't stop them, because the kingdom of Heaven belongs to people who are like these children." He wasn't too busy after all! Our frowns turned upside down into smiles again. Our feet felt like hopping and skipping and jumping again. As we raced toward Jesus, our parents were right behind us. Jesus gently lifted some of us into His lap. He gave us hugs. He prayed for us. And He showed us how much He loved children. We will always remember that Jesus is a special friend to children.

Option: If you think this song is appropriate for your children, pretend to be the children singing on their way home: "Jesus loves the little ones like me, me, me."

Give each child a red balloon and a green balloon. The children can hold up the red ones for statements that are false and hold up the green ones for true statements. (Use other red and green items if balloons are not available.)

Only grandpas and grandmas came to see Jesus.
Parents wanted Jesus to touch and pray for the children.
The followers said, "Come."
Jesus said, "Come tomorrow."
The children said, "Let's just go home."
Jesus touched the children and prayed for them.
Jesus showed He was a friend to the children.

Summary questions: **What did the parents and children need?** (to see Jesus, to have Him touch them and pray for them) **What did Jesus do to be a friend?** (He invited the children to come; He touched them and prayed for them.)

▼ Bible Verse ▲

In 3 John 11, one of Jesus' apostles wrote some words to help a friend follow Jesus. The friend is whoever reads the verse. Let's find out what it says.

Guide the children to find and read 3 John 11 in their Bibles. Ask for volunteers to recite it from memory. If any children need help, use the footprint puzzle (Lesson 28, page 185).

To help children explain the verse, distribute copies of page 191. Children should cut out the word blocks and glue them to the correct places in the puzzle to match the verse phrases to their explanations. Then use the following questions to help the children explain the verse.

Who wrote this verse? What two instructions does this verse give? What does (a phrase) **mean?** (Children can report the explanation they matched to the phrase.) **What does the whole verse mean?**

Purpose
Recite and explain 3 John 11.

Materials
Bibles
copies of page 191
scissors
glue

▼ Bible and Me ▲

Following Jesus means doing the kinds of things Jesus did to be a friend. Our verse helps us remember not to follow what is bad, but to follow what is good—Jesus! But sometimes it is hard to be a friend like Jesus.

On page 192, guide children to match each reason it's hard (on the left) with a child on the right. In the blank spaces, help them add their own reasons it is sometimes hard to be a friend.

For each situation on page 192, focus the conversation on how it can be hard to be a friend. **When is it hard to be a friend? What might you be thinking about in this situation? What would you do if you chose to be a friend to Jesus?**

Option: Divide children into four groups and let each group act out a situation from page 192. The group can decide which reason each situation shows.

Purpose
Tell what makes it hard to be a friend.

Materials
copies of page 192
pencils

▼ Bible Project ▲

We are preparing to make new friends—just like Jesus did. We are going to talk to, hug and pray for, and help the people we will visit. Let's think about the kind words we can say as we complete our projects today.

Help the children complete the last details of their Making Friends gifts or presentations. Allow time for the children to display and tell about their gifts or practice the presentations. Emphasize the importance of keeping the needs of their new friends in mind. That's what Jesus did!

What do you think the people we are going to visit need? What might make it hard to be friends with these people? What will you do if you choose to be a friend like Jesus?

Purpose
Follow Jesus by being a friend.

Materials
materials necessary to complete gifts or presentations (see page 166)

▼ Bible Sharing ▲

Spread the blanket on the floor like a picnic and have children sit on the blanket to eat their snack.

Let's pretend we are going to see Jesus. We are eating our picnic lunch on the trip to see Jesus. Why do you want to see Jesus? How do you think Jesus will be a friend to you? Give each child a turn to share.

Close with guided prayer. Ask the children to pray what you suggest. Pause between sentences. **Dear God, thank You for Jesus. Thank You that Jesus was a friend to children. Help us to be more and more like Jesus this week. In Jesus' name, amen.**

Purpose
Share ways Jesus helps you be a friend.

Materials
crackers and cheese, pretzel sticks, or another picnic-type snack
a blanket

Lesson Goals
- Describe Zacchaeus.
- Tell how Jesus was a friend.
- Recite and explain 3 John 11.
- Report times and ways they followed Jesus by being a friend.
- Follow Jesus by being a friend.

Memory Block
"My dear friend, do not follow what is bad; follow what is good. He who does what is good is from God" (3 John 11).

▼ Bible Search ▲

In today's story, Jesus was a friend to someone who was not kind. Let's find words that describe this person.

Guide the children to find Luke 19:2, 3, 7 in their Bibles. Ask them to look for words that describe the man to whom Jesus was a friend. Circle those words on page 193. Then sing a song about Zacchaeus or act out what Zacchaeus did.

Let the children describe Zacchaeus. **Where did he live? What did he do? What did he look like? Why didn't people like him?**

Purpose
Describe Zacchaeus.

Materials
Bibles
copies of page 193
pencils

▼ Bible Story ▲

Before the session, print the name *Zacchaeus* on the piece of paper and keep it to use during review.

What kinds of things do people stand on so they can be taller? (tree stump, step stool, ladder, table, cabinet, chair, steps, platform) **Listen to see if someone used one of these in our story.** Unveil a stepladder. Use it as you tell the story from Zacchaeus' point of view.

"Jesus Eats with Zacchaeus"

I heard someone say I was short, fat, and not pretty. That's a good way to describe me. They also said I was the richest man in the city. Being rich used to be important to me. But something happened and changed the way I feel.

My name is Zacchaeus, and I'm in charge of all the other tax collectors in Jericho. In my job, I took money from the people in Jericho to pay tax money to the Romans. But I always took extra money from the people so I would have lots of money just for myself. Because tax collectors cheated people, no one liked us. So even though I had lots of money, I didn't have any friends.

Maybe that's why I wanted to see Jesus when He came to town. I heard He treated people differently. Everyone in Jericho must have had the same idea. Soon so many people were bumping and pushing each other, I couldn't even see the road. No one in the crowd liked me. No one would let me through. But I didn't give up. I had to think of something. And then I did!

My short legs hobbled down the road to a sycamore tree. It had grown up by the road where Jesus was coming. Huffing, puffing, I pulled myself up into the branches. Finally I was up above the crowd, high enough to see where Jesus would walk. A smile crept across my face. My tricky ways helped me get what I wanted again.

Purpose
Tell how Jesus was a friend.

Materials
stepladder
paper
marker
tape

Soon, Jesus walked right toward my sycamore tree. What would He look like? Would He speak to the crowd? I watched and listened. And then, as Jesus walked right under my tree, He stopped. His face looked up and His eyes smiled. At me! He looked at me! But that wasn't all. Jesus didn't say mean, unkind words like other people. He spoke kindly, "Zacchaeus, hurry and come down. I must stay at your house today!"

I felt like jumping right down from that tree to get to Jesus as fast as I could. When my feet hit the dirt, I turned to Jesus and told Him how much I wanted Him to come home with me. As we started walking to my house, people were grumbling and complaining, "Jesus is staying with a sinner!" But all that mattered to me now was my new friend, Jesus.

I gave Jesus a fancy place to stay and fine food to eat that day. But Jesus gave me something even more important. As Jesus and I talked, I realized I must stop cheating people. I must stop tricking people to get what I wanted. I began to feel sorry for all the times I took things that were not mine. To show that I was truly sorry, I decided to change. I stood up before Jesus and told Him, "I will give half of my money to the poor. If I have cheated anyone, I will pay that person back four times more!" And then Jesus let me know that because I believed what He said, someday I would get to live with Him in Heaven. I think Jesus is the best friend I've ever had.

Tape the word *Zacchaeus* to the top of the stepladder. For each correct answer, move Zacchaeus down one step (or half-step) to get him down to go with Jesus.

What was Zacchaeus's job?
What did people think of Zacchaeus?
What was Zacchaeus's problem when Jesus came?
What did Zacchaeus do to solve his problem?
What did Jesus say to Zacchaeus?
What did Zacchaeus say he would do to show he was sorry?

Summary questions: **What did Jesus do to be a friend to Zacchaeus? What was Zacchaeus like before and then after he met Jesus?** (Everything was the same except the way he acted.)

▼ Bible Verse ▲

Purpose
Recite and explain 3 John 11.

Materials
Bibles
construction paper
footprint pattern (can use footprint puzzle on page 185)
scissors
marker
tape

Before class, cut construction paper footprints. On one footprint, print 3 John 11. Attach the footprints to the floor in a circle (two per child; no more than eight children in one circle).

In 3 John 11, one of Jesus' apostles wrote words to help a friend follow Jesus. Let's see how many of us can say this verse by ourselves.

Ask for volunteers to find the verse in their Bibles and then recite the verse from memory. If anyone needs a review, use the footprint puzzle (Lesson 28, page 185). Play a game to recite and explain the verse. Place footprints in a circle. Children will step on the footprints, saying the verse as they walk around the circle. At the end, whoever stands on 3 John 11 gets to explain the verse. If the child has already explained it twice, he can choose someone else to explain it.

After the game, talk about the verse. **Who wrote this verse? What two instructions does this verse give? What is one way not to follow what is bad? What is one way to follow what is good? What does this verse help you remember to do?** (Children give their explanation.)

▼ Bible and Me ▲

Before the session, make a masking-tape game grid (triangle with three sections) on the floor. Print one of the following directions on each piece of paper and tape the papers inside the masking tape sections: Name a time or way to be a friend like Jesus at school. Name a time or way to be a friend like Jesus when playing. Name a time or way to be a friend like Jesus at home.

Following Jesus means doing the kinds of things Jesus did to be a friend. Our verse helps us remember not to follow what is bad, but to follow what is good—Jesus! Let's play a game to help us tell about times and ways when we can follow Jesus by being a friend.

Children will toss a bean bag at the game grid. The directions taped to the floor will help the children report times and ways to follow Jesus.

After the game, talk about what it means to follow Jesus. **What does it mean to follow Jesus?** (do what He did or said) **How do you know if you are being a friend or not?** (Ask, "What would Jesus do?") **Why should we be a friend?** (That's one way to follow Jesus.) **What makes it hard to be a friend sometimes?** (It takes time, people might laugh.)

▼ Bible Project ▲

Provide finalized details of the Making Friends project and, if necessary, permission slips for parents to complete.

Following Jesus means being the kind of friend Jesus would be—doing the kinds of things Jesus did to be a friend. Let's use what we have prepared to act out our visit.

Encourage each child to participate in a role play of the visit. Adult leaders can pretend to be the person visited as children offer their gifts and presentations. Ask the children questions that might be asked during the visit. This kind of practice will help the children think of the needs of their new friends. If you are visiting elderly people, encourage the children to speak clearly and loud enough to be heard.

▼ Bible Sharing ▲

Serve the strawberry shortcake as a snack, or let children make their own. Bring a sheet cake, whipped cream, and strawberries. Each child can choose a piece of cake, put on a squirt of whipped cream, and add a couple of strawberries on top.

Ask volunteers to share in one of these ways: tell how Jesus was a friend to Zacchaeus; tell how they will be a friend like Jesus this week; recite the memory block. Each child who shares can stand on the stool to address the group. Close by singing favorite songs about following Jesus.

Bible Search

Read John 3:1.
Circle the name of the man who went to see Jesus.
Read John 3:2. Tell when he visited Jesus.
Work the maze to find out what Jesus told the man.

that he left

much

gave his

so

only Son.

Jesus

world the world

loved you us

For

God made

Nicodemus

 Unit 7, Lesson 27

Bible Verse

Find and read 3 John 11.
Fill in the blanks below.
Then sing it to the tune of
"Three Blind Mice."

My dear _____, do not _____

what is _____; fol-low what is _____.

He who _____ what is _____

is from _____. Third _____ e-lev-en.

Bible and Me

Find and circle the answers to
   the questions.
Print each answer in the correct
   blank below.

T A L K

A B C I

L D E N

K I N D

✏️ What did Jesus do to be a friend? _____

_____

_____

✏️ What can we do to be a friend like Jesus? _____

_____

_____

Bible Verse

Count the coins. How many pages equal 500 coins?
Cut out the footprint as directed in Lessons 28 and 29.

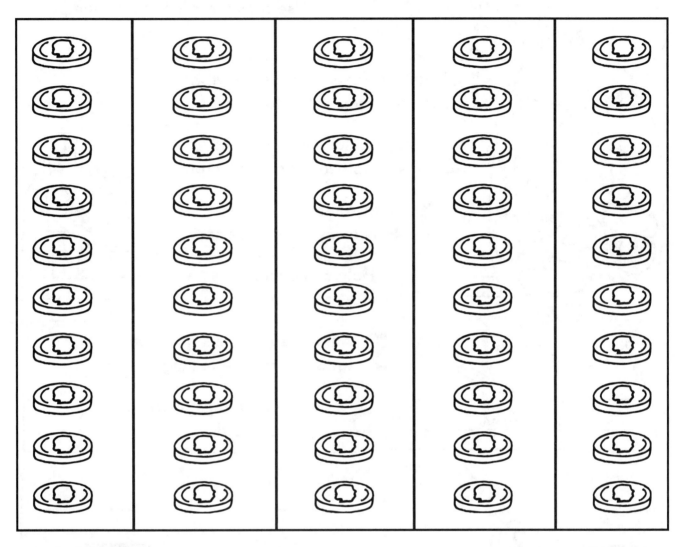

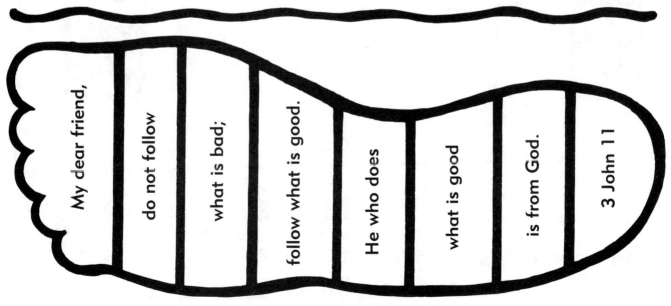

My dear friend, do not follow what is bad; follow what is good. He who does what is good is from God. 3 John 11

Bible and Me

Cross out what Jesus would not do.
Circle what Jesus would do.
Use those words to finish the puzzle.

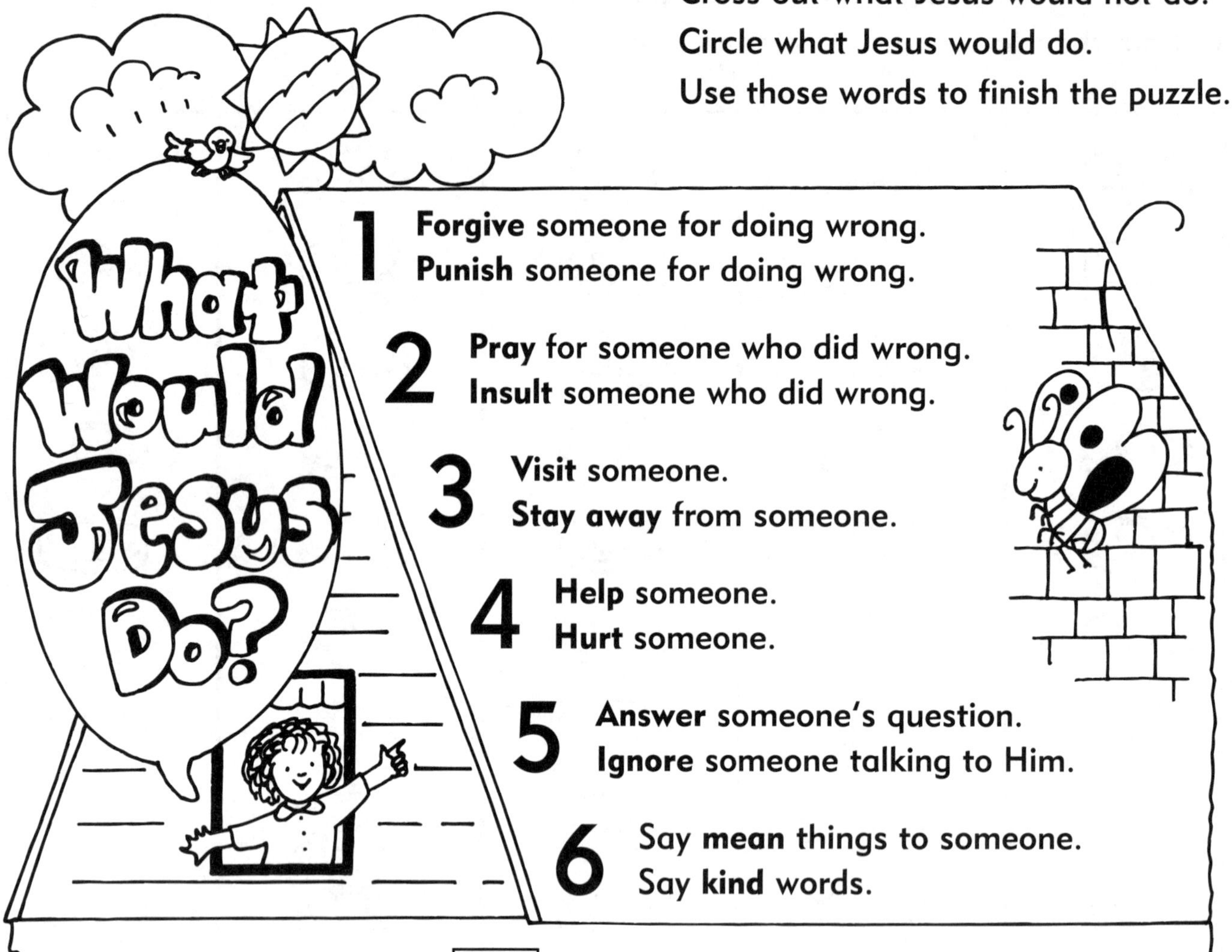

What Would Jesus Do?

1 Forgive someone for doing wrong.
Punish someone for doing wrong.

2 Pray for someone who did wrong.
Insult someone who did wrong.

3 Visit someone.
Stay away from someone.

4 Help someone.
Hurt someone.

5 Answer someone's question.
Ignore someone talking to Him.

6 Say mean things to someone.
Say kind words.

①
②
③
④
⑤
⑥

What would Jesus do?
Jesus would be a

UNIT 7, LESSON 28

Bible Search

Find and read Luke 10:38, 39.
Find the names of three people
who were in Bethany.
Finish the puzzle with the names.

B E T H A N Y

Bible Verse

Find and read 3 John 11.
Say it with a friend.
Then connect the correct arrows
to say it again.

is from God.

what is
boring

what is good

is for
God.

3
John
11

He
who
does

He
who
is

follow
what is
good.

Start

what
is
goofy

what is bad;

My dear
friend,

do not follow

UNIT 7, LESSON 29

Bible and Me

Cut apart, roll up, and tape questions into little
paper rolls.
Make one set of three questions for each child.

Why should we be a friend?
What is a way to be a friend like Jesus?
What is a way NOT to be a friend like Jesus?

Why should we be a friend?
What is a way to be a friend like Jesus?
What is a way NOT to be a friend like Jesus?

Why should we be a friend?
What is a way to be a friend like Jesus?
What is a way NOT to be a friend like Jesus?

Why should we be a friend?
What is a way to be a friend like Jesus?
What is a way NOT to be a friend like Jesus?

Why should we be a friend?
What is a way to be a friend like Jesus?
What is a way NOT to be a friend like Jesus?

Why should we be a friend?
What is a way to be a friend like Jesus?
What is a way NOT to be a friend like Jesus?

Bible Search

Find and read the Bible verses.
Answer the questions.

1. Find and read Matthew 19:13.
What did people want Jesus to do for the children?

_____

- -

_____

2. Find and read Mark 10:13.
What did people want Jesus to do for the children?

_____

- -

_____

3. Find and read Luke 18:15.
What did people want Jesus to do for the children?

_____

- -

_____

4. Circle the words that mean the same as your answers.

hug   push   tickle   hold   pinch   talk to God

5. What would doing these things show the children?

 UNIT 7, LESSON 30

Bible and Me

Find and read 3 John 11.

Say it from memory.

Cut out these word blocks and glue them to the
   blank puzzle pieces in the correct order.

The puzzle will help you memorize the verse.

do what is right.	To my friend,	is like God.	based on 3 John 11	what is wrong;	A person doing	do not do	the right things

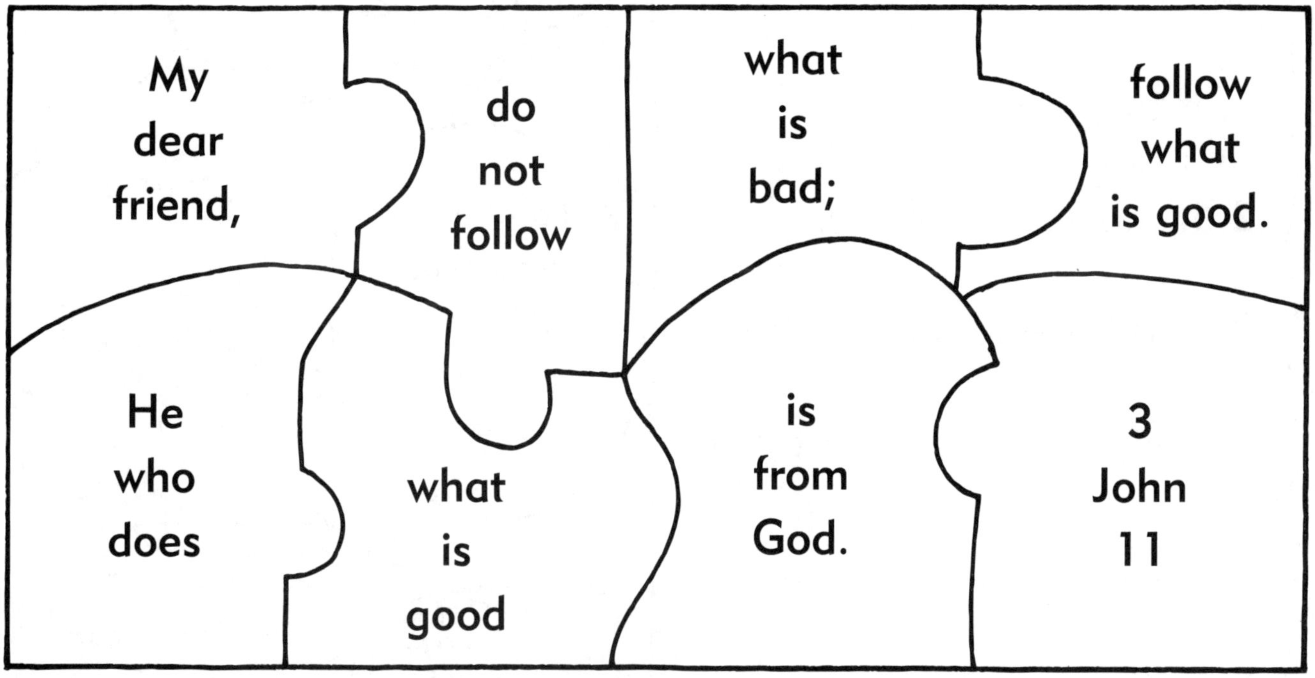

My
dear
friend,

do
not
follow

what
is
bad;

follow
what
is good.

He
who
does

what
is
good

is
from
God.

3
John
11

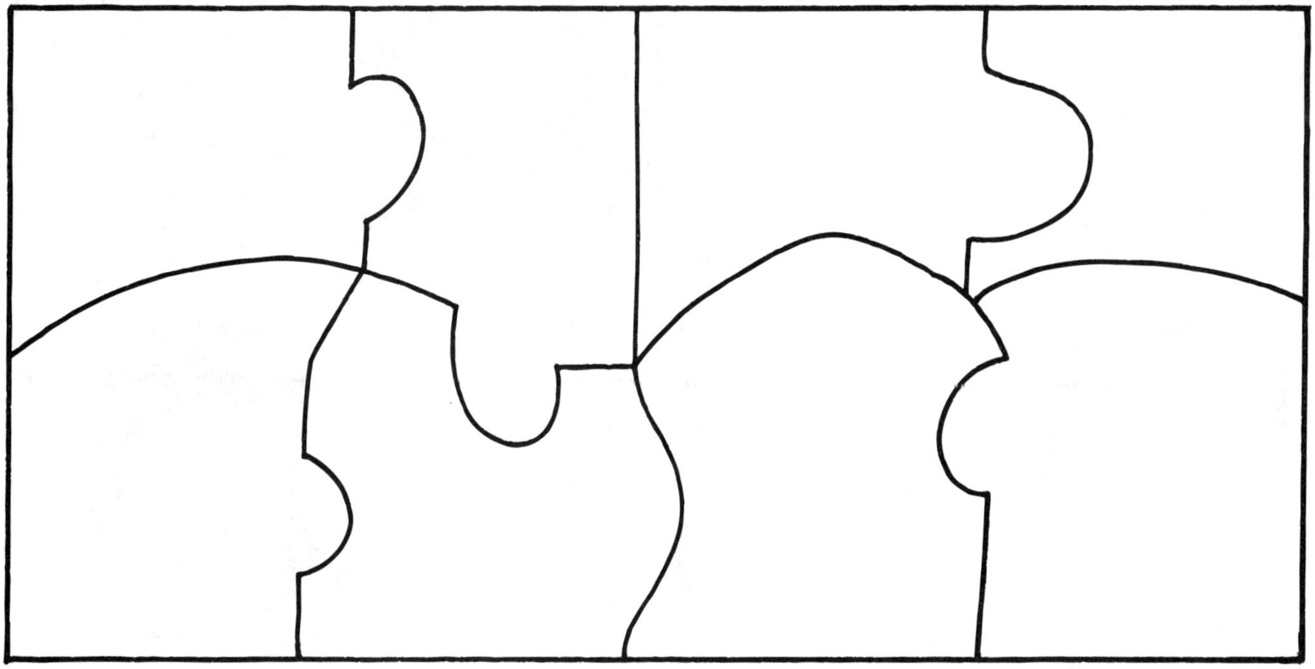

Bible and Me

Read the words below.
These are reasons why it is hard to
  be a friend like Jesus.
Match each reason to a child.
Add a reason for number 5.

Reasons

1. It takes your time.

2. It makes you share.

3. You have to think right.

4. People may laugh at you.

5. _____

   _____

   _____

The other kids will laugh at me if I talk to the new girl no one likes.

I'd sure like to eat these cookies before my cousin gets here.

It will take more time if I stop to give my teacher a thank-you hug.

She is so rude to me. I feel like saying rude things to her.

 UNIT 7, LESSON 30

Bible Search

Find and read Luke 19:2, 3, and 7. Then circle the words that describe Zacchaeus.

from Bethlehem

woman

wanted to see Jesus

tax collector

fisherman

wealthy

very tall

poor

man

loved by all

from Jericho

sinner

short

did only good

Zacchaeus

very important

Just for Fun

Sing a song about Zacchaeus.

Act out what Zacchaeus looked like and what he did.

Jesus Helps Me Bring Friends to Him

Lessons 32–35

32 Jesus Talks to a Samaritan

John 4:5-42

A Samaritan woman who learned about Jesus invited many other people to come to meet Him also. We follow Jesus when we invite people to meet Jesus.

33 Jesus Heals a Man Who Can't Walk

Matthew 9:1-8; Mark 2:1-12; Luke 5:17-26

Four men brought their friend to Jesus to be healed. We follow Jesus when we bring our friends to Jesus.

34 Jesus Heals a Centurion's Servant

Matthew 8:5-13; Luke 7:1-10

A Centurion cared about his servant-friend so much that he asked Jesus to help him get well. We follow Jesus when we care about our friends and bring them to Jesus.

35 Jesus Heals a Man Who Can't Hear

Mark 7:31-37

People brought a deaf man to Jesus to be healed. The people couldn't help telling everyone what Jesus could do. We follow Jesus when we bring friends to Jesus so they can know what Jesus can do.

By the end of this unit, the leaders and learners will

KNOW times Jesus helped people.

FEEL eager to allow Jesus to help friends.

DO Bring friends to Jesus.

Unit Value

The goal of all of Jesus' work on earth was bringing people back into a relationship with God. This unit helps children grow in their awareness of how they fit into Jesus' plan for evangelism. Jesus helped people who brought their friends to Him. And He will help us do the same, because it is God's will for all people to come to Him.

In the first lesson, Jesus is a friend to the Samaritan woman. When she learned who Jesus was, she invited the people in her town to come meet Jesus, too. Many came and many believed. Her example introduces the theme for the unit. The unit memory block comes from her story. The other three stories continue with the example of people bringing friends to see Jesus. Four friends brought a paralyzed man to Jesus. A Centurion asked Jesus to heal his servant-friend. And in the final story, people brought a deaf friend to Jesus to be healed. They couldn't help talking about what Jesus could do.

Just like Bible people brought friends to Jesus, the children in your class can bring their friends to Jesus. This unit will challenge them to identify what it means to bring friends to Jesus. They will learn why it is so important and how to know when their actions are or are not helping to bring people to Jesus. The unit closes with helping children think about what they can say when it's hard to bring friends to Jesus.

▼ Bible Project ▲

Jesus and Me Party

The learners will plan a Follow Jesus party to which they can invite their friends. Help the children show their eagerness for bringing their friends by involving them in every part of the planning. Plan big and make this party a great opportunity for outreach! Use the *Follow Jesus* logo to make invitations, decorations, and T-shirts to give to the invited guests.

Let the theme center around fun, food, and friends. Plan games, but also include skits about Jesus (the four Bible stories for the unit). The skits will be a fun and informal way for your children to introduce Jesus to their friends.

Week 1: Plan the party theme, time, and place. Make invitations.

Week 2: Plan food, decorations, games, and skits. Ask children to help.

Week 3: Make T-shirts with the *Follow Jesus* logo to give to guests.

Week 4: Practice Bible story skits. Make final preparations.

Materials
copies of the *Follow Jesus* logo
   from page 166
construction paper for
   invitations
planning board
plain T-shirts for each person
   invited (more if you want
   your children to wear them
   also)
fabric markers

Paste this *Follow Jesus* logo on the cover of a folded construction paper card and paste this ◆▶ inside to make your invitations!

You're Invited to Our *Follow Jesus* Party!

When: _____

Where: _____

What to bring: _____

_____

Fun! Food! Entertainment!

Jesus Talks to a Samaritan

John 4:5-42

Purpose
Tell what Jesus did to help the Samaritan woman.

Materials
trash bag or old shower curtain
trash can
large container of water
small bucket
six-foot length of rope
gallon plastic jug
brown wrapping paper (brown paper bags)
brown spray paint
small paper cups
tape
markers

Purpose
Tell what the Samaritan woman did for her friends.

Materials
a drink of water in a glass
the Bible times well made in Bible Search
an empty soup can wrapped in brown paper
slips of paper
marker

Lesson Goals

- Tell what Jesus did to help the Samaritan woman.
- Tell what the Samaritan woman did for her friends.
- Begin to memorize John 4:28-30.
- Tell what it means to bring friends to Jesus.
- Bring friends to Jesus.

▼ Bible Search ▲

Before the session, spray paint the gallon jug brown. Tie the six-foot rope to the small bucket.

In today's story, Jesus met a Samaritan woman who was coming to get a drink of water. Jesus was kind to her and talked to her. Let's find the verse in our Bibles. Then we will see what she had to do, just to get a drink!

Follow these instructions to make a Bible times well.

1. Set the trash can on the trash bag or shower curtain.
2. Place the large container of water in the trash can.
3. Tape brown wrapping paper to the outside of the trash can.
4. Draw stones on the paper to look like a well.
5. Practice dipping the small bucket into the large container of water.
6. Try pouring the water into your "water jar" (gallon jug).
7. Let each child use a cup to get a drink from the "water jar."

How did Bible times people get a drink of water? What parts would be fun? What parts would be hard? Would you rather get a drink in Bible times or today? What did Jesus do to help the Samaritan woman? (He was kind; He talked to her.)

▼ Bible Story ▲

For review, make a "well" out of a soup can wrapped in brown paper. Print the review questions on slips of paper and put them in the "well."

Sip a drink of water. **What's the difference between how I got this drink and how Bible people got water to drink?** (Children report.) **Listen for why a woman forgot to take her drink back home with her.**

"Jesus Talks to a Samaritan"

The tired, thirsty travelers saw Jacob's well on down the dusty road. That would be a great place to stop and rest. And they could get food for a noon meal in the nearby town of Sychar. While His followers went into town, Jesus stopped to rest at the well. Jesus knew Jacob had dug this well. And it still had cool water to drink—if you had something to get water with!

Soon, someone else came to the well—a Samaritan woman. Most Jews hated Samaritans. They spoke unkindly or else they didn't speak to them at all. But Jesus was different. He asked kindly, "Please give me a drink." The shocked woman couldn't understand why a Jew was being kind to her, a Samaritan.

Jesus decided to help her learn who He was. First, He explained how He could give her something even better than the water she would get from Jacob's well. That puzzled her. What could be better to drink than cool water from the well? Jesus explained, "Every person who drinks this water I give will never be thirsty again. It will give him eternal life." Jesus was talking about Heaven.

The woman liked the idea of not being thirsty, so she said, "Sir, give me this water," but she still didn't understand what Jesus meant.

So Jesus said, "Go get your husband and come back here." Jesus knew she had no husband. He said this to show her that He knew what kind of life she had lived. He wanted her to see that He was willing to be her friend in spite of all the wrong things He knew she had done.

When she heard Jesus tell about things she had done, she realized He was from God. So she decided to ask Him some questions, "Where do you think we should worship?"

Jesus gave her a good answer to help her learn about worship. He said, "Soon people will worship God all the time, and not just when they are in special places for worshiping."

The woman was still confused, so she said, "I know that the Messiah is coming. He will explain everything to us." That's when Jesus told her who He was, the Messiah, the Son of God.

Wow! The woman could hardly believe what she heard. But she did believe it, and she couldn't wait to tell everyone in Sychar. She was in such a hurry she left her water jar back at the well. She had something more important to take back to town: this news about Jesus. She told the people, "Come, see a man who told me everything I ever did. Could this be the Christ?"

Many Samaritans who came out believed Jesus was from God. They begged Jesus to stay. He didn't leave for two more days. Then the people said, "We no longer believe just because of what you said; now we have heard for ourselves, and we know that this man really is the Savior of the world."

The children can pull questions out of a "well" (a soup can covered with brown paper).

When Jesus was traveling, where did He stop to rest? (Sychar, well) **What did the followers go to do?** (buy food) **Who else came to get a drink in the middle of the day?** (woman) **What unusual thing did Jesus do?** (spoke to a Samaritan; asked her for water) **Why was it unusual for Jesus to speak kindly to this woman?** (Jews hated Samaritans.) **What did the woman do when she learned who she was talking to?** (went to bring people to Jesus) **Why did she forget to take her water jar?** (She was excited to tell about Jesus.) **Why did people in Sychar decide to follow Jesus?** (The woman invited them to come see Jesus; then they listened to Jesus and decided to follow Him.)

Summary questions: **What did Jesus do to help the Samaritan woman?** (spoke, asked for water, was a friend, told her how to live in Heaven) **What did the Samaritan woman do for her friends?** (invited them to meet Jesus) **What happened because she brought them to Jesus?** (Many believed what Jesus said and learned how to follow Jesus.)

▼ Bible Verse ▲

Before the session, follow the instructions on page 208 to make one verse baton to use in class.

John 4:28-30 tells how a Samaritan woman brought friends to Jesus. We help our friends follow Jesus when we bring them to Jesus.

Guide the children to find and read John 4:28-30. Find the page number for John in the table of contents. Then find the big 4 for the chapter and the small 28 for the verse. Read the verses aloud. Sing "There Was a Woman at a Well" from

Purpose
Begin to memorize John 4:28-30.

Materials
Bibles
copies of page 208
copy of page 215
empty paper towel rolls
tape
scissors

page 215. (The tune is "B-I-N-G-O.") Pass the verse baton around the circle of children as you sing the song again. At the end of each stanza, the child with the verse baton can use it to say the verses aloud. Repeat several times.

If you have time, let each child make a 3-section verse baton as suggested on page 208.

Who wrote these verses in the Bible? Are these verses in a story Jesus told or did they really happen? What did the woman do in the first verse? What did she say in the second verse? What happened in the last verse?

▼ Bible and Me ▲

Bringing a friend to Jesus means you help a friend know who Jesus is so they will want to be His friend too. Let's work on how we can do it.

Use page 209 to help children identify who Jesus is, what He can do, and how we can tell people what we know about Jesus. Then let each child pull an item from the sack and show/tell how to use it to help a friend meet Jesus.

What does it mean to bring a friend to Jesus? Who is Jesus? What can Jesus do? What can we do to help people meet Jesus?

▼ Bible Project ▲

Bringing friends to Jesus means you help them know who Jesus is. We're going to plan a party so we can help our friends know Jesus.

Spend as much time as you need planning the *Follow Jesus* party and infusing into the children enthusiasm for the big event. Plan the theme, time, and place. Use the *Follow Jesus* logo to make invitations. List friends to bring on the planning tablet. Include parents as you plan (or inform them ahead of time) so they will be excited about bringing their children's friends to the party.

▼ Bible Sharing ▲

Serve Popsicles® or another water-based snack, or put a fruit drink in the well from Bible Search and allow children to serve themselves drinks from the well.

Ask the children to think about friends they want to bring to the *Jesus and Me* party. Write down the names to obtain addresses later. Review the questions from the Bible and Me section. **What does it mean to bring a friend to Jesus? Who is Jesus? What can Jesus do? What can we do to help people meet Jesus?** Close by singing songs about Jesus.

Purpose
Tell what it means to bring friends to Jesus.

Materials
copies of page 209
pencils
paper sack with these items:
Bible story paper, Bible with a verse marked, CD or cassette of songs about Jesus, picture of a church building, Bible story book, invitation to church postcard, phone, party hat with a sticker of Jesus on it

---

Purpose
Bring friends to Jesus.

Materials
planning tablet
enlarged copies of the *Follow Jesus* logo from page 166 for everyone
construction paper
markers, colored pencils

Purpose
Share how Jesus helps you bring your friends to Him.

Materials
Popsicles® or fruit flavored ice (water-based snack) or a fruit drink
the well made in Bible Search
CD or cassette of songs about Jesus
CD or cassette player

Jesus Heals a Man Who Can't Walk

Matthew 9:1-8; Mark 2:1-12; Luke 5:17-26

Lesson Goals

- Tell what the four men did for their friend.
- Tell what Jesus did to help the man who couldn't walk.
- Memorize John 4:28-30.
- Tell why we bring friends to Jesus.
- Bring friends to Jesus.

▼ Bible Search ▲

In today's story, Jesus was teaching in a house when four men lowered their friend down through the roof. Let's learn how that could happen—on purpose!

Guide the children to find and read Mark 2:3, 4 in their Bibles. Then talk about Bible times houses using page 210. Help the children understand what the houses were made of and how they were built.

How did Bible times people build their houses? What parts would be the same as your house? What parts would be different from your house? What did the four men do for their friend? How could they do that?

▼ Bible Story ▲

Ask one child to lie on the sleeping bag. **How would it feel if you could never get up off your sleeping bag? What would you not get to do? Listen to see how four friends helped someone who couldn't get off his mat.**

"Jesus Heals a Man Who Can't Walk"

"He's back," someone said. "Jesus is back in Capernaum today. He came across Lake Galilee in a boat." I wished I could have followed the crowd headed to the house where Jesus was. But my paralyzed legs kept me from standing up to get off my mat. I never went anywhere unless someone carried me on that old mat. Then, right before my eyes stood four of my friends. They wanted to take me along with them to see Jesus. What a great idea! They yanked that old mat up off the ground, and all five of us headed for Jesus.

At the house there were people everywhere. They were crowding to get in, crowding around the door. We'd never get through. But my friends were determined to bring me to Jesus. After thinking and figuring, they came up with a plan. Up on the roof they made an opening. Then they hoisted me up next to the hole. What a great idea! Carefully they lowered me, on my mat, into the room where Jesus was teaching. The mat inched down, down, down, until I was lying right in front of Jesus.

People were all over the room. There were even Pharisees and Jewish teachers of the law sitting near Jesus. But when Jesus saw how much my friends wanted to help me, He spoke clearly and simply to me, "Young man, your sins are forgiven." Jesus could say that because God had given Him the power to both forgive sins and heal people.

Memory Block

"Then the woman left her water jar and went back to town. She said to the people, 'A man told me everything I have ever done. Come see him. Maybe he is the Christ!' So the people left the town and went to see Jesus" (John 4:28-30).

Purpose
Tell what the four men did for their friend.

Materials
Bibles
copies of page 210

Purpose
Tell what Jesus did to help the man who couldn't walk.

Materials
a sleeping bag

But the teachers and Pharisees didn't like what Jesus said. They were thinking that only God could forgive sins. And they didn't think Jesus was from God. They thought Jesus was doing something wrong. So Jesus said, "Why are you thinking that?" He told them He could both forgive my sins and tell me to stand up and walk. To prove it, He spoke to me again, "I tell you, stand up. Take your mat and go home." My legs felt strong. I bounced up off my mat. I took a step and realized I could make my legs walk. While everyone watched, I picked up my mat and walked right out of the house.

Jesus showed the crowd He really was from God by using God's power to heal me. But the people could hardly believe what they saw. They said, "We have never seen anything like this," and "Today we have seen amazing things!" It was amazing, but it was true. And it happened because of my friends. They were determined to bring me to Jesus. And Jesus did the rest!

Group the children in four areas of the room. Give each group a name (people, four men, paralyzed man, Jesus). When the group's name answers a riddle, they can stand and answer, "We did!"

Who came to the house? (all groups)

Who brought someone on a mat? (four men)

Who needed to get into the house to see Jesus? (paralyzed man)

Who solved the problem of how to get in to see Jesus? (four men)

Who said, "Your sins are forgiven"? (Jesus)

Who said, "Stand up. Take your mat and go home"? (Jesus)

Who said, "Today we have seen amazing things"? (people)

Who carried the mat home? (paralyzed/healed man)

Summary questions: **What did the four men do for their friend who was paralyzed?** (brought him to Jesus) **What did Jesus do to help the paralyzed man?** (forgave his sins, healed him)

▼ Bible Verse ▲

Purpose
Memorize John 4:28-30.

Materials
Bibles
the verse baton (made in Lesson 32)
a card for each child cut from page 211
blindfold

John 4:28-30 tells how a Samaritan woman brought friends to Jesus. We can be like that woman when we bring friends to Jesus.

Let the children find and read John 4:28-30 in their Bibles. Together read the verses aloud. Play a game with the verse baton. Put a blindfold on one child and give him the baton. The children march around him in a circle, saying the verses. Each marcher has a card from page 211. When the verses end, the blindfolded child points the verse baton toward someone. That child reads his card and follows the directions. If the verses are said correctly, the blindfolded child switches places with the one to whom he pointed. Let every child have a turn to say the verses or hold the baton.

Focus the conversation on John 4:28-30. **Who wrote these verses in the Bible? What did the woman do in the first verse? What did she say in the middle verse? What happened in the last verse?**

▼ Bible and Me ▲

Bringing a friend to Jesus means you help a friend know who Jesus is so they will want to be His friend too. Let's learn why this is important.

Follow instructions on page 212 to help the children tell why we bring friends to Jesus. After completing the top of the page, use the following questions to focus the conversation on why we bring friends.

What does bringing a friend to Jesus mean? What reasons do you think are the best? Why? Are there any reasons you don't understand? (If so, explain.) **Do you add any reasons?** (If so, what?)

Sing about bringing friends to Jesus. Each time you sing, ask a child this question. **What reason makes you want to bring friends to Jesus?**

Purpose
Tell why we bring friends to Jesus.

Materials
copies of page 212
pencils

▼ Bible Project ▲

You may want to ask parents to come to this planning session.

Bringing a friend to Jesus means you help a friend know who Jesus is so they will want to be His friend too. We want to plan more of our *Follow Jesus* party so we can help our friends learn about Jesus.

Plan the kinds of food and decide who you need to ask to bring food. Plan simple decorations (perhaps the *Follow Jesus* logo on posters). Ask the children to suggest their favorite games; decide who will lead the game at the party. Plan the Bible skits—who will play which parts and the props needed. You may want to consider recording the stories on cassette and letting the children act them out. (If you prepared skits for the Making Friends project for Unit 7, present those skits at the party.) Once again, your enthusiastic example and excitement about introducing friends to Jesus will be contagious!

Purpose
Bring friends to Jesus.

Materials
materials for planning food, decorations, games, and skits for the *Follow Jesus* party

▼ Bible Sharing ▲

The children can make faces on their hot dogs with ketchup or mustard to remind them of the man on the mat. It might be fun to eat on sleeping bags or mats on the floor.

Spend the sharing time listening to and singing songs about Jesus.

Close with prayer. Ask volunteers to pray sentence prayers. Suggest they pray for their friends and pray that many friends will come to the *Follow Jesus* party.

Purpose
Share how Jesus helps you bring your friends to Him.

Materials
hot dogs on open-faced buns
ketchup and mustard
sleeping bags or mats
CD or cassette of songs about Jesus
CD or cassette player

Jesus Heals an Army Officer's Servant

Matthew 8:5-13; Luke 7:1-10

Memory Block
"Then the woman left her water jar and went back to town. She said to the people, 'A man told me everything I have ever done. Come see him. Maybe he is the Christ!' So the people left the town and went to see Jesus" (John 4:28-30).

Purpose
Tell what the army officer did for his servant.

Materials
Bibles
copies of page 213
pencils

Purpose
Tell what Jesus did to help the army officer's servant.

Materials
army items (helmet, khaki hat, medal, stripes, picture of military officer from a news magazine)

Lesson Goals

- Tell what the army officer did for his servant.
- Tell what Jesus did to help the army officer's servant.
- Recite John 4:28-30.
- Tell the difference between bringing and not bringing friends to Jesus.
- Bring friends to Jesus.

▼ Bible Search ▲

In today's story, an army officer in Capernaum had built a synagogue. What do all these big words mean? Let's find out.

Guide children to find Luke 7:2, 3 in their Bibles. Read the verses. Ask the children to repeat the name of the man (army officer) and town (Capernaum). Find Luke 7:5 and repeat the word *synagogue*. Complete page 213 by matching each picture to its description and its meaning for this story.

What is an army officer? What is Capernaum? What is a synagogue? What did the army officer do for his servant? (Luke 7:2, 3)

▼ Bible Story ▲

Display items. **If these were yours, what might your job be? Listen to see how Jesus helped the friend of someone who served in an army.**

"Jesus Heals an Army Officer's Servant"

The face of the army officer in Capernaum was frantic. Even his armor couldn't hide his worry. His dear servant lay quietly on his bed, suffering. If he didn't start getting better soon, he would die. The army officer could command his 100 soldiers to do anything he wished, and it would be done. But there was nothing he or any of his soldiers could do to help his friend—his servant.

Later, the army officer heard about a man called Jesus who had done many miracles. Jesus had been teaching on a mountain in Galilee and had just arrived at the gate of Capernaum. The army officer knew he could not command Jesus to heal his servant, but he believed Jesus could help. But even though the army officer was an important man, he didn't feel that he was good enough to speak to Jesus himself. Quickly, he sent for older Jewish leaders who were his friends. After he explained what he needed, they left to find Jesus. They begged Jesus to help the army officer's servant, saying, "This officer is worthy of your help. He loves our people, and he built us a synagogue."

Jesus was glad to be able to help. He said, "I will go and heal him." Down the streets of Capernaum they walked, closer to the house where the servant lay dying. As they got near, the army officer sent out more friends with another message: "I am not good enough for you to come into my house. That is why I did not come to you myself. All you need to do is command that my servant be healed, and he will be healed. I too am a man under authority of other men. And I have soldiers under my authority. I tell one soldier, 'Go,' and he goes. I tell another soldier, 'Come,' and he comes. I say to a servant, 'Do this,' and my servant obeys me." The army officer believed that Jesus' power was great enough just to speak and the servant would be healed.

Jesus was amazed. The army officer believed Jesus didn't have to touch his servant to help him. He could do a miracle just by speaking about it. In all of the miracles Jesus had done, He had never seen anyone believe that His power was that great. Jesus was so amazed that He said to the crowd around him, "This man has more faith than any other person I have found."

Without waiting any longer, Jesus said to the messengers, "Go home. The servant will be healed." When the messenger got back, they learned that the servant was healed at the same time. The army officer's servant got well because the army officer cared enough to go to Jesus for help.

Play the game "Officer, May I?" For each question you ask, a child must first say, "Officer, may I?" If you say, "Yes, you may," the child may give his answer.

Where did Jesus arrive when the story began? (Capernaum)

Who wanted Jesus to come help? (the army officer)

What was wrong with the servant-friend? (sick, nearly dead)

Who did the officer send to talk to Jesus? (Jewish leaders)

What did Jesus decide to do? (come to servant)

When Jesus came near the house, who met Him? (friends with message)

What did the officer want Jesus to do? (speak and heal his servant)

Why was Jesus so surprised? (The army officer's faith was great.)

When was the servant healed? (same time Jesus spoke)

Summary questions: **What did the army officer do for his servant-friend?** (sent to Jesus for help) **What did Jesus do to help the servant-friend?** (made him well when He spoke)

▼ Bible Verse ▲

Before the session, print *town* on one piece of paper. Print *well* on the other piece of paper. Display the pieces of paper at opposite ends of your classroom.

John 4:28-30 tells how a Samaritan woman brought friends to Jesus. We can be like that woman when we bring friends to Jesus.

Find and read John 4:28-30. Then play a relay game with the verse baton. Label one side of the room *town* and the opposite side *well*. Use a stopwatch to see how long it takes groups of 4-6 to relay everyone from the town to the well. A "Samaritan woman" holds the verse baton at the well. Everyone is in town. She runs to town, says the verses to someone, and brings them to the well. That child runs the baton back to town, says the verses to someone, and brings them to the well. That child runs the baton back to town, says the verses to someone, and brings them to the well. Continue until everyone is at the well. Focus on the best times of each group instead of the fastest group. (Start groups 30 seconds apart.) Repeat the activity.

What did the woman do in the first verse? What did she say in the middle verse? What happened in the last verse? What do these verses help us remember to do?

Purpose
Recite John 4:28-30.

Materials
verse baton (Lesson 32)
a stopwatch
paper
marker
tape

▼ Bible and Me ▲

Bringing a friend to Jesus means you help a friend know who Jesus is so they will want to be His friend too. Let's see if we can tell the difference between bringing and not bringing friends to Jesus.

Complete page 214 to help the children tell the difference between bringing and not bringing friends to Jesus. Then use the following conversation questions to talk about bringing friends.

What does bringing a friend to Jesus mean? (Review Lesson 32.) **Why do we want to bring friends to Jesus?** (Review Lesson 33.) **What are some things to say that help friends learn about Jesus? What is a good thing to do that doesn't help your friend learn about Jesus? What is the difference? Which child in the bottom picture is most likely to get his friend to come with him later to learn about Jesus?**

Purpose
Tell the difference between bringing and not bringing friends to Jesus.

Materials
copies of page 214

▼ Bible Project ▲

Before the session, trace the *Follow Jesus* logo on each T-shirt.

Bringing a friend to Jesus means you help a friend know who Jesus is so they will want to be His friend too. Let's make T-shirts to give to our friends when we bring them to the *Follow Jesus* party.

Guide the children to use the fabric markers to color the *Follow Jesus* logo on T-shirts. Encourage them to do their best work for their friends. If you have time, allow children to make T-shirts for themselves. The *Follow Jesus* T-shirts can build relationships in your group and give your children a team identity. While children work, ask questions about the friends they plan to bring.

Purpose
Bring friends to Jesus.

Materials
plain T-shirts
fabric markers
copies of the *Follow Jesus* logo from page 166

▼ Bible Sharing ▲

Serve a snack of army rations. Play songs about Jesus. While the songs play, pass the three cards around the circle. When the music stops, each child who holds a card stands up and shares about what is printed on the card (story—share something about the Bible story; verse—recite or tell about the Bible verses; friend—tell about a way to bring a friend to Jesus or name a friend to bring). Close by singing songs printed on page 215 or other favorite songs about Jesus.

Purpose
Share how Jesus helps you bring your friends.

Materials
Copies of page 215
a snack of army rations (beef jerky, trail mix)
three index cards on which you have printed the following words: *story, verse, friend*
CD or cassette of songs about Jesus
CD or cassette player

Jesus Heals a Man Who Can't Hear

Mark 7:31-37

Lesson Goals
- Tell what the people begged Jesus to do.
- Tell what Jesus did to help the man.
- Recite and explain John 4:28-30.
- Tell what makes it hard to bring friends to Jesus.
- Bring friends to Jesus.

Memory Block
"Then the woman left her water jar and went back to town. She said to the people, 'A man told me everything I have ever done. Come see him. Maybe he is the Christ!' So the people left the town and went to see Jesus" (John 4:28-30).

▼ Bible Search ▲

In today's story, some friends bring a man to Jesus. Let's find out what they wanted Jesus to do and why.

Guide the children to find Mark 7:32 in their Bibles. Read the verse together. **What did the people beg Jesus to do? What things would you miss out on if you couldn't hear? What would be hard to do if you couldn't talk? What can we say in signs to talk to a person who can't hear?**

Make up or teach motions for the sentence, "Jesus makes the deaf to hear." Suggested signs:

Jesus—Touch tips of middle fingers to opposite palms (signifying nail prints).

Makes—hold fists on top of each other and twist opposite ways.

The deaf—hold ears with palms.

To hear—stick index fingers in ears.

Purpose
Tell what the people begged Jesus to do.

Materials
Bibles

▼ Bible Story ▲

If I couldn't talk with my voice, you would hear me speak with my hands. Ask the children to sign with you or do motions for the sentence "Jesus makes the deaf to hear." **Listen to see who said this in the story.**

Purpose
Tell what Jesus did to help the man.

"Jesus Heals a Man Who Can't Hear"

I used to be a deaf man. That also meant I couldn't talk. When you can't hear people speaking, you can't learn how to make sounds into words that people understand. Many times I pointed to what I wanted or made faces to show how I felt. It was very hard to get people to understand me. Many times no one understood me. But I did have some friends who cared about me. One day, they gave me the best gift anyone could ever give a friend.

It happened on a day when a man named Jesus came to our area—the area of the Ten Towns. While He was in our area by Lake Galilee, my friends found me and hustled me off to see Him. A crowd was around Jesus, so they led me through the crowd and took me right up close. I watched as they patiently waited their turn to speak to Jesus. I couldn't hear what they were saying, but I could tell they were very serious about whatever they were asking. I wondered if Jesus could help me. Would it be too much to ask?

When my friends finished speaking to Jesus, He turned to me with His kind eyes. His gentle touch led me away from the crowd. My heart nearly burst out of my chest—it was beating so wildly. What was Jesus going to do? Could He help me? Would it be too much to ask?

When Jesus and I were standing off by ourselves, He showed me that He understood my problems. He put His fingers in my ears that would not hear. And He touched my tongue that would not speak. Oh, maybe He could help me! Maybe it wouldn't be too much to ask?

I watched as Jesus looked up into Heaven. I saw His chest heave out in a deep breath. And then He said, "Ephphatha." It means "Be opened!" Oh, He did help me! It wasn't too much to ask! Immediately I could hear—the wind, the birds, the people, and best of all, I could hear Jesus. But that wasn't all. I could use my tongue—not just to grunt and make sounds, but to speak words clearly. People could understand me, and I could hear and understand them.

Jesus commanded us not to tell anyone about what had happened, but we were so excited, we couldn't keep quiet. Everyone was so amazed. We said, "Jesus does everything well. Jesus made the deaf hear. And those who can't talk—Jesus makes them able to speak." Today I can hear and speak because my friends cared enough to bring me to Jesus. Now I can listen to Jesus, learn how to follow Him, and tell more people what He can do.

Show the sign for yes (shake head up and down) and no (shake head from side to side). Children will use the sign to answer.

Did today's story take place in the area of the Ten Towns?
Did children beg Jesus to heal the deaf man?
Did Jesus heal the man in the middle of the crowd?
Did Jesus put His fingers in the man's ears?
Did Jesus look up to Heaven just before He healed the man?
Did Jesus say, "Do not open"?
Did Jesus command the people not to tell what happened?
Did the people keep quiet?
Did the people say, "Jesus makes the deaf to hear"?

Summary questions: **What did the people beg Jesus to do?** (heal the deaf man) **What did Jesus do to help the man?** (helped him hear and speak)

▼ Bible Verse ▲

Purpose
Recite and explain John 4:28-30.

Materials
Bibles
chalkboard and chalk or marker board and marker

John 4:28-30 tells how a Samaritan woman brought friends to Jesus. We can be like that woman when we bring our friends to Jesus.

Find and read John 4:28-30. Ask for volunteers to recite the verses. If some children need help, print the words of the verses on a chalkboard. Let them read and erase words, read and erase, until they can say the verses.

Let children who know the verses dramatize them to explain them. A narrator recites the beginning (v. 28). A "Samaritan woman" recites what she said (v. 29). The other children are townspeople. They recite the last sentence (v. 30). Let the children choose places for characters to stand and then recite the verses as they act out the verses. Encourage using lots of feeling and enthusiasm. Trade roles several times!

Help children explain the verses. **What did the woman do in the first verse? What did she say in the middle verse? What happened in the last verse? What do these verses help us remember to do?**

Option: Provide mural paper, markers, and crayons. Print the three parts of the verses across the length of mural paper. Children can use markers and crayons to picture what happens in each of the verses.

▼ Bible and Me ▲

Before the session, cut apart the cards on pages 216 and 217. Provide at least one set of cards from both pages for every 2-3 children.

Bringing a friend to Jesus means you help a friend know who Jesus is so they will want to be His friend too! Jesus promised He would always be with us, even when it's hard. Let's learn what we can say when it's hard to bring friends to Jesus.

Use pages 216 and 217 to help the children talk about times when it is hard to bring friends to Jesus. Give groups of 2-3 a set of cards from page 216 to put in one column. Then give them the cards from page 217 with conversation to match to each "hard time." Use the situations as a guide for acting out what to say when it's hard to bring friends to Jesus. After the game, use the following questions to focus the conversation on what we have learned about bringing friends.

What does bringing a friend to Jesus mean? Why do we want to bring friends to Jesus? How can you tell if what you are saying will bring friends to Jesus? (Does it say something about Jesus?) **What are some things to say that help friends learn about Jesus? What can make it hard to bring friends to Jesus?** (Use pages 216 and 217; for each situation, talk about what to say or do.)

Purpose
Tell what makes it hard to bring friends to Jesus.

Materials
copies of pages 216 and 217
scissors

▼ Bible Project ▲

Bringing a friend to Jesus means you help a friend know who Jesus is. What are some things to say that help friends learn about Jesus? (Let children answer.) **Let's practice skits for our *Follow Jesus* party. That's a way to help our friends learn about what Jesus did.**

Practice skits for the party. Finalize party details. Go over with the children what will happen at the party. Talk about ways to make sure friends feel a part of the group. Review the reason for bringing friends to Jesus and show your enthusiasm for the big event!

Purpose
Bring friends to Jesus.

Materials
props and materials to practice Bible story skits

▼ Bible Sharing ▲

During the first part of snack time, ask the children to pretend to be hearing impaired—don't talk. Then talk about what it felt like.

Pretend you are a part of the crowd. You just saw a man healed by Jesus! I am a reporter for the Ten Town Tribune. (Interview different children for each question.) **What did you see? Do you really believe that happened? What are you going to do now? Who will you tell? Why?**

Close by singing favorite songs about Jesus.

Purpose
Share how Jesus helps me bring friends to Him.

Materials
a favorite snack
a toy microphone
CD or cassette of songs about Jesus
CD or cassette player

Bible Verse

Find John 4:28-30 in your Bible. Then make a memory verse baton. You will need tape and an empty paper towel roll.

cut

3. Put the strips on a paper towel roll.

2. Tape each paper strip together.

1. Cut on the heavy lines on this page.

She said to the people,

Maybe he is the Christ!"

—John 4:28-30

Overlap top to line and tape.

jar and went back to town.

I have ever done. Come see him.

and went to see Jesus.

Overlap top to line and tape.

Then the woman left her water

"A man told me everything

So the people left the town

Overlap top to line and tape.

UNIT 8, LESSON 32

Bible and Me

Answer the questions about Jesus.

1. **Who is Jesus? Jesus is the Son of God.**
   Write another sentence about Jesus.

   _____

   -

   _____

2. **What can Jesus do?**

   Put a star by all the right answers.

   Miracles!

   Teach me how to live the best way.

   Prepare a special place for me in Heaven.

   Help me bring other friends to meet Him.

3. **What can I do to tell people what I know about Jesus?**
   Draw a picture.

Bible Search

Find Mark 2:3, 4 in your Bible. What did four men do for their friend?

Bible Times House

Our story takes place in the town of Capernaum. The houses in that town have been discovered by people called archaeologists.

The houses were simple. The walls were made of stone. The roofs were flat. They were made of mud mixed with straw.

It would have been easy for the four friends to make a hole in the roof. They just pulled apart a section of the roof.

Most houses in Capernaum had courtyards. There were also outside stairways leading to the roof.

The friends probably carried their friend up the outside stairs onto the roof.

 UNIT 8, LESSON 33

Bible Verse

Cut apart the cards. Play a matching game with the cards.

Say the verses by yourself.

Ask someone behind you to say the verses.

Ask all the girls to say the verses.

Ask someone in front of you to say the verses.

Ask all the boys to say the verses.

Say the verses with a friend.

Bible and Me

- Mark **B** by the 3 reasons you think are the best.
- Mark **?** by any reason you don't understand.
- Mark **X** by the reason you want to bring a friend to Jesus.

Reasons

____ Jesus wants our friends to know He loves and cares about them.

____ Jesus wants our friends to know His good news about Heaven!

____ Bringing friends to Jesus helps them learn who Jesus is.

____ Bringing friends to Jesus shows you think Jesus is important and special.

____ Bringing friends to Jesus shows you care about friends.

Why Bring a Friend?

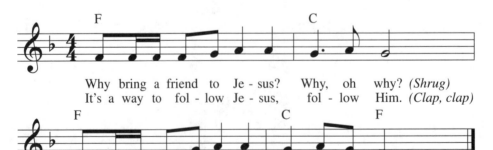

F   C

Why bring a friend to Je - sus?   Why,   oh   why? *(Shrug)*
It's a way to fol - low Je - sus,   fol - low Him. *(Clap, clap)*

F   C   F

Why bring a friend to Je - sus?   Why, why, oh why? *(Shrug)*
It's a way to fol - low Je - sus.   I'll fol - low Him. *(Clap, clap)*

Bible Search

Find Luke 7:2, 3 in your Bible.
Find the name of a town and the name
   of a person who lived there.
In Luke 7:5, find what he built.
Then match each picture to 2 squares.

It was a town near Lake Galilee. Roman soldiers lived there.	\n**Army officer**	In our story, this place was built by an army officer in town.
He was an army officer. He was in charge of 100 men.	\n**Capernaum**	In our story, Jesus went to this town to teach and heal people.
It was a place where Jesus came to read and study God's Word.	\n**synagogue**	In our story, this man built a synagogue. He loved the people of Capernaum.

Bible and Me

Look at the pictures.
Read what the children are saying.

Which children are bringing friends to Jesus?
How can you tell?

I've got a great new CD called "Follow Jesus." Can you come over on Saturday to listen to it?

Can you come stay overnight with me this weekend?

There's a great story in my paper about what Jesus can do. Do you want to take it home and read it?

We're having a "Follow Jesus" party at church Sunday night. Can you come?

Which child is doing things that will help
bring friends to Jesus?

Looks like you really hurt yourself when you fell. Let me help you up.

Oh, shut up, baby face. You're always crying about something.

UNIT 8, LESSON 34

Bible Sharing

Learn these songs about bringing friends to Jesus.

There Was a Woman at a Well

Carla Crane   Traditional "Bingo"

1. There was a wo-man at the well who met a man named Je-sus.
2. The wo-man was not liked by some, but Je-sus showed He cared.

J - E - S - U - S, J - E - S - U - S, J - E - S - U - S. Yes, Je-sus was His name-oh!
C - A - R - E - D, C - A - R - E - D, C - A - R - E - D. Yes, Je-sus showed He cared-oh!

©1989 Standard Publishing

We tell our friends that
    Jesus loves them,
And to Jesus bring them.
B-R-I-N-G, B-R-I-N-G, B-R-I-N-G,
To Jesus we can bring them.

Tell Your Friends

Traditional "Row Your Boat"

Tell, tell, tell your friends of Je-sus and His love.

Tell them how He died for you and lives in Heav'n a-bove.

©1989 Standard Publishing

Bible and Me

Cut apart the cards.
Think about ways to answer.

You want to bring someone to Jesus and **he laughs.**

What can you say**?**

You want to bring someone to Jesus and **she asks hard questions.**

What can you say**?**

You want to bring someone to Jesus and **he has other plans.**

What can you say**?**

You want to bring someone to Jesus and **her parents say "No."**

What can you say**?**

You want to bring someone to Jesus and **you forget what you want to say.**

What can you say**?**

You want to bring someone to Jesus and **you feel shy.**

What can you say**?**

UNIT 8, LESSON 35

Cut apart the cards.
Use these answers to help you bring friends to Jesus.

Bible and Me

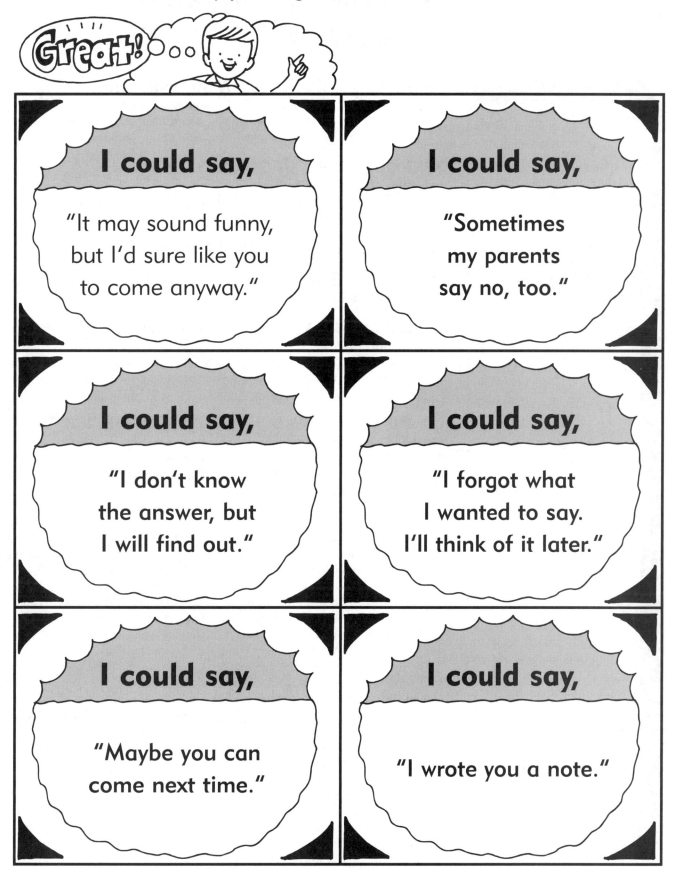

I could say,

"It may sound funny, but I'd sure like you to come anyway."

I could say,

"Sometimes my parents say no, too."

I could say,

"I don't know the answer, but I will find out."

I could say,

"I forgot what I wanted to say. I'll think of it later."

I could say,

"Maybe you can come next time."

I could say,

"I wrote you a note."

UNIT 9

Jesus Helps Me Love My Family

Lessons 36–39

Unit Memory Block

"My children, our love should not be only words and talk. Our love must be true love. And we should show that love by what we do" (1 John 3:18).

Memory Challenge

"So comfort each other and give each other strength, just as you are doing now" (1 Thessalonians 5:11).

"Do everything without complaining or arguing" (Philippians 2:14).

36 Jesus Heals Peter's Mother-in-Law
Mark 1:29-34; Matthew 8:14, 15; Luke 4:38, 39

Jesus showed love to Peter when He helped his mother-in-law get well. We follow Jesus when we show love to people in our families.

37 Jesus Heals an Official's Son
John 4:43-54

Jesus showed love to a father when He helped his son get well. We follow Jesus when we show love to people in our families.

38 Jesus Heals a Widow's Son
Luke 7:11-17

Jesus showed love to a mother when He made her only son come back alive. We follow Jesus when we show love to people in our families.

39 Jesus Heals Jairus's Daughter
Matthew 9:18-26; Mark 5:22-43

Jesus showed love to a father when He made his daughter come back alive. We follow Jesus when we show love to people in our families.

By the end of this unit, the leaders and learners will

KNOW times Jesus showed love to someone in a family.
FEEL willing to show love to people in their families.
DO Follow Jesus by showing love to people in their families.

Unit Value

Saying you love someone and actually showing love can often be miles apart. The Bible verse for this unit challenges us to close the gap between saying we love our family and showing our love. Home, the greatest source of conflict for children, may be the place where loving each other is the biggest, hardest challenge. This unit focuses on what children can do to show love both to parents and siblings. The Bible stories provide Jesus' example of showing love to 1) Peter's mother-in-law, 2) an official and his son, 3) a widow and her son, and 4) Jairus and his daughter. We follow Jesus when we love our families.

The unit has a two-fold application. First, in the words of the unit Bible verse, "Our love should not be only words and talk. Our love must be true love. And we should show that love by what we do." This unit focuses on what it means to show love to people in a family. It guides the children to be able to tell when they are and are not showing love to family members. It helps them know why this is important and then helps them deal with the fact that it is sometimes very hard to show love to people in their families.

Second, take the application a step further to include showing love by the way they speak. The optional verses to memorize can challenge the children to show their love not just by obeying and by helping, but also by the way they talk. In Paul's words, "Encourage one another and build each other up" (*NIV*). And again, "Do everything without complaining or arguing." Help the children see that love starts at home; it doesn't stop when they come home.

▼ Bible Project ▲

Family Album

The learners will make a family album to help them show love to family members. Each child's family album should include pictures of family members, a prayer calendar, an inside pocket with coupons to help him show love, items that remind him of the specialness of each person in his family, and anything else to remind him to follow Jesus at home.

The learners will compile the albums together during the project time. Use the last week to allow children to share their albums with the large group.

Take a picture of each child in your group and make a class family album, or use those photos to send each child a reminder to show love to family members.

Week 1: Plan contents of album; make a prayer calendar.

Week 2: Add pictures to album; make coupon pocket and coupons.

Week 3: Complete album with more pictures and descriptions of parents and siblings.

Week 4: Share family albums with each other.

Materials
inexpensive photo albums for each child (if needed, ask parents to purchase)
copies of page 238
colored pencils
construction paper or poster board
clear tape

Jesus Heals Peter's Mother-in-Law

Mark 1:29-34; Matthew 8:14, 15; Luke 4:38, 39

Memory Block
"My children, our love should not be only words and talk. Our love must be true love. And we should show that love by what we do" (1 John 3:18).

Lesson Goals
- Tell how Peter's mother-in-law felt.
- Tell what Jesus did to show love.
- Begin to memorize 1 John 3:18.
- Tell what it means to show love to people in your family.
- Follow Jesus by showing love to people in your family.

Purpose
Tell how Peter's mother-in-law felt.

Materials
Bibles
copies of page 232
a family tree (optional)

▼ Bible Search ▲

In our story, Jesus showed love to Peter when He helped his mother-in-law. Let's find out how Peter's mother-in-law felt and how she fit in Peter's family.

Guide the children to find and read Mark 1:30 in their Bibles. Find the page number for Mark in the table of contents. Then find the big 1 for the chapter and the small 30 for the verse. Together read the verse aloud. **How did Peter's mother-in-law feel?**

Distribute page 232. Look at and talk about what a mother-in-law is. Display another family tree, if you have one you can bring.

In our story, who is Jesus going to help? How did she feel? What is a mother-in-law? Who is your father's mother-in-law? (your grandma)

▼ Bible Story ▲

Purpose
Tell what Jesus did to show love.

Materials
a thermometer
copies of the top of page 233
pencils

What does your dad or mom do to see if you have a fever? Display the thermometer. **If they didn't have a thermometer, how could they tell?** (red face, hot skin) **Listen to see what Jesus did when someone had a fever.**

"Jesus Heals Peter's Mother-in-Law"

Lots of us were going with James and John to Peter and Andrew's home. We had all been at the synagogue, and now we laughed and talked as we headed to their house. We might eat together there and talk some more. It was great when we could all eat together and learn from Jesus.

But at Peter and Andrew's house, things were not so great. Inside, there was a sick woman. She was Peter's mother-in-law. (That means she was the mother of Peter's wife.) Her fever was so high that she was in her bed. Her head was hot to touch. Sometimes her body felt hot with sweat and sometimes it felt cold with chills. She felt terrible. And nothing seemed to help. The people at the house were worried.

When Jesus and the rest of the followers arrived at the house, we heard about the sick woman, and our laughing and talking stopped. We became concerned. The people in the house talked to Jesus about how sick she was because they knew Jesus had power from God to make her well. They asked Jesus to please help her.

Jesus, in His kind way, walked over to her bed. He could see how hot she was and how much she needed His help. Gently He touched her hand and commanded the sickness to leave. And right then, the fever left, just as the people believed it would happen. She wasn't hot anymore. She wasn't chilled anymore. She wasn't feeling terrible anymore. She felt great!

Peter's mother-in-law stood up with Jesus' help. She wasn't sick now. She was ready for work. She must have felt very thankful for what Jesus had done. Immediately she began serving Jesus and His followers. Jesus had shown love to someone in a family. And she followed His example. She showed love to Jesus and His followers.

Help the children fill in the blanks on the top of page 233. The underlined words are blank on page 233.

Jesus and His followers left the synagogue. Everyone went to the home of Simon and Andrew. At the house, Simon's mother-in-law was sick in bed with a fever. Jesus walked to her bed and touched her hand. The fever left, and Jesus helped her up. Then she began serving them.

Summary questions: **How did Peter's mother-in-law feel?** (sick) **What did Jesus do to show love to her?** (He commanded the sickness to leave.)

▼ Bible Verse ▲

Before the session, learn the verse song on page 235. (The tune is "O Be Careful Little Hands What You Do.") Print the words to the verse on 12 index cards. Divide up the words as follows: My children; our love; should not; be only; words and talk.; Our love; must be; true love.; And we should show; that love; by what we do.; 1 John 3:18. Make a set of verse cards for every 3-4 children in your class.

One of Jesus' followers, John, wrote some words to tell us how to show love. Let's find those words in 1 John 3:18.

Let the children find and read 1 John in the table of contents. Then find a big number 3 for the chapter and a small number 18 for the verse.

Give groups of 3-4 children a Bible and a set of twelve verse cards. They will look in their Bibles to see how to put the cards in order on a wall. Help them sing the verse song (page 235). Each time you sing it, let a child remove a card. Continue to sing again and remove a card to help children begin to memorize the verse. Then ask the following questions.

Who wrote this verse in the Bible? (John) **In what book can we find this verse?** (John's first letter) **What does John say love should not be?** (only words and talk) **What does John say love must be?** (true love) **How do we show true love?** (by what we do)

Keep the verse cards to use next session.

> **Purpose**
> Begin to memorize 1 John 3:18.
>
> **Materials**
> Bibles
> index cards
> marker
> copy of page 235

▼ Bible and Me ▲

Jesus showed love to Peter's mother-in-law. We follow Jesus when we show love to people in our families. Showing love does not mean just doing what we feel like doing. Showing love to people means giving them what they need. People need things like your *kind words*, your *helping hands*, your *obedient feet*, your *"I spy" eyes*, and your *"cheer up" ears*. Let's work on ways to show love to our families.

Print the italicized ways to show love on a chalkboard. Use the list on the chalkboard and game cards from page 233 to play a "Showing Love" game. For example, if a child draws a "Dad" card, she should give a situation where she can show love for Dad. Ask, **"What does he need?"** (helping hands) **"So how could you show love to your dad?"** (Pick up and carry away what he raked and pruned.) Make up more situations to fit your children.

> **Purpose**
> Tell what it means to show love to people in your family.
>
> **Materials**
> copies of the people cards on page 233 cut apart
> chalkboard and chalk

Starter situations: **Dad** (is working to finish lawn—raking, mowing, pruning), **Mom** (wants to take everyone swimming after supper is cleaned up), **Sister** (dropped and broke her favorite doll in her collection), **Brother** (can't go swimming until he get his newspapers delivered), **Grandma** (is looking for her glasses so she can read the newspaper), **Grandpa** (is feeling sad because his doctor said he can't swim today).

What does it mean to show love to people in your family? What does showing love to people <u>not</u> mean? (just doing what you feel like) **What are some things people in your family often need? Which is your favorite way to show love?**

▼ Bible Project ▲

We are learning about ways to show love to people in our families. We're each going to complete a family album to help remember ways to show love to people in our families.

Ask volunteers to name one person in their families and tell something they need. This will help all the children begin to think about ways to show love. Then describe what the children can include in their albums; see the explanation on page 219. Work together on the prayer calendar. The children can write the name of each family member on a different day of the month to remember to pray for them. Put the calendar on the first page of the album.

Ask parents to find photos the children can include in the album, or let children draw pictures of their families and favorite activities.

▼ Bible Sharing ▲

For the snack time, each child will get a snack if someone else serves him. This will require the children to use their "I spy" eyes to see to whom they can show love.

Ask children to share ways they can show love to someone in their family this week. Then sing praise songs to Jesus.

Purpose
Follow Jesus by showing love to people in your family.

Materials
an inexpensive photo album for each child
copies of page 238
colored pencils
scissors
photos of children from parents or drawing paper

Purpose
Share how Jesus helps you love your family.

Materials
an easy snack for the children to carry, such as animal-shaped cookies on a napkin and juice
CD or cassette of songs about Jesus or about showing love
CD or cassette player

Jesus Heals an Official's Son

John 4:43-54

Lesson Goals
- Tell how the official's son felt.
- Tell what Jesus did to show love.
- Memorize 1 John 3:18.
- Tell the difference between showing and not showing love in your family.
- Follow Jesus by showing love to people in your family.

Memory Block
"My children, our love should not be only words and talk. Our love must be true love. And we should show that love by what we do" (1 John 3:18).

▼ Bible Search ▲

In our story, two people did a lot of traveling. One man traveled because his son was sick. Let's find out where these people went.

Guide the children to find John 4:46, 47 in their Bibles. Read the verses slowly while the children follow along. Distribute page 234 and colored pencils. After you ask each question on page 234, allow children time to connect the footprints. Suggest the children use one color for Jesus' travels and another color for the official's travels.

Where did Jesus travel? Where did the official travel? Why did the official travel? (His son was sick.) **How would the official's son have felt?**

Purpose
Tell how the official's son felt.

Materials
Bibles
copies of page 234
colored pencils

▼ Bible Story ▲

What's your favorite way to travel? Where's your favorite place to go when you travel? People did lots of traveling in today's story. Display map, page 234. **Listen to see why a father traveled to see Jesus.**

"Jesus Heals an Official's Son"

People in Galilee were excited when the news spread that Jesus had come to see them. They had seen Jesus at the Passover in Jerusalem, so they knew the wonderful things He could do. After the Passover, Jesus had stopped for a few days at Sychar where He met a woman at a well. And now, finally, Jesus had come to Galilee. The people welcomed Him. The people in Cana were especially glad because Jesus came to their town first. *(Show town on map.)*

One of the king's important officials lived in Galilee in the town of Capernaum. He wished Jesus had come to Capernaum first. *(Show town on map.)* This man's son was so sick that he was almost dead. The official believed that Jesus could make him well. But he also knew that Jesus might not come to Capernaum soon enough. His son might die anytime. So the official decided to go to Cana and bring Jesus back.

When the official left for Cana, he had to travel over 20 miles. He didn't waste any time. All he could think about was hurrying to get there quickly. He had to find Jesus before it was too late.

As soon as the official found Jesus in Cana, he explained that his son was almost dead. The official begged Jesus to come to Capernaum. Jesus knew if He went to Capernaum, it would help the official believe in Him. Jesus said, "You people must see miracles and wonderful works before you believe in me." But the

Purpose
Tell what Jesus did to show love.

Materials
completed map from Bible Search
paper
scissors
marker

official didn't give up. He pleaded again, "Sir, come before my child dies." This time, Jesus gave the man another answer he was not expecting. Jesus said, "Go, your son will live." What wonderful news! Jesus said his son would live—even if Jesus didn't come to Capernaum to heal him. And the official did believe that whatever Jesus said would happen.

On the trip back to Cana, the official hurried again, eager to see his son. As he traveled, he saw someone he knew coming in the distance. It was the official's servants. His heart must have beat a little faster, and his mind must have wondered why they were coming to meet him. But their first words were just what he hoped to hear. The servants said, "Your son is well."

And then, the official asked a very important question, "What time did my son begin to get well?" The servant's answer was not a surprise. He said, "It was about one o'clock yesterday when the fever left him." The official must have felt like throwing his hands up in praise to God. One o'clock was the exact time when Jesus had said his son would live!

The official told everyone in his house what had happened. He wanted them to know how Jesus had shown love to his family. Jesus had used His power to just speak—and now his son was well. Because of that miracle, the official and all the people of his house believed that Jesus was from God.

Give each child or pair of children a strip with a sentence from the story on it. (If you have fewer than 8 children, only use strips 1, 3, 5, 7. Then play again, using strips 2, 4, 6, 8.) Ask children to arrange themselves to stand in story order and then read the strips. If you have time, collect the strips and play again. Story sentences follow:

1. Jesus went to Cana in Galilee.
2. An official traveled from Capernaum to Cana to find Jesus.
3. The official begged Jesus to come to Capernaum and heal his son.
4. Jesus told the official his son would live.
5. The official believed what Jesus said and started back home.
6. On the way, the official's servants told him, "Your son is well."
7. The official learned his son became well at the exact time Jesus spoke.
8. The official and all the people of his house believed in Jesus.

Summary questions: **How did the official's son feel?** (sick) **What did Jesus do to show love to the boy and his family?** (spoke and healed him)

▼ Bible Verse ▲

Purpose
Memorize 1 John 3:18.

Materials
Bibles, verse cards used in
    Lesson 36
copies of the song on page 235
two index cards on which you
    print "1 John 3:18"

In the Bible, one of Jesus' followers told us how to show love. John said we show love by how we talk and what we do. Together, read or sing the verse (music on page 235).

Arrange in a line one chair per child, every other chair facing the same direction. Tape the index cards on two chairs. The children will march around the chairs, singing the verse to you. When you stop spontaneously at various points in the song, the children can scramble for a seat. The two children sitting on "1 John 3:18" get to read (or recite) the verse aloud.

Who wrote this verse in the Bible? (John) **In what book can we find this verse?** (John's first letter) **What does John say love should not be?** (only words and talk) **What does John say love must be?** (true love) **How do we show true love?** (by what we do)

▼ Bible and Me ▲

Jesus showed love to an official when He helped someone in his family. We follow Jesus when we show love to people in our families. Showing love does not mean just saying what we feel like saying—arguing and complaining. Showing love to people means saying what helps people. Let's see if we can tell when we are and are not showing love by what we say.

Let the children find and read Philippians 2:14. "Do everything without complaining or arguing." Play a game (cards from page 233 and game sheet from page 235) to help the children tell the difference between right and wrong responses to what family members say. If appropriate, let two children act out the loving and complaining responses for each situation. Use the questions on the game sheet for each situation.

What does it mean to show love to people in your family? (say what helps) **What does showing love not mean?** (just saying what you feel like—arguing and complaining) **How can you tell if you are showing love with you words?** (Is it helpful or was it complaining or arguing?)

Purpose
Tell the difference between showing and not showing love in your family.

Materials
Bibles
people cards from the bottom of page 233 and game sheet from the bottom of page 235

▼ Bible Project ▲

We are learning about ways to show love to our families. To do that, we need to think about what the people in our families need. Let's work on our family albums.

Ask parents to find photos the children can include in the album, or let children draw pictures of their families and favorite activities. Guide the children to make and decorate a pocket using construction paper to attach to the front inside cover of the album. Help the children complete coupons from page 238 and keep them in the pocket until they use them at home. Suggestions for completing coupons: hugs every day, kind words, happy smiles, help with dishes, helping words, good attitude, less arguing.

Purpose
Follow Jesus by showing love to people in your family.

Materials
an inexpensive photo album for each child (if you have not already done so)
copies of page 238
construction paper
colored pencils
scissors
clear tape

▼ Bible Sharing ▲

Ask the children to share coupons they completed for their family albums. This will help them name ways they can follow Jesus by loving people in their families.

Sing songs that reinforce the unit concept of showing love. Close with prayer for family members. Ask each child to pray for someone in her family.

Purpose
Share ways Jesus helps you love your family.

Materials
Provide a travel snack of GORP (good old raisins and peanuts)
CD or cassette of songs about Jesus
CD or cassette player

Jesus Heals a Widow's Son

Luke 7:11-17

Memory Block
"My children, our love should not be only words and talk. Our love must be true love. And we should show that love by what we do" (1 John 3:18).

Purpose
Tell how the mother felt.

Materials
Bibles
copies of page 236

Purpose
Tell what Jesus did to show love.

Materials
a box of tissues

Lesson Goals
- Tell how the mother felt.
- Tell what Jesus did to show love.
- Recite 1 John 3:18.
- Tell why we should show love to people in our families.
- Follow Jesus by showing love to people in our family.

▼ Bible Search ▲

In our story, Jesus showed love to a mother who was very sad. Let's find out why she was so sad and learn about life in Bible times.

Guide the children to find and read Luke 7:12. Read the verse slowly. **What does the verse say happened in the town of Nain? How do you think the mother felt?**

Distribute copies of page 236 and talk about what a funeral might have been like in Bible times.

How do you think the mother felt in our story? How can you show love to someone who is sad? (listen, hug, send a card) **How do you think Jesus might show love to his mother?**

▼ Bible Story ▲

When someone cries, it shows he might be feeling sad. One way to show love when someone cries is to offer him a tissue. Display tissue box. **Listen to see what Jesus did to show love when He saw a mother crying.**

"Jesus Heals a Widow's Son"

"First, my husband died, and now my son is gone too," I sobbed to myself. (Sniff-sniff; dab eyes with tissue.) "The men near me carried the coffin box where my son lay. (Sniff-sniff; dab eyes.) Many people were walking around me in my son's funeral procession. But even though I was walking in a large crowd, I felt so sad and alone. (Sniff, sniff; dab eyes.) Without a man in my family, I was sure to become a beggar, because women like myself had no way to earn money. It was the saddest day of my life.

"As we walked out of Nain to bury my son, another large crowd was coming from Capernaum toward Nain. A man seemed to be leading the people into town. But my eyes were swollen from crying and it didn't matter to me who was coming or going out of Nain right now. I trudged on in silence.

"When the other crowd met us, a man came toward me. I could tell by His kind eyes and gentle ways that He was a good man. I could also tell He sincerely felt sad with me. He spoke simply, 'Don't cry.' And then He went to the coffin box and touched it. Why should I not cry? Why did He touch the coffin box? The men holding the box paused for a moment. They were probably as surprised as I was to see what was happening.

"The surprise went on. We were all amazed when we heard this kind, gentle man say to my son, 'Young man, I tell you, get up!' Did He say, 'Get up'? I couldn't believe what I was hearing. He told my son, my dead son, to get up. He acted as if my son were alive. As I watched with my own eyes, I saw my own son sit up in the coffin box. Not only did he sit up, but he began to talk. It was almost more than I could believe. And then, as if to show it really was happening, He gave my son back to me. My son was alive!

"The people around us were amazed along with me. Some people began giving praise to God for this wonderful miracle. The man who did this miracle was Jesus. The people said, 'A great prophet has come to us! God is taking care of His people.' After a miracle like this, the news about Jesus spread through all Judea. Jesus had certainly shown love to my family. What had started out to be the saddest day became the gladdest day of my life."

Ask the children to make sad faces if the statement is false, a glad face if the statement is true.

Jesus traveled to Capernaum from Nain. (glad)
Some men were carrying a coffin into town. (sad)
A large crowd was with the mother whose son died. (glad)
Jesus felt sorry for this mother. (glad)
When Jesus went to the coffin, the men carrying it stopped. (glad)
When Jesus spoke, the young man jumped out of the coffin. (sad)
The young man began to talk. (glad)
The people were frightened by what Jesus did. (sad)
Summary questions: **How did the mother feel on the way out of Nain?** (sad)
What did Jesus do to show love to her? (made her son alive)

▼ Bible Verse ▲

In the Bible, one of Jesus' followers told us how to show love. John said we show love by how we talk and what we do. Let's find his words in 1 John 3:18.

Let the children find and read 1 John 3:18. Sing it together (song on page 235) for review. Then give each group of 3-4 children a set of verse cards, clothespins, and yarn. Tie the yarn between two chairs. The children will work together to pin the cards on the yarn. (Many clothespins are so heavy they hang down and the card is hung above the yarn.) Option: Let groups race to put their cards in order, or use a stopwatch to see if groups can improve their own speeds. For memory practice, children can remove a card and say the verse until they know it well.

At the end of the activity, focus the conversation on the verse. **Who wrote this verse in the Bible?** (John) **In what book can we find this verse?** (John's first letter) **What does John say love should not be?** (only words and talk) **What does John say love must be?** (true love) **How do we show true love?** (by what we do)

Purpose
Recite 1 John 3:18.

Materials
Bibles, copy of page 235
verse cards used in Lesson 36
spring-type clothespins
six-foot pieces of yarn

Purpose
Tell why we should show love to people in our families.

Materials
a set of people cards from page 233
copies of page 237
paper fasteners
pencils

▼ Bible and Me ▲

Jesus showed love to a mother in our story today. We follow Jesus when we show love to people in our families. Showing love does not mean just saying or doing what we feel like. Showing love means saying or doing what helps people. People need things like your kind words, your helping hands, your obedient feet, your "I spy" eyes, and your "cheer up" ears. But why should we do these things to show love in our families? (It's a way to follow Jesus.)

Sing the song from last unit (page 212) using the following words:
Why should I love my family? Why? Oh, why?
Why should I love my family? Why, why, oh, why?
It's a way to follow Jesus. Follow Him.
It's a way to follow Jesus. I'll follow Him.

Let the children use the game card and spinner from page 237 and the people cards from page 233 to tell why we show love.

What does it mean to show love to people in your family? (say and do what helps) **What does not showing love mean?** (saying or doing what you feel like) **Why do we want to show love to people in our families?** (to follow Jesus) **How can you tell if you are showing love with your words?** (Was it helpful or was it complaining or arguing?) **Which way to show love is the easiest in your family?**

Purpose
Follow Jesus by showing love to people in your family.

Materials
inexpensive photo albums (if children do not have them already)
copies of page 238
construction paper
colored pencils
scissors
clear tape

▼ Bible Project ▲

Showing love means saying or doing what helps people. Think about using your kind words, your helping hands, your obedient feet, your "I spy" eyes, and your "cheer up" ears to love your family. Write about how you will use these things in your family album.

Help children complete the albums with more photos or drawings of their families and favorite activities. Guide the children to write a sentence or two about each family member on paper and add it to the album. Some children will need to dictate their sentences to you. Next week they can share their albums with each other.

Purpose
Share ways Jesus helps you show love to your family.

Materials
items for salad faces: half slices of pineapple, grape halves, peach chunks, banana slices, raisins
paper plates and napkins
CD or cassette of songs about Jesus
CD or cassette player

▼ Bible Sharing ▲

Let the children make their own salad faces (half slice of pineapple for mouth, grape halves for eyes, peach chunk nose, banana slice ears, raisin hair).

Ask children to name ways to show love. Guide them to choose and tell a way to use kind words, helping hands, obedient feet, "I spy" eyes, or "cheer up" ears. Then sing favorite songs about Jesus.

Jesus Heals Jairus's Daughter

Matthew 9:18-26; Mark 5:22-43; Luke 8:40-56

Lesson Goals

- Tell how the father felt.
- Tell what Jesus did to show love.
- Recite and explain 1 John 3:18.
- Tell what makes it hard to show love to people in your family.
- Follow Jesus by showing love to people in your family.

Memory Block
"My children, our love should not be only words and talk. Our love must be true love. And we should show that love by what we do" (1 John 3:18).

▼ Bible Search ▲

In our story, Jesus showed love to a father whose daughter died. Let's find out who the father was and the names of the other people in the story.

Guide the children to find Luke 8:41, 42a. Read the verses for the children. Talk about how the father must have felt. Then distribute page 239 and help the children find Luke 8:51. They can use the names in the verse to complete the puzzle.

How do you think the father felt when he went to Jesus? Who did Jesus help? Who was with Jesus when He helped the father and his daughter?

Purpose
Tell how the father felt.

Materials
Bibles
copies of page 239
pencils

▼ Bible Story ▲

Display the pillow. **What do most people use these for?** (pillow fights, resting, sleeping) **I use mine for sleeping. In our story, Jesus talks about sleeping. But He wasn't talking about normal sleeping. Listen to see what He said.**

"Jesus Heals Jairus's Daughter"

A crowd of people pressed around me as I watched a boat sailing across Lake Galilee. I knew Jesus was in that boat. It was hard to wait patiently for the boat to hit the shore. The moment it struck the sand, the whole crowd surrounded Him, each of us trying to get closer.

I was an important ruler of the synagogue, but I knew Jesus was even greater than me. So when I got to Him, I bowed at His feet. What I wanted to say was the most important thing I had ever said. Back at home, my only daughter was sick. In fact, we thought she was dying. She was only twelve years old. Our only hope was that Jesus would come to our house and make her well. I begged Jesus, "My daughter is dying. Please come and put your hands on her. Then she will be healed and will live."

A huge smile of hope filled my face when Jesus agreed to come. Many people followed us to my house. On the way, Jesus stopped to talk to another woman who was sick. While He was talking, someone arrived from my house with the worst possible news. "Your daughter is dead. Don't bother the teacher now." Tears came to my eyes as I realized my only daughter was gone. My heart went from hopeful to horrified. But Jesus paid no attention to what the messenger said. He spoke hopeful words again, "Don't be afraid; only believe and your daughter will be well." Quietly we walked on.

Jesus and three of His followers, Peter, James, and John, went in the house

Purpose
Tell what Jesus did to show love.

Materials
a bed pillow

with me. Already many other people were at the house, crying loudly and showing sadness for my family. In the noise and confusion, people were already playing funeral music.

But when Jesus went in, He acted differently. His calm voice spoke again, "Don't cry. She is not dead; she is only sleeping." The people didn't understand what Jesus was talking about. They laughed at what Jesus said, because they knew my little girl had died.

Jesus asked the noisy crowd to stay outside. Only Jesus, the three followers, my wife, and I went in to where my little girl lay. We watched and wondered what would happen. Then Jesus took my little girl's hand and said, "Little girl, stand up!" As we looked lovingly at her, her spirit came back into her. Immediately she stood up and began walking. She wasn't dead anymore! Jesus had made her come back alive. The people playing funeral music could stop. The people crying could stop. The people who laughed at Jesus could stop. She was alive!

Jesus told us to get her something to eat. And He asked us not to tell anyone what happened. But news of this amazing miracle spread all around the area. Jesus showed great love to my family when He made my daughter come back alive.

Read the following statements, one at a time. Let the children correct what you said wrong. The wrong words are italicized.

A small crowd waited for Jesus when He crossed *Street* Galilee.
Jerry, the *mother*, was an important man in the Jewish synagogue.
The *boy* who was *eight* years old was so sick that *he* was going to die.
On the way to the *synagogue*, someone said the little girl was *better*.
Jesus said, "Don't be *angry*. Just *smile* and your daughter will be well."
James and John wanted the crowd to stay *inside* the house.
Jairus took the girl by the hand and said, "Little girl, *sit up!*"
The little girl *rolled over* immediately and *stopped* walking.
Summary questions: **How did Jairus feel when he went to get Jesus?** (sad) **What did Jesus do to show love to him?** (healed his daughter)

▼ Bible Verse ▲

Purpose
Recite and explain I John 3:18.

Materials
Bibles, copies of page 240, copy of page 235, buttons or pennies for markers, and a coin

In the Bible, one of Jesus' followers told us how to show love. John said we show love by how we talk and what we do. Let's find his words in 1 John 3:18.

Let the children find and read 1 John 3:18. Sing it together for review (song on page 235). Give groups of 2-3 children a game board (page 240) to help them recite and explain the verse. Provide buttons or pennies for markers and a coin. For each turn, a child flips a coin. Heads means move two spaces. Tails means move one space. After the game, use the following questions to review what they know about showing love.

What does 1 John 3:18 say? (Give each child a turn to recite.) **What does 1 John 3:18 help us remember to do? What is a way to do 1 John 3:18?**

▼ Bible and Me ▲

Jesus showed love to a father in our story today. We follow Jesus when we show love to people in our families. Showing love means saying and doing what helps people. But sometimes it is just plain hard work to show love in your family.

Complete page 241 to help the children tell what makes it hard to show love. Then play a game to review what they are learning about showing love in their families. Tape people cards from page 233 to six plastic tubs. Let the children take turns tossing a bean bag toward the tubs. They can work together to answer the following questions when a bean bag lands in a tub.

What does it mean to show love to (name on tub)**?** (do what helps them)
What kinds of things will you say if you don't show love? (complain or argue)
What makes it hard to show love to this person? Why do you want to show love to this person? (to follow Jesus)

> **Purpose**
> Tell what makes it hard to show love to people in your family.
>
> **Materials**
> copies of page 241
> pencils
> six plastic tubs
> people cards from page 233
> clear tape
> bean bag (a size to fit in the plastic tub)

▼ Bible Project ▲

Provide a fun place to share family albums (cozy room, room with family-room furniture).
We have learned many ways to show love to people in our families. Showing love means saying or doing what helps people. Who would like to show his album and tell about his special family?
Encourage each child to share his album. Then share your album or the class family album, if you made one.

> **Purpose**
> Follow Jesus by showing love to people in your family.
>
> **Materials**
> completed family albums
> class family album (if you made one)

▼ Bible Sharing ▲

This will be an important sharing time. It will be a time for you to encourage the children to use their family albums at home and report back progress they are making. Ask each child to share one way she will use the album this week to show love to someone in her family.
Close by singing the children's favorite songs about following Jesus.

> **Purpose**
> Share ways Jesus helps you show love to your family.
>
> **Materials**
> a "raised" snack, such as doughnuts or soft pretzels
> CD or cassette of songs about Jesus
> CD or cassette player

Bible Search

Find Mark 1:30 in your Bible.
How did Peter's mother-in-law feel?

What is a "mother-in-law"?
Look at Peter's family tree. Talk about it with your teacher.
Peter's mother-in-law was his wife's mother. Circle her.

| Peter's father | Peter's mother | Wife's father | Wife's mother |

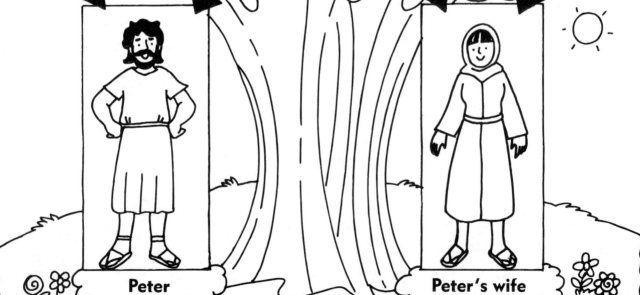

| Peter | Peter's wife |

Fill in the blanks.
Use the words from
the word bank.

Jesus and His followers left the _____ .

Everyone went to the home of Simon and _____ .

At the house, Simon's mother-in-law was sick in bed with

a _____ .

Jesus walked to her bed and touched her _____ .

The fever _____ , and Jesus helped her up.

Then she began _____ them.

Word Bank

Andrew

left

serving

synagogue

fever

hand

Cut apart the cards.
Use them to play a game.

father	**mother**	**sister**
brother	**grandfather**	**grandmother**

Bible Search

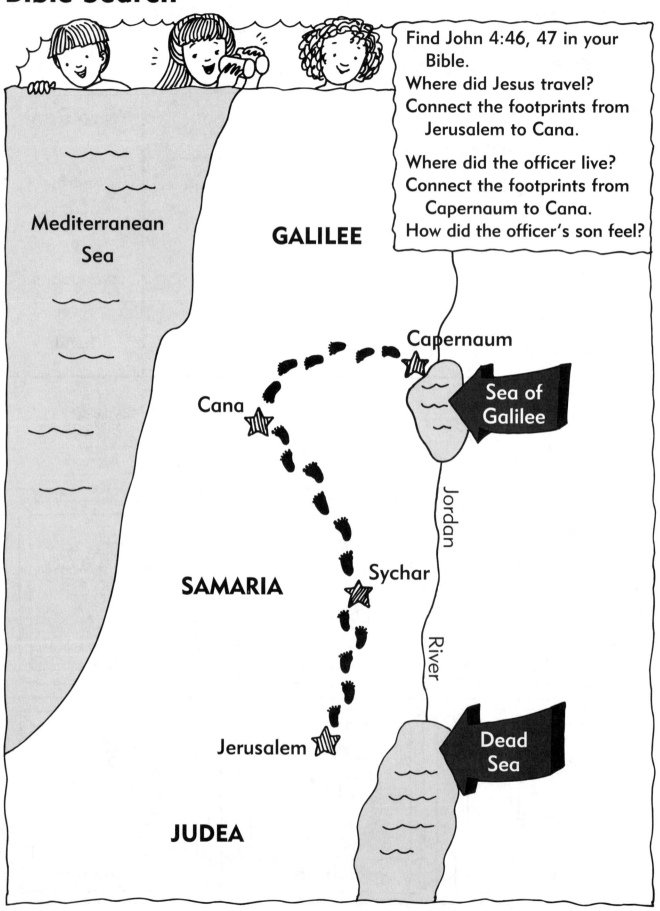

Find John 4:46, 47 in your Bible.
Where did Jesus travel?
Connect the footprints from Jerusalem to Cana.

Where did the officer live?
Connect the footprints from Capernaum to Cana.
How did the officer's son feel?

Mediterranean Sea

GALILEE

Capernaum

Cana

Sea of Galilee

Jordan

Sychar

SAMARIA

River

Jerusalem

Dead Sea

JUDEA

Find and read 1 John 3:18.
Sing the song.

Bible Verse

F   C

(Spoken) My children, our   love   should   not   be   on - ly   words   and   talk.

F   B♭

Our   love   must   be   true — love.   And   we   should   show   that

F   C7   F

love by what we do. Our love should not be on-ly words and   talk. *(Spoken) 1 John 3:18*

1. Shuffle cards and place them facedown.

2. Read a situation for the card you choose.

Dad says: It's time to clean the garage again.

Mom says: Here's your broccoli.

Sister says: Please leave when my friends are here.

Brother says: It's not my turn to do dishes tonight.

Grandma says: My windows could use washing.

Grandpa says: I sure could use some fishing worms.

Place cards here

3. Answer two questions.

What could you say if you wanted to show love?

What might you say if you felt like complaining or arguing?

Bible Search

Find and read Luke 7:12.
How do you think the mother felt?

When Jesus came to the town of Nain, He saw a funeral. In Bible times, what was a funeral like?

When a person died, the body was washed carefully. Spices that smelled sweet were placed on the body. Then it was wrapped in long, linen cloths.

People were paid to cry and mourn for the person who died. They were very loud. The loud crying was the way people showed how much the person had been loved.

A funeral procession formed. The paid mourners sang a funeral song. Friends carried the body on a mat or in a coffin box. Family and friends came last in the procession.

A funeral was a sad time. For the mother in our story, it was a very sad time until Jesus came.

 UNIT 9, LESSON 38

Bible and Me

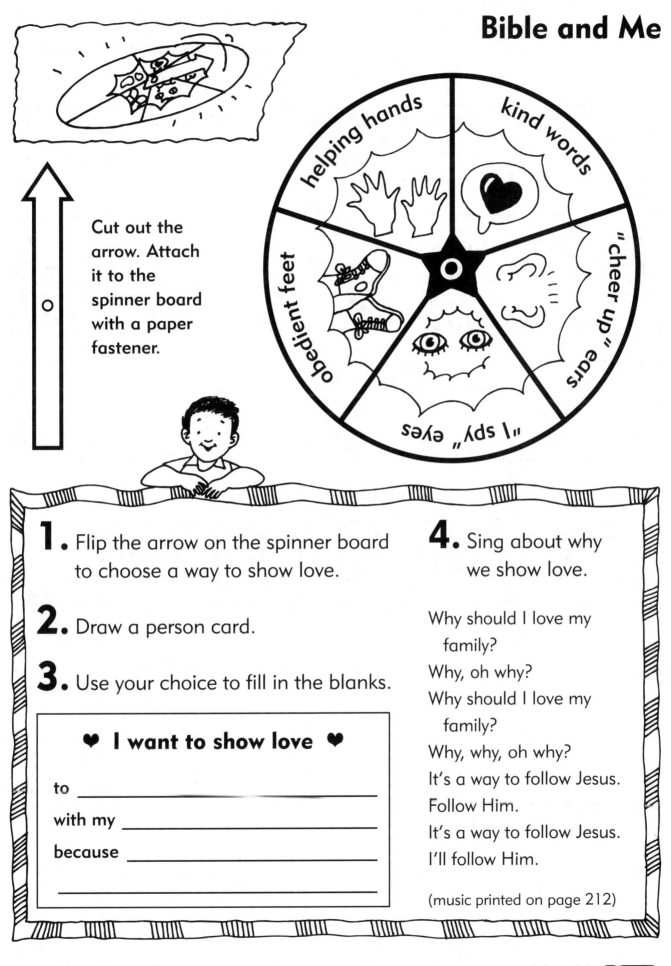

Cut out the arrow. Attach it to the spinner board with a paper fastener.

helping hands

kind words

"cheer up" ears

"I spy" eyes

obedient feet

1. Flip the arrow on the spinner board to choose a way to show love.

2. Draw a person card.

3. Use your choice to fill in the blanks.

♥ **I want to show love** ♥

to _____

with my _____

because _____

_____

4. Sing about why we show love.

Why should I love my
  family?
Why, oh why?
Why should I love my
  family?
Why, why, oh why?
It's a way to follow Jesus.
Follow Him.
It's a way to follow Jesus.
I'll follow Him.

(music printed on page 212)

© 2004 Standard Publishing. Permission is granted to reproduce this page for ministry purposes only—not for resale.

Bible Project

Use the coupons to show love to people in your family.

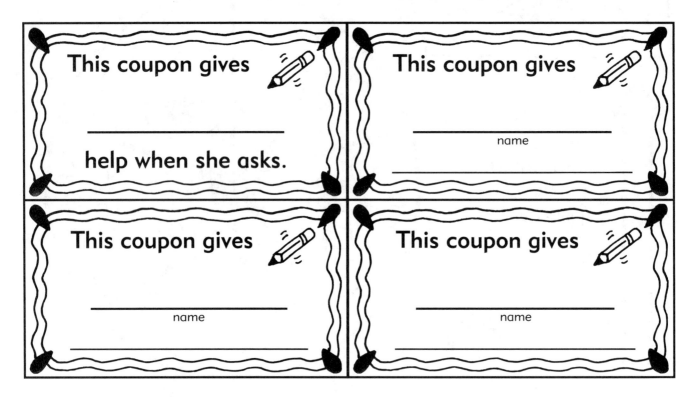

This coupon gives

_____

help when she asks.

This coupon gives

_____
name
_____

This coupon gives

_____
name
_____

This coupon gives

_____
name
_____

Make a prayer calendar to add to your Family Album.

Prayer Calendar

Sunday	Monday	Tuesday	Wednesday	Thursday	Friday	Saturday

Unit 9, Lessons 36–38

Bible Search

Find and read Luke 8:41, 42.
How do you think Jairus felt?

Find and read Luke 8:50, 51.
Who went into the house?
Use the names to finish the puzzle.

M

J

J

J

P

Bible Verse

Find 1 John 3:18 in your Bible.
Play the game to learn the verse.

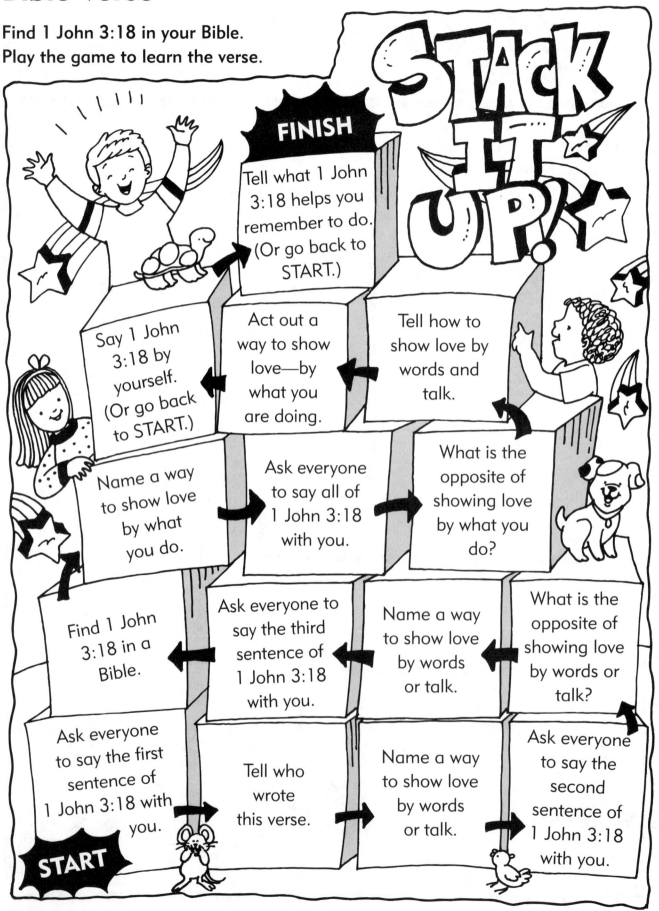

STACK IT UP!

FINISH

Tell what 1 John 3:18 helps you remember to do. (Or go back to START.)

Act out a way to show love—by what you are doing.

Tell how to show love by words and talk.

Say 1 John 3:18 by yourself. (Or go back to START.)

Name a way to show love by what you do.

Ask everyone to say all of 1 John 3:18 with you.

What is the opposite of showing love by what you do?

Find 1 John 3:18 in a Bible.

Ask everyone to say the third sentence of 1 John 3:18 with you.

Name a way to show love by words or talk.

What is the opposite of showing love by words or talk?

Ask everyone to say the first sentence of 1 John 3:18 with you.

Tell who wrote this verse.

Name a way to show love by words or talk.

Ask everyone to say the second sentence of 1 John 3:18 with you.

START

UNIT 9, LESSON 39

Bible and Me

It's hard to show love in my family when . . .

Mark ✘ by things that make it hard to show love in your family.

_____ someone speaks unkind words to me.

_____ someone complains or argues with me.

_____ someone asks me to do something I don't like to do.

_____ I would rather go play.

_____ I feel like doing what I want.

_____ I feel like saying how I feel.

When it's hard for me to show love, I can . . .

Mark ✘ by what you can do next time it is hard to show love.

_____ remember that showing love is a way to follow Jesus.

_____ say or sing Philippians 2:14 to myself.

_____ pray, "Dear God, please help me show love right now."

_____ say or sing 1 John 3:18 to myself.

Talk about showing love to your family.

❤ 1. What does it mean to show love?

❤ 2. What kinds of things will you say if you don't show love?

❤ 3. Why do you want to show love to your family?

❤ 4. What makes it hard to show love to your family?

❤ 5. What can you do next time it is hard to show love?

UNIT 10

Jesus' Power Helps Me to Worship Him

Lessons 40–43

Unit Memory Block
"You do great and wonderful things, Lord God, the God of heaven's armies. Everything the Lord does is right and true, King of the nations" (Revelation 15:3).

Memory Challenge
"Everyone will respect you, Lord. They will honor you. Only you are holy. All people will come and worship you. This is because he is a faithful God who does no wrong. He is right and fair" (Revelation 15:4).

40 Jesus Stops a Storm
Matthew 8:18, 23-27; Mark 4:35-41
Jesus' power stopped a storm with just His words. We worship Jesus because He has all power from God.

41 Jesus Heals Ten Lepers
Luke 17:11-19
Jesus' power healed ten men with leprosy. We worship Jesus because He has all power from God.

42 Jesus Walks on Water
Luke 17:11-19
Jesus had power to walk on top of water. We worship Jesus because He has all power from God.

43 Jesus Heals a Man Born Blind
John 9:1-38
Jesus' power healed a man born blind. That man worshiped Jesus. We worship Jesus because He has all power from God.

By the end of this unit, the leaders and learners will

KNOW four amazing things Jesus can do.
FEEL a sense of awe because of what Jesus can do.
DO Worship Jesus.

Unit Value

The four Bible stories in this unit show that Jesus is the Son of God. In each story, Jesus uses His power from God to do an amazing thing. And in each story, the people who were affected by the miracle responded in worship or praise (praise is one form of worship). These stories provide a concrete model for the children's relationship with Jesus. They will be motivated to worship Him only as they are awe-struck by who Jesus is and what He can do. The four miracles in this unit, Jesus stops the storm, Jesus heals ten lepers, Jesus walks on water, and Jesus heals a man born blind, can help the children grow in their own motivation to worship. If we fail to worship Jesus after hearing these stories, then we have not yet accepted who Jesus is.

This unit builds on previous opportunities to develop worship skills. It guides the children to 1) tell what they know about worship, 2) tell why they want to worship Jesus, 3) grow in their ability to tell when they are and are not worshiping, and 4) demonstrate a variety of ways to worship. The unit memory block provides an example of speaking worship to the Lord. For many people, it is difficult to see the difference between speaking about the Lord and speaking to Him. This unit can help your children address their worship to Jesus.

▼ Bible Project ▲

Praising Jesus

The learners will worship Jesus by writing a worship song, rap, or psalm. Then let the children arrange (with the help of rhythm instruments) and produce (record on cassette) what they write. As a bridge between stanzas or parts of the worship song or rap, let each child say a worship prayer to Jesus. This Praising Jesus project will help the children use what they know about worship and provide a fun time to praise Jesus for His power.

Week 1: Explore ways to worship. Decide which rhythm instruments to make and what to write—song, rap, psalm. Collect materials for instruments during the week.

Week 2: Group students into worship teams. One team can make instruments; another team can work on the song, psalm, or rap.

Week 3: Complete instruments. Put finishing touches on worship song. Prepare worship sentence prayers.

Week 4: Combine song and instruments. Record on cassette; include worship prayers between stanzas.

> **Materials**
> paper
> pencils
> rhythm instruments or materials
>   for making instruments (see
>   instructions below)
> blank cassette
> cassette player

Rhythm Instruments

Kazoos: Cover an 8-inch length of paper-towel tube with adhesive-backed plastic. Tape or use a rubber band to put a square of wax paper over one end. Make a small hole in the side of the tube. Hum into the open end of the tube.

Sand blocks: Staple coarse sandpaper to two 2-inch thick blocks of wood. Rub the sandpaper sides together.

Drum: Glue the lid on an empty oatmeal box and decorate the box. Use an unsharpened pencil, a dowel rod, or a wooden spoon to beat the drum.

Bell stick: Use yarn or string to tie two jingle bells on a non-snap clothespin. Shake the bells when you sing.

Shaker: Put rice, dried beans, or button between two sturdy paper bowls or plates. Staple the edges together. Decorate with stickers, markers, or yarn.

These ideas can be used as printed, or used to spark creativity. The song could easily be spoken in rhythm (rap), repeating words and phrases necessary to fit the meter you choose.

Use Psalm 150 as a model for writing a psalm. Record it as a choral reading. Some sentences can be spoken by all, by individuals, or by pairs or trios of children. The following is an example.

Praise the Lord!
Praise Jesus!
Praise Him in His mighty Heaven.
Praise Him for His power.
Praise Him for His greatness.
Praise Him for stopping the winds and the waves.
Praise Him with drums and blocks.
Praise the Lord!
Praise Him for healing the men with leprosy.
Praise Him with bells and kazoos.
Praise the Lord!
Praise Him for walking on the water.
Praise Him with tambourines and shakers.
Praise the Lord!
Praise Him for healing the man who couldn't see.
Praise Him with all instruments.
Let everyone praise the name of Jesus.
Praise the Lord!

We Worship You
(tune: "Camptown Races")

Jesus, You're the Son of God.
  We will praise You!
Only You can stop the storm.
  We worship You!

Only You could heal the man
  who could not see.
Only You could heal the men
  with leprosy.

Jesus, You are wonderful.
  We praise You!
Only You can walk on water.
  We worship You!

Jesus Stops a Storm

Matthew 8:18, 23-27; Mark 4:35-41

Memory Block
"You do great and wonderful things, Lord God, the God of heaven's armies. Everything the Lord does is right and true, King of the nations" (Revelation 15:3).

Lesson Goals
- Tell how Jesus' friends felt when Jesus stopped the storm.
- Tell what Jesus did that shows He is powerful.
- Begin to memorize Revelation 15:3.
- Tell what it means to worship Jesus.
- Explore ways to worship Jesus.

▼ Bible Search ▲

Purpose
Tell how Jesus' friends felt when Jesus stopped the storm.

Materials
a piece of butcher paper for each child
blue finger paint (see recipe in activity)
paint shirts
water and paper towels for clean-up

Recipe for finger paint for 4-5 children:
1. Mix together 2 tablespoons of sugar and 1/3 cup of cornstarch in a small pan, then slowly add 2 cups of cold water.
2. Cook over low heat, stirring until the mixture becomes a smooth, almost clear gel (about 5 minutes).
3. Cool the mixture, then stir in 1 cup clear dishwashing liquid and food coloring or paste.
4. Store in an airtight container for up to a week.
In our story, Jesus helps His followers in the middle of a storm. Let's find out how the followers felt.
Guide the children to find Matthew 8:26 in their Bibles. Find the page number for Matthew in the table of contents. Then find a big number 8 for the chapter and a small number 26 for the verse. Ask children to find the word that describes how the followers felt (afraid). Then find and read Matthew 8:27. Find the word that describes the followers' feeling (amazed). Distribute paint supplies and have the children finger-paint a boat in a storm.
Who made the followers feel afraid? What made the followers feel amazed? Tell us about your picture. How would you have felt in the storm? After the storm?

▼ Bible Story ▲

Purpose
Tell what Jesus did that shows He is powerful.

Materials
a toy boat
copies of page 256
scissors

Before the session, cut out the boats from page 256. Fold the sails so the questions can't be seen.
Would it be easier to fall asleep in an airplane, car, or boat? Listen for what happened after Jesus fell asleep in a boat. Display toy boat.

"Jesus Stops a Storm"
The gentle ripples in the water made me think it would be a quick, easy trip across the lake. Jesus had asked us to go across with Him. So we left the crowd and stepped into the boat where Jesus was waiting. As we walked to our places in the boat, the water made little splashing noises against the boat's hull. Jesus went to the back of the boat. He was so tired that He laid His head on a pillow and fell asleep. The rest of us set sail for the other shore.
I grew up by Lake Galilee and became a fisherman. After Jesus chose me to be one of His followers I didn't spend as much time on the lake. So I looked forward

to sailing these waters again. However, as we crossed the lake that day, one of those furious storms hit us with its full force. In moments, the wind was biting right through our rain-soaked cloaks. The rain was coming so fast and the waves were so big that our little boat began filling with water. Wave after wave crashed over the side and into the boat. Our attempts to bail out the boat were useless. First the water was ankle deep, then it was halfway to our knees. The coldness of the water made our legs numb as it got closer to our knees. Our own power was too small to fight a storm like this. We were afraid. We were going to drown.

In the midst of all our fear and frantic bailing, we noticed Jesus was still asleep, on His pillow, in the back of the boat! How could He sleep when we were going to drown! We screamed above the noise of the storm, "Master! Master! We will drown! Lord, save us! Or we will drown!"

When Jesus opened His eyes and saw what was happening, somehow He managed to stand up in that rocking, rolling boat. When He saw the fear on our faces, He asked, "Why are you afraid? Where is your faith?" Then He showed us we really had nothing to fear. With simple words, He commanded the wind and waves, "Quiet. Be still." And immediately the whistling, biting wind stopped blowing. The soaking rain and crashing waves were gone. And once again, the lake gently rippled against the hull of the boat.

In just one moment, everything had changed. Our feelings of fear turned into feelings of amazement at what Jesus' power could do. We exclaimed our thoughts of worship, "What kind of man is this? He commands the wind and the water, and they obey Him! Even the wind and the sea obey Him." Jesus' words stopped the storm. Jesus' power gave us a reason to worship Him.

Show children the boats from page 256 you prepared before class. Let the children take turns choosing a boat question to answer.

Summary questions: **What did Jesus do to show He is powerful?** (stopped a storm) **How did Jesus' followers feel when He stopped the storm?** (amazed)

▼ Bible Verse ▲

Depending on your time limitations, you may wish to cut out the strips on pages 257 and 258 before class. You will need one set for every 2-3 children.

The words of our new Bible verse are words that worship Jesus. They speak to Jesus about the kinds of things He does and the kind of person He is.

Let the children find and read Revelation 15:3 (and 4). Find the page number for Revelation in the table of contents. Then find a big number 15 for the chapter and a small number 3 for the verse. Start with the word *You*.

Give groups of 2-3 a set of puzzle strips from page 257 and 258, or ask children to cut out the strips themselves. Children can use their Bibles to put the puzzle together; then glue it on construction paper. The children can begin to memorize the verse(s) by reading it together.

Focus the conversation on the verse. **Where do we find this verse in the Bible?** (Revelation; not Revelations) **What kinds of things does this verse say Jesus does?** (great, wonderful) **What names for Jesus are in this verse?** (Lord God, God of heaven's armies, King of the nations) **What does the verse say about what Jesus does?** (right, true)

Keep the verse strips from pages 257 and 258 to use in later lessons.

Purpose
Begin to memorize Revelation 15:3.

Materials
Bibles
copies of pages 257 and 258
scissors
construction paper
glue sticks

▼ Bible and Me ▲

In our story, Jesus' followers talked to Him about how special He was after His power stopped a storm. Our Bible verse also talks to Jesus about how special He is. When we tell Jesus how special He is, that is called worship.

Use the song on page 259 to sing about ways to tell Jesus how special He is. Then ask the children to name the four ways that were in the song. They can use the words they list to fill in the blanks on that same page.

What is worshiping Jesus? (talking to Jesus to tell Him how special He is) **What are four ways to tell Jesus He is special?** (write, draw, sing, pray) **Which is your favorite way to tell Jesus He is special?**

Purpose
Tell what it means to worship Jesus.

Materials
copies of page 259
pencils
CD or cassette of songs about Jesus
CD or cassette player

▼ Bible Project ▲

Our Bible verse talks to Jesus about how special He is. When we tell Jesus how special He is, that is called worship. What are some ways we can tell Jesus how special He is? (write, draw, pray) **Let's plan a Praising Jesus time.**

Display rhythm instruments and decide which ones to make. Discuss writing a song, rap, or psalm. (See examples on page 243.) Help children choose one to write. Ask children to suggest facts about Jesus and words that describe who Jesus is. Print these on the tablet. Include their suggestions in whatever they choose to write.

Use time this week to plan, explore, and encourage children. Your enthusiasm will make this project a real time of prayer and praise.

Purpose
Explore ways to worship Jesus.

Materials
samples of rhythm instruments (see page 243)
a list of tunes familiar to your children
planning tablet
marker

▼ Bible Sharing ▲

After snack time, let the children share the finger-painted pictures made in Bible Search. Each child can display his picture and complete the following sentence: "Jesus, You are powerful because…"

Close by singing songs of praise to Jesus.

Purpose
Share how Jesus' power helps you worship Him.

Materials
a snack of a boat cake (see illustration) and milk
plates and napkins
pictures made in Bible Search
CD or cassette of songs about Jesus
CD or cassette player

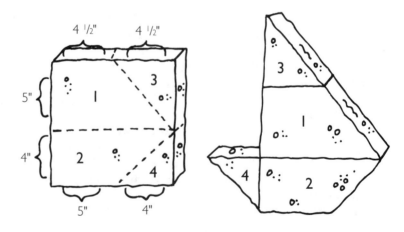

Boat Cake (from a 9-inch square cake)

Jesus Heals Ten Lepers

Luke 17:11-19

Lesson Goals

- Tell what Jesus did that shows He is powerful.
- Tell what one leper did when he saw he was healed.
- Recite Revelation 15:3.
- Tell why we worship Jesus.
- Worship Jesus.

Memory Block
"You do great and wonderful things, Lord God, the God of heaven's armies. Everything the Lord does is right and true, King of the nations" (Revelation 15:3).

▼ Bible Search ▲

In our story, Jesus helps ten men who were very sick. Let's use our Bibles to find out what was wrong with them.

Guide the children to find Luke 17:12 in their Bibles. Read the verse slowly. Distribute copies of page 260. Ask the question at the top of the page. Ask the children what they know about leprosy. Then read together the information about leprosy printed on page 260.

What disease did the ten men have? What would it be like to have leprosy? How would you feel if you had leprosy today? What could Jesus do to help the men with leprosy?

Purpose
Tell what Jesus did that shows He is powerful.

Materials
Bibles
copies of page 260

▼ Bible Story ▲

Hold up ten fingers. **How would my fingers look if I had leprosy? How would they feel? Why? Listen to see who praised God for healthy fingers.**

"Jesus Heals Ten Lepers"

Ten sick men huddled together outside a small town. "Unclean, Unclean," they cried whenever anyone came toward them. The priest had told them they must do this because they had an awful skin disease called leprosy. People got leprosy by touching someone who had it. Leprosy made parts of the skin die. Then that skin could not feel it was being bumped or if it was getting burned. Lepers had terrible sore places on their hands and feet—because their hands and feet got bumped or burned the most often. Sometimes parts of their fingers or toes would fall off.

In that group of ten men, one leper was a Samaritan. Usually Jews and Samaritans stayed away from each other. But since these men all had leprosy, they had no choice but to stick together. They all had the same troubles. They could not live with their families anymore. They missed their mom and dads and boys and girls. They had to scrounge for food and old cast-off clothes. And there were always the warnings they must yell, "Unclean, Unclean," so people would stay far enough away.

One day, on His way to Jerusalem, Jesus came to this little town along the border between Samaria and Galilee. As Jesus entered the town, He did not come toward the lepers so they didn't have to yell, "Unclean, Unclean." But even from a distance they could tell who He was. Instead of yelling a warning, they yelled a desperate request, "Jesus, Master, help us." Those men knew that unless Jesus

Purpose
Tell what one leper did when he saw he was healed.

Materials
ten paper men for the review time

used His power to heal them, they would suffer as lepers for the rest of their lives.

When Jesus saw the men, He did not hesitate to help them. He gave them hope. He said, "Go and show yourselves to the priest." The men knew the priest could look at them and give them permission to go back to their homes and families. They believed in Jesus' power, so they left at once to find a priest. When they started out, they still had their leprosy. But on the way, they noticed their fingers, and feet, and arms, and legs were "clean" and healthy, not "unclean" with leprosy. The joy they felt must have made them run and jump on their way to the priest.

But one man, the Samaritan, turned right around in the middle of the road. As he ran in the opposite direction, he praised God at the top of his voice. And when he reached Jesus, he threw himself down at Jesus' feet. He knew Jesus had used power from God to make him well. Only Jesus could do such a miracle. Praising God for what Jesus had done was even more important than hearing a priest say he could go home to his family.

Jesus was glad for the praise and thanks the Samaritan spoke to Him. But He was also sad because the other nine did not take time to go back to give their praise to God. Jesus said, "Ten men were healed. Where are the other nine? Is this Samaritan the only one who came back to praise God? Stand up and go on your way. You were healed because you believed." Jesus' power healed ten men with leprosy. And the one who came back to praise God was the one who pleased Jesus.

Place ten paper men in a row. Let a child remove one for each correct answer.
Where was Jesus traveling?
Who met Him?
Why did they stay away?
What did they ask?
What was Jesus' answer?
When were the men healed?
How many praised God?
What was different about the Samaritan?
What did Jesus say when the Samaritan came back?
Who pleased Jesus?
Summary questions: **What did Jesus do that shows He is powerful?** (healed lepers) **What did one leper do after he was healed?** (praised God)

▼ Bible Verse ▲

Purpose
Recite Revelation 15:3.

Materials
copy of pages 257 and 258
scissors
mural paper
glue sticks
markers

The words of our Bible verse worship Jesus. John wrote these words after he had heard people speak them to Jesus.

Let the children find and read Revelation 15:3 (and 4). Start with "You." Give children a copy of pages 257 and 258 and ask them to cut apart the verse strips. Then glue the strips on the mural paper into complete sentences. Let children work together to draw pictures on the mural to illustrate the verses.

When the mural is completed, gather the students in a group and say the verse together several times. Focus the conversation on the verse. **Who are people talking to in this verse?** (Jesus) **What kinds of things does this verse tell Jesus He does?** (great, wonderful) **What names for Jesus are in this verse?** (Lord God, God of heaven's armies, King of the nations) **What does the verse say about what Jesus does?** (right, true) **What are we doing when we sing this verse to Jesus?** (worshiping Jesus)

▼ Bible and Me ▲

In our story, a leper praised God when Jesus' power made him well. Our Bible verse also talks about how wonderful He is.

We worship Jesus because He has the same power as God. We worship Him because He is God. He is the Son of God.

Use the words on page 261 to rap (or sing) about why we worship Jesus (tune: "London Bridge"). At the end of the rap, the children will mark an *X* by reasons we worship Jesus. Mark *O* by the ways to worship Jesus. Circle what it means to worship Jesus.

What does it mean to worship Jesus? (talk to Him to tell how special He is) **Why do we worship Jesus? What are some ways to tell Jesus how special He is?** (sing, draw, write, pray)

Purpose	Tell why we worship Jesus.
Materials	copies of page 261 pencils

▼ Bible Project ▲

When we tell Jesus how special He is, we worship Him. **What are some ways we can tell Jesus how special He is?** (write, draw, pray) **Let's work on Praising Jesus.**

Group children into worship teams. Allow them to choose the part of the project in which to participate. This will keep each child's interest at a higher level. One worship team will begin making rhythm instruments (page 243). The other worship team will begin writing the song, rap, or psalm. Use the song chart to begin putting lyrics together. Unit page 243 includes a song or rap and a psalm (based on Psalm 150) to help you get started.

Purpose	Worship Jesus.
Materials	materials to make rhythm instruments (see page 243) song chart black marker

▼ Bible Sharing ▲

Use the time after the snack to sing favorite songs of praise to Jesus. Or learn another worship song. Sing the following words to the tune of "Jesus in the Morning."

Jesus, Jesus, we will worship You, Lord.
We will praise You, Jesus.
Jesus, Jesus, we will praise and worship You.

Jesus, Jesus, only You can heal men.
Only You are pow'rful.
Jesus, Jesus, we will praise and worship You.

Purpose	Share how Jesus' power helps you worship Him.
Materials	a snack of gingerbread men or smaller snacks in bundles of ten (such as chocolate candies, mini crackers, or cookies) CD or cassette of songs about Jesus CD or cassette player

Jesus Walks on Water

Matthew 14:22-33; Mark 6:45-51; John 6:15-21

Memory Block
"You do great and wonderful things, Lord God, the God of heaven's armies. Everything the Lord does is right and true, King of the nations" (Revelation 15:3).

Lesson Goals

- Tell what Jesus did that shows He is powerful.
- Tell what people in the boat did and said after the wind was calm.
- Recite and explain Revelation 15:3.
- Tell the difference between worshiping and not worshiping Jesus.
- Worship Jesus.

▼ Bible Search ▲

In our story, Jesus does another miracle so He can help His followers. We're going to do an experiment with water and then discover what Jesus did that shows He is powerful.

Distribute copies of page 262. Give each child a turn to experiment with an object in the water. Then search for Matthew 14:25 and find out what Jesus did that shows He is powerful (walked on water).

What did Jesus do to help His followers? What is so unusual about what Jesus did? What would happen if you stepped out on some water? What does that tell us about Jesus?

Purpose
Tell what Jesus did that shows He is powerful.

Materials
Bibles
copies of page 262
materials listed on page 262

▼ Bible Story ▲

Show tub of water. **What happens when people step into a tub of water? (They get wet, foot goes to the bottom.) Listen for what happened when Jesus stepped on a lake of water.**

"Jesus Walks on Water"

Whew! Jesus' followers were tired. They had just finished passing out food to a crowd of 5,000 men, plus women and children. It was getting late, so Jesus asked them to go ahead to Bethsaida on the other side of Lake Galilee. Then Jesus dismissed the crowd and slipped away into the hills to pray by himself. Meanwhile, in the dark, the followers began to row their boat across the lake.

Later in the night, the boat was far out onto the lake, but it was getting hard to go any further. The waves were splashing higher and higher against the boat. The force of the blowing wind made it nearly impossible to row. Between three and six in the early morning, Jesus' followers were still trying to get across the lake. They had only rowed between three and four miles. After a long day with Jesus and a long night without sleep, they were exhausted. Their eyes wanted to fall shut and their feet wanted to step onto solid ground, but they were still far from shore.

As they struggled and strained against the oars, they saw something moving past them on the water. Their tired voices cried out in terror. What was that thing on the water? Then a voice they knew called, "Have courage! It is I! Do not be afraid." It was Jesus. He had seen them struggling to row the boat across the lake. So He had come out to help them. But He wasn't in a boat. He was walking on top of the water!

Purpose
Tell what people in the boat did and said after the wind was calm.

Materials
ten lids (milk jug lids) numbered 1 to 10
tub of water

When Peter saw Jesus walking on the water, he spoke up quickly. "Lord, if that is really You, then tell me to come to You on the water."

Jesus knew Peter very well. Jesus wanted to help Peter believe in His power. Jesus said, "Come, Peter." The other followers watched with wide eyes as Peter stepped over the side of the boat into the boisterous waves. Their eyes got wider when they saw Peter start taking steps toward Jesus, on top of those waves.

But then, Peter must have felt the sting of lake water and the force of the waves crashing around him. As Peter's fear began to grow, his feet began to sink beneath the waves. "Lord, save me!" he cried. That's when Jesus reached out His strong hand and caught Peter.

The rest of the followers were glad to have Jesus get into the boat. As soon as Jesus and Peter stepped in, the wind became calm and the waves disappeared back into the lake. The followers were amazed again. They spoke words of worship to Jesus, "Truly You are the Son of God!" And at once the boat was across the lake where they wanted to go. Jesus' power had helped Him to walk on the water, calm the storm, and get the boat across the lake. Jesus truly was the Son of God.

Float ten lids, numbered from 1-10, in a tub of water, numbered side down. Let the children take turns choosing lids. When someone finds lid #1, they can answer question #1, and so on.

1. **Where did Jesus send His followers?**
2. **What did Jesus plan to do in the hills?**
3. **What trouble did the followers have in the boat?**
4. **When did Jesus come to help the followers?**
5. **What did the followers do when they saw Jesus?**
6. **What did Jesus say to the followers?**
7. **What did Peter want to do?**
8. **What happened when Peter got out of the boat?**
9. **What did the followers say when Jesus got into the boat?**
10. **How much longer did it take to cross the lake?**

Summary questions: **What did Jesus do that shows He is powerful? What did the followers do after the wind was calm? What did the followers say when they worshiped Jesus?**

▼ Bible Verse ▲

Put a large blue dot on one card and large red dots on the rest of the cards.

The words of our Bible verse tell Jesus how special He is. John wrote these words after he had heard people speak them to Jesus. We can use these same words to worship Jesus too.

Let the children find and read Revelation 15:3 (and 4). Start with "You." Give one child the card with a large blue dot. Give everyone else a card with a large red dot. While you sing (or recite) the verse together, everyone passes the cards around the circle—behind their backs. At the end of the verse, whoever has the blue dot tells what this verse is about.

Focus the conversation on the verse. **What kinds of things does this verse say Jesus does?** (great, wonderful) **What names for Jesus are in this verse?** (Lord God, God of heaven's armies, King of the nations) **What does this verse help us do?** (worship Jesus) **Who can say this verse by himself?**

Purpose
Recite and explain Revelation 15:3.

Materials
Bibles
an index card for each child
blue and red marker

▼ Bible and Me ▲

Cut apart one set of cards from page 263.

In our story, the followers worshiped Jesus (told Jesus how special He was) after He used His power to walk on water. Our Bible verse also worships Jesus because it talks to Jesus about how special He is. Let's see if we can tell when we are or are not worshiping Jesus.

Each child can select a card from the set on page 263. For each card, let the child answer two questions: **Is this worship? How can you tell?**

Then focus the conversation on what they are learning about worshiping Jesus. **What does it mean to worship Jesus?** (talk to Him to tell Him how special He is) **Why do we worship Jesus? What are some ways to tell Jesus how special He is?** (sing, draw, write, pray) **How can you tell if your song or prayer is worshiping Jesus?** (Worship talks to Jesus about special things He has done.)

Purpose
Tell the difference between worshiping and not worshiping God.

Materials
copy of page 263
scissors

▼ Bible Project ▲

When we tell Jesus how special He is, we worship Him. We have been learning to worship Jesus in many ways. Let's work on Praising Jesus with our songs, instruments, and prayers.

Worship teams should complete the rhythm instruments (page 243) and the song, rap, or psalm. Allow enough time for each child to prepare a worship prayer. This can be done individually while worship teams complete other parts of the Praising Jesus project. Children may write their own sentences or have them dictate a sentence prayer to you or another leader. Suggest worship sentences that begin like the following: "Jesus, You are special. Only You can . . . ," or "Dear Jesus, I worship You because You . . . ," or "Jesus, You are powerful. I praise You for . . . "

Purpose
Worship Jesus.

Materials
materials to complete rhythm instruments
song chart
black marker
writing paper
pencils

▼ Bible Sharing ▲

After snack time, allow the children to take turns throwing a lid into the tub of water. For every lid they get in the water, they should tell something about Jesus that makes Him special. They can tell things Jesus did or tell names that describe Jesus.

Close by asking each child to say a sentence prayer of praise to Jesus. They may use the ideas from the Bible Project time if they need help forming their prayers.

Purpose
Share how Jesus' power helps you worship Him.

Materials
a snack of ice cream floats (soda pop over scoops of ice cream)
tub of water and lids used in Bible Search

Jesus Heals a Man Born Blind

John 9:1-38

Lesson Goals
- Tell what Jesus did that shows He is powerful.
- Tell what the blind man did after Jesus healed Him.
- Recite and demonstrate Revelation 15:3.
- Demonstrate ways to worship Jesus.
- Worship Jesus.

Memory Block
"You do great and wonderful things, Lord God, the God of heaven's armies. Everything the Lord does is right and true, King of the nations" (Revelation 15:3).

▼ Bible Search ▲

In our story, Jesus helps a man who had always been blind.

Guide the children to find and read John 9:1 in their Bibles. Distribute page 264 and ask them to find the answer to the question at the top of the page. Talk about what it might be like to be unable to see. Then make a message in Braille. Practice "reading" the messages with your fingertips.

Who did Jesus see? What parts of being blind would not be fun? What would you miss the most if you were blind? What did the man say Jesus did that shows how powerful Jesus is? (the Braille message: Jesus healed me)

Purpose
Tell what Jesus did that shows He is powerful.

Materials
Bibles
copies page 264
materials listed on page 264 to make Braille

▼ Bible Story ▲

Before the session, print the review clues on strips of paper and attach them to the wall.

Mix dirt and water to make mud. **What are some fun things to do with mud? Jesus made some mud one day. Listen to see what He did with it.**

"Jesus Heals a Man Born Blind"

I had never seen clouds floating in a blue sky or yellow flowers bending in the breeze. I had never seen myself or any other person, but I could hear. One day when I was begging by the side of the road, I heard Jesus talking to His followers. They wanted to know why I had always been blind. Jesus told them it wasn't because my parents or I had done anything wrong. But now, because I was blind, people could see God's power heal me.

Then I heard Jesus spit on the ground and in a few moments He smoothed something cool and gooey over my eyes. It smelled like mud! I was glad when He told me to wash it off in the Pool of Siloam. Carefully, I made my way to the pool. As soon as I splashed the water in my face, I could see! All the way back, I marveled at the blue sky, the green trees, and all the other colors around me. But mostly I marveled at the power of Jesus to make me see.

Some people recognized I was the man who had been blind. But others thought I was someone who looked like me. I was so excited to tell them, "I am the man." When they asked me what happened, I explained, "The man named Jesus made some mud and put it on my eyes. Then He told me to go to Siloam and wash. So I went and washed and came back seeing." When the people wanted to know where Jesus was, I had to tell them, "I don't know."

The people who didn't believe it was really me took me to the Pharisees and

Purpose
Tell what the blind man did after Jesus healed him.

Materials
dirt and water to make mud
blindfold
strips of paper
marker
tape or Plasti-Tak® reusable adhesive

told them what happened. The Pharisees asked me to explain, so I told them, "He put mud on my eyes. I washed and now I can see." They asked who made me see. But when I said, "He is a prophet," they didn't believe me.

The Pharisees were determined to find someone to say Jesus was not from God, so next they asked my parents, "Is this your son? You say that he was born blind. Then how does he see now?"

My parents were afraid what might happen if they said that Jesus was from God. They answered, "Ask him. He is old enough to answer for himself."

Those Pharisees didn't give up. Next they tried to get me to say that Jesus was a sinner. That would show he wasn't from God. They urged me to tell the truth. So I did. I said, "I don't know if He is a sinner. But one thing I do know. I was blind, and now I see." The Pharisees were angry because I wouldn't say what they wanted to hear. They didn't believe Jesus was from God. They didn't believe Jesus could heal me. So they threw me out!

Later Jesus found me and told me He was the Son of God. He wanted to know if I believed He was the Son of God. I said, "Yes, Lord. I believe." I bowed and worshiped Jesus because of who Jesus was. Jesus' power had helped me see. My worship told Jesus I believed only He could heal me.

Let the children take turns wearing a blindfold and "feeling" for a clue taped to the wall. Each answer is a person in the story.

We asked why this man had always been blind. (followers)
I said people would see God's power because the man was blind. (Jesus)
I put mud on the man's eyes. (Jesus)
I washed in the Pool of Siloam. (man)
We took the man to the Pharisees. (people)
I told the Pharisees, "I was blind, and now I can see." (man)
We refused to believe Jesus had power from God. (Pharisees)
I worshiped Jesus because I believed he was the Son of God. (man)
Summary questions: **What did Jesus do to show He has power from God?** (healed the blind man) **What did the blind man do after Jesus healed him?** (bowed, worshiped)

▼ Bible Verse ▲

Purpose
Recite and demonstrate Revelation 15:3.

Materials
rhythm instruments made for the Bible Project (see page 243)
slips of paper
marker
a sack
verse strips used in Lesson 40

Before the session, print the names of the rhythm instruments on slips of paper and put them in a sack.

The words of our Bible verse tell Jesus how special He is. John wrote these words after he had heard people speak them to Jesus. We can use these same words to worship Jesus too.

Let the children find and read Revelation 15:3 (and 4). Start with "You."

Children who have not memorized the verse can do the verse strip puzzle (used in Lesson 40). Children who can say the verse can take turns using a variety of rhythm instruments to sing the verse to Jesus. Each time they sing it, pull a slip of paper from the sack. Whoever has that instrument gets to say the verse alone or tell what the verse helps him to do. Pass instruments to the person on the left before singing it again.

What kinds of things does this verse say Jesus does? (great, wonderful) **What names for Jesus are in this verse?** (Lord God, God of heaven's armies, King of the nations) **What were we doing when we sang this verse to Jesus?** (worshiping Him)

▼ Bible and Me ▲

In our story, the man Jesus healed worshiped Jesus (told Jesus how special He was). Our Bible verse also worships Jesus because it talks to Jesus about how special He is. Let's show how we can worship Jesus too.

Each child may select a way to worship from page 265. Or each may think of an idea of his own. Guide those who choose to be creative by asking these questions: **Which way to worship will you show us? What do you want to say to Jesus in your worship?** (For example, Jesus, only You can . . . ; Jesus, You are special because . . . ; Jesus, Your power is great because . . .)

Review ways to worship and ask the children to worship with you in Bible Sharing. **What does it mean to worship Jesus?** (talk to Him to tell Him how special He is) **Why do we worship Jesus? What are some ways to tell Jesus how special He is?** (sing, draw, write, pray) **How can you tell if your song or prayer is worshiping Jesus?** (Worship talks to Jesus about special things He has done.)

Purpose
Demonstrate ways to worship Jesus.

Materials
copies of page 265
materials to complete the worship cards

▼ Bible Project ▲

When we record the Praising Jesus project, let's worship Jesus with our songs, instruments, and prayers.

Practice the song, rap, or choral reading based on Psalm 150 using the instruments. Allow children time to practice reading their sentence prayers. Then record the Praising Jesus project.

If you will be duplicating the tapes for each child, remind them to use them at home to worship. If you can, plan a time to take the worship project to people who are home bound. The children can tell them about worship and then worship together with them.

Purpose
Worship Jesus.

Materials
items created for the Praising Jesus project (rhythm instruments, songs, choral readings, and prayers)
a blank cassette and cassette player with microphone

▼ Bible Sharing ▲

To make dirt pudding, layer vanilla pudding, whipped cream, and crushed chocolate cookies. Give each child a sturdy paper plate with glob of dirt pudding or instant chocolate pudding. Let them finger-paint something from the story on the plate. After telling about it, they can use their fingers to eat it.

Worship together using the worship cards from page 265. Give each child a turn to participate. Close by singing favorite songs about Jesus.

Purpose
Share how Jesus' power helps you worship Him.

Materials
Dirt pudding (see instructions in the activity) or instant chocolate pudding
sturdy paper plates
soapy water and towels for washing
worship cards from page 265
CD or cassette of worship songs
CD or cassette player

Bible Story

Cut out the boats.
Fold the sails and use the
questions to review the
Bible Story.

cut

How did Jesus
plan to get to
the other side
of the lake?

1.

Who was sailing
with Jesus
in the boat?

2.

What did Jesus do
after the boat
left the shore?

3.

What happened
to the boat
during the storm?

4.

How did the
followers feel
during the storm?

5.

What did the
followers say
when they
woke Jesus?

6.

What did Jesus
say to the storm?

7.

What did Jesus'
followers say
when Jesus did
this miracle?

8.

Fold left half
of the sails
over, so that
the questions
are inside.

UNIT 10, LESSON 40

Cut apart the verse strips.
Put them in order to make a puzzle.
Mount the puzzle on construction paper.

You do great

and wonderful things, Lord God,

the God of heaven's armies.

Everything the Lord does

King of the nations.

is right and true,

respect you, Lord.

Everyone will

They will honor you.

Bible Verse

You do great and wonderful things, Lord God, the God of heaven's armies. Everything the Lord does is right and true, King of the nations. Everyone will respect you, Lord. They will honor you. Only you are holy. All people will come and worship you. This is because he is a faithful God who does no wrong. He is right and fair. —Revelation 15:3, 4

—Revelation 15:3, 4

Only you are holy.

All people will come

and worship you.

This is because he is

a faithful God

who does no wrong.

He is right and fair.

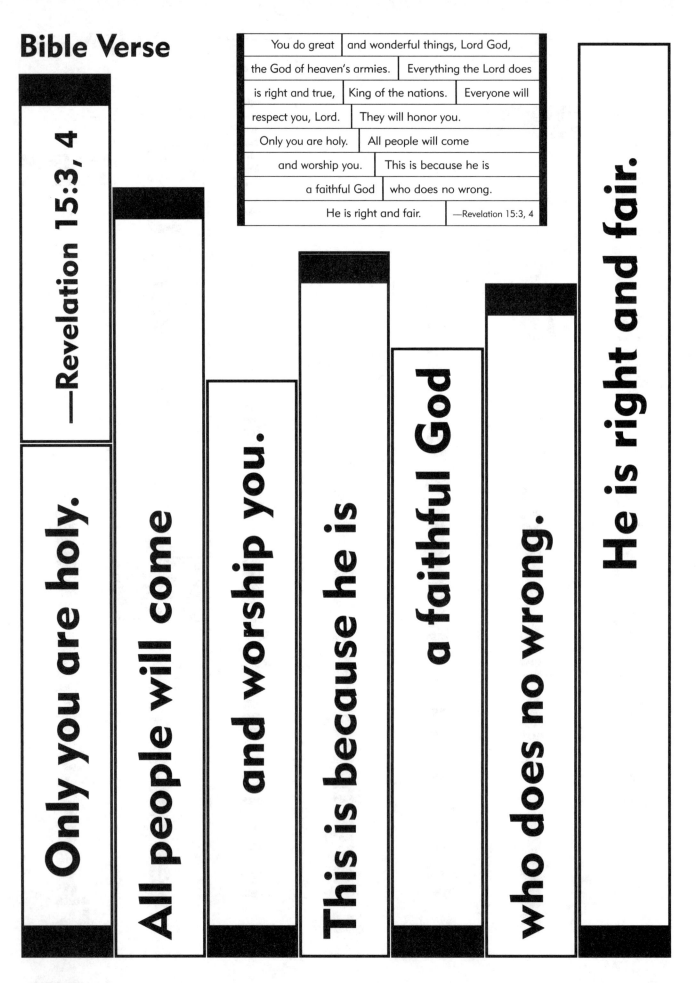

Unit 10, Lesson 40

Bible and Me

Sing the song.
Fill in the blanks at the bottom.

I will sing, I will sing, I will sing. I will sing my wor - ship

to___ the Lord.___ I will sing, I will sing, I will sing. I will

sing___ to___ the Lord.

Verse 2. I will write . . .
Verse 3. I will draw . . .
Verse 4. I will pray . . .

These children know lots of ways to tell Jesus He is special.

Joel and Sarah like to _____ poems to Jesus.

Micah, Joshua, and Laura are going to _____ pictures of how special Jesus is.

Kayla and Emily want to _____ a song to Jesus.

And Steven and Andrea like to tell Jesus He is special when they _____.

Bible Search

Find Luke 17:12 in your Bible.

What kept ten men from coming close to Jesus?

The harmful skin disease was called leprosy.

When a person had leprosy, he had to live away from healthy people. Healthy people were not allowed to touch a person with leprosy.

Leprosy made parts of a person's skin die. The skin with leprosy could not feel if it was being bumped or if it was getting burned.

People with leprosy had terrible sore places on their hands and feet. Sometimes parts of their fingers or toes would fall off.

Only a priest could look at a person who had been sick with leprosy to see if he was healed. The priest could give the person permission to go back to his home and family.

 UNIT 10, LESSON 41

Bible and Me

Sing or speak in rhythm why we worship Jesus.

Je - sus is the Son of God, Son of God, Son of God.

Je - sus is the Son of God. That's why we wor - ship Je - sus.____

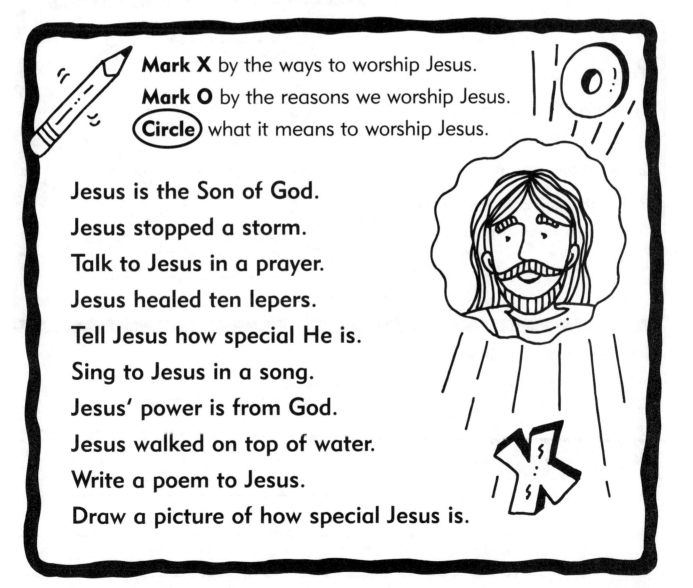

Mark X by the ways to worship Jesus.

Mark O by the reasons we worship Jesus.

(Circle) what it means to worship Jesus.

Jesus is the Son of God.

Jesus stopped a storm.

Talk to Jesus in a prayer.

Jesus healed ten lepers.

Tell Jesus how special He is.

Sing to Jesus in a song.

Jesus' power is from God.

Jesus walked on top of water.

Write a poem to Jesus.

Draw a picture of how special Jesus is.

UNIT 10, LESSON 41 261

Bible Search

Do the experiment.
Then find out what Jesus did
  that shows He is special.

Experiment

You will need

dishpan of water

several small objects—
  rock, small ball, leaf, penny,
  quarter, plastic building block,
  spoon, plastic lid, crayon

You will do

1. Choose one object to
   put in the water.

2. Ask the question: Will it sink or will it float?

3. Put the object in the water
   and see what happens.

Find and read Matthew 14:25.

What did Jesus do that shows He is powerful?

Jesus

 UNIT 10, LESSON 42

Cut apart the cards. Choose one.
Read the card and answer
these two questions:

Bible and Me

1. Is this worship?   2. How can you tell?

Song

I will sing,
I will sing,
I will sing!

I will sing
my worship
to the Lord!

Song

Jesus, You healed
the sick.
You healed the
deaf and blind.

You are
God's Son.
You're the
best friend
I will find.

Prayer

Dear God,
help me have a
good day at school.

Prayer

Dear God,
You are special
because You sent
Jesus to be our friend.

Poem

Jesus,
You are special,
I know.

You stopped
the waves
and the winds
that blow.

Poem

"Jesus, help us,"
called the
sick men.

They did what
He said and
got well again.

Picture

Jesus, You are
the Son of God.

Picture

"I'm going to
your house today."

Bible Search

Find and read John 9:1
in your Bible.
Who did Jesus see?

In Bible times, a person who could not see
could not read either.

But today, people who cannot see use their
fingers to read. They read a code called Braille.

Braille is a code of small raised dots on paper
that can be read by touch.

Make a Message in Braille

You will need

- tagboard
  (file folder)
- dull pencil
- kitchen towel

You will do

1. Cut out the Braille message below. (It is printed backwards.)
2. Fold the kitchen towel once. Put the tagboard on the towel.
3. Put the Braille message on top (so you can see the dots).
4. Use the dull pencil to press on each dot. Be careful not to
   make a hole in the tagboard.
5. Turn the tagboard over and read the message with your
   finger tips.

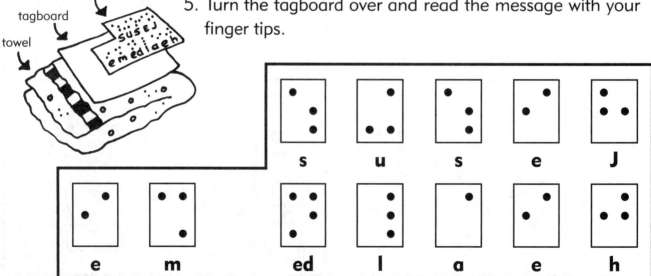

Braille message

tagboard

towel

s   u   s   e   J

e   m   ed   l   a   e   h

 Unit 10, Lesson 43

Choose a way to worship Jesus. Use one of the cards or think of your own idea.

Sing Revelation 15:3, 4 to tell Jesus how special He is.

OR

Think of worship words to sing to a favorite tune ("This Old Man," "Row Your Boat," "London Bridge," "Are You Sleeping?").

Draw a picture of the blind man bowing to worship Jesus. Write what he might have said to worship Jesus.

OR

Draw your own picture. Write a sentence to tell Jesus how special He is.

Plan a prayer to tell Jesus how special He is because He healed the blind man.

OR

Plan a prayer with your own ideas to tell Jesus He is special.

Finish this poem to tell Jesus how special He is:

Jesus, You're the only one

_____.

OR

Write your own ideas in a free verse poem to tell Jesus He is special. (The poem doesn't have to rhyme.)

UNIT 11

Jesus' Miracles Help Me Tell About Him

Lessons 44–47

Unit Memory Block
"The man that Jesus had healed begged to go with him. But Jesus sent him away, saying, 'Go back home and tell people what God did for you.' So the man went all over town telling how much Jesus had done for him" (Luke 8:38, 39).

Memory Challenge
"Jesus did many other miracles before his followers that are not written in this book. But these are written so that you can believe that Jesus is the Christ, the Son of God. Then, by believing, you can have life through his name" (John 20:30, 31).

44 Jesus Helps a Gadarene
Mark 5:1-20; Luke 8:26-39
A Gadarene man told everyone how Jesus made demons leave him. We tell the amazing things Jesus can do because He is the Son of God.

45 Jesus Feeds 5,000
Matthew 14:13-21; Mark 6:32-44; Luke 9:10-17; John 6:1-14
Jesus used five loaves and two fishes to feed more than 5,000 people. We tell about Jesus because of the amazing things He can do.

46 Jesus Heals a Man at a Pool
John 5:1-15
A man at a pool told people that it was Jesus who helped him walk. We tell about Jesus because of the amazing things He can do.

47 Jesus Brings Lazarus Back Alive
John 11:1-45
Jesus brought Lazarus back alive to show that He (Jesus) is from God. We tell about the amazing things Jesus can do because He is from God.

By the end of the unit, the leaders and learners will
KNOW four things they can tell about Jesus.
FEEL eager to tell about Jesus.
DO Tell about Jesus.

Unit Value

This unit helps children learn four more amazing things Jesus did. The stories show that Jesus' power can solve whatever problems people have. Because Jesus is the answer to people's problems, we want to tell everyone what we know about Jesus. That's what the Gadarene did in the first story. He told people from ten towns what Jesus had done. In the second story, over 5,000 people went home able to tell what they had seen Jesus do. In the third story, the man at the pool told the Jews what Jesus had done for him. In the final story, we are reminded that Jesus' miracles were not just to help solve problems. Jesus' miracles prove He is the Son of God—the one we follow, the one we obey, the one we are eager to tell about.

In this unit you can help children develop an eagerness to tell about Jesus. First, you can help them identify what it means to tell about Jesus. Then they can learn to recognize when they are or are not telling about Jesus. Third, they can focus on why it's important to tell about Jesus. And finally, you can help them develop the attitude that it is easy to tell about Jesus. Other units have dealt with the difficulties of following or worshiping Jesus. In contrast, this unit can help them feel that telling about Jesus is as easy as talking about any other person they love. Your own enthusiasm for evangelism will be mirrored in the faces and voices of the children. Allow your own eagerness to talk about Jesus to show. Then be amazed as the children grow in their abilities to tell about Jesus.

▼ Bible Project ▲

Sandwich Boards

The learners will make sandwich boards to tell amazing things about Jesus. Guide the learners to decide what to write and draw on the boards—amazing things Jesus did, what Jesus said, who Jesus is. Page 284 can be enlarged and reproduced for the children to use.

Provide cord or string and two pieces of poster board for each child. Old Sunday school visuals and teaching pictures can be used as well as original drawings, designs, and lettering. Since sandwich boards are usually read at a distance or read quickly, guide the children to use large letters and designs to fill each piece of poster board. The goal is to tell about Jesus! Then when the students have completed their boards, they can punch holes in the top of each board and use the string to tie the boards together as shown in the illustration.

Week 1: Plan and sketch designs on drawing paper.

Week 2: Sketch design and letter words on poster board.

Week 3: Color design and add finishing details.

Week 4: Wear sandwich boards to tell about Jesus. (Or plan when and where the group will wear them.)

You may want to use overhead transparencies to trace the smaller designs the children create, and then to project the design onto the piece of poster board using the overhead projector.

Materials
copies of page 284
poster board (two pieces for each child)
string or cord
drawing paper
crayons
colored pencils
markers
rulers
scissors
old Bible story art/pictures

Play Dough

1 cup flour
2 teaspoons cream of tartar
1 tablespoon cooking oil
1/2 cup salt
1 cup water

Mix flour, salt, and cream of tartar in a saucepan. (Do not omit cream of tartar.) Add water, oil, and food coloring. Cook, stirring for 3 minutes or until mixture pulls away from the pan. Knead immediately. Store in an airtight container. This recipe makes enough dough for six children.

Memory Block

"The man that Jesus had healed begged to go with him. But Jesus sent him away, saying, 'Go back home and tell people what God did for you.' So the man went all over town telling how much Jesus had done for him" (Luke 8:38, 39).

Purpose
Tell what miracle Jesus did near Gadara.

Materials
Bibles
two large index cards
marker

Purpose
Tell how the Gadarene man changed.

Materials
a telephone
copies of page 280
scissors
clear tape

Lesson Goals

- Tell what miracle Jesus did near Gadara.
- Tell how the Gadarene man changed.
- Begin to memorize Luke 8:38, 39.
- Tell what kinds of things to say to tell about Jesus.
- Tell about Jesus.

▼ Bible Search ▲

Before class, print a set of three questions on each card. (Use the questions at the end of the activity.)

In our story, Jesus helps a wild man who lived near Gadara. Let's find out what Jesus did for him and what Jesus asked him to do.

Group children into two search teams. Guide one team to find Luke 8:38, 39; the other team will find Mark 5:18-20. Give each team a question card, and help them find the answers in Luke or Mark. Then compare the verses.

How did Jesus help the wild man? What did Jesus tell the man to do? What did the man do after Jesus talked to him?

▼ Bible Story ▲

Before the session, cut out the story strips on page 280.

Who do you want to tell when something wonderful happens to you? Display telephone. **Listen to see who wanted to tell people in ten towns what had happened to him.**

"Jesus Helps a Gadarene"

Herding 2,000 pigs is not an easy job, especially when you have to protect your pigs from a wild man. This wild man had made a terrible mistake of letting demons live in him. The demons made him do dreadful things. Day and night he wandered around caves where we buried people. For a long time he had worn no clothes. Sometimes we saw him wander near us, cutting himself with stones and shrieking long, painful wails and screams. We were terrified of what he might do to us. But whenever any of us tried to tie him or chain his hands and feet, he just broke the ropes and chains.

One day we took the pigs to a hill near Lake Galilee. From up on the hill we watched a boat coming across the lake to Gadara from Galilee. As some men got out of the boat, we saw that wild man screaming and racing toward them. We were relieved he wasn't headed our way. But to our amazement, he didn't attack the men. When he got to them, we saw him fall down in front of the man named Jesus. This man, Jesus, didn't seem to be afraid of the wild man. He just spoke to him, "You evil spirit, come out of that man."

Then the wild man screamed again. That was normal. But the words the demon made him scream were not normal, "What do you want with me, Jesus, Son of the Most High God? I beg you, please don't punish me." When Jesus asked for his name, the man answered, "My name is Legion, because I have many spirits in me." Never before had we seen anyone who could frighten the demons in this wild man. What was happening?

Those demons were so afraid of Jesus that they begged him again and again not to make them leave our area. Instead, they wanted Jesus to let them go live in our pigs. It all happened so quickly. One minute the pigs were rooting and snorting in the grass. The next minute all 2,000 pigs squealed and rushed headlong into the lake, sank to the bottom, and drowned. We were shocked. How could we explain this to the owners of the pigs? We started running the other way, back to town. Along the way we told everyone what had happened.

People in town rushed out to see what we were talking about. By the time we got back, the wild man was sitting by Jesus. His clothes were on, he was thinking in his right mind, and the demons were gone! Some of the people wondered what power could be strong enough to make demons leave. We explained how Jesus made the demons leave the man and how the pigs ran into the lake. Some people began to feel afraid, because they didn't understand how Jesus could do this miracle. Instead of being glad, more and more began to be afraid. Soon all the people in our country of Gadara were so afraid that we begged Jesus to leave.

But the man who was free from demons was not afraid. He begged to sail back to Galilee with Jesus. But instead, Jesus gave him a special job. Jesus said, "Go home to your family and friends. Tell them how much the Lord has done for you and how he has had mercy on you. Go back home and tell people what God did for you." The man was eager to do what Jesus asked. He told people in ten of our towns about the great thing Jesus had done for him. The people who heard him were amazed at what Jesus had said and done.

Help the man from Gadara tell about Jesus. Help children cut out and put the strips from page 280 in story order. Then they can tape the strips together to make a paper chain. The story order follows:

1. Man lives in caves and breaks out of chains.
2. Man runs and falls down before Jesus.
3. Jesus commands demons to leave.
4. Demons beg to live in some pigs.
5. 2,000 pigs rush into the lake and drown.
6. People are afraid and ask Jesus to leave.
7. Man wants to go with Jesus.
8. Jesus asks the man to go and tell what God has done.
9. Jesus sails across the lake to Galilee.

Summary questions: **What miracle did Jesus do?** (made demons leave a man) **What did the man do after his miracle?** (put on clothes, listened to Jesus, told people from ten towns what Jesus had done with God's power)

Option: For younger children, use only sentences number 2, 3, 7, and 8. Or have the children work as a group to order the strips and make the paper chain.

▼ Bible Verse ▲

Before the session, cut out a verse pyramid from page 281 for every 3 to 4 children.

One of Jesus' followers was a doctor. He wrote a book to tell people what Jesus did and said. Our Bible verses are in this book, and it was in our story.

Let the children find and read Luke 8:38, 39. Find the page number for Luke in the table of contents. Then find a big number 8 for the chapter and a small number 38 for the first verse. Show children the verse pyramids. Let them work in groups of 3 to 4 to use their Bibles to number and learn the sentences on the pyramid. Then fold each pyramid and let groups help you tape it together.

Purpose
Begin to memorize Luke 8:38, 39.

Materials
Bibles
copy of page 281
marker
scissors
clear tape

Play a game in the small groups to help the students learn the verses. Take turns tossing the verse pyramid. The student who tosses the pyramid will read (or say from memory) the sentence on the side that lands facing up. Then the child to her left will try to say the next sentence of the verse in order, and so on, until the verses are completed. Students may leave their Bibles open to Luke 8:38, 39, and use them if they need help.

Who wrote the verses? Where can we find the verses? What happened first? (man begged) **What happened second?** (Jesus sent him away.) **What happened next?** (Jesus said to go, tell.) **What happened last?** (man told)

Option: If you are limited on time, give each child a copy of page 281 and have them number the verse sentences in order. They may cut out and assemble the verse pyramid at home.

▼ Bible and Me ▲

Purpose
Tell what kinds of things to say to tell about Jesus.

Materials
copies of page 282
scissors

Before the session, cut apart a set of cards from page 282.

Telling about Jesus means talking about the things Jesus did or said in the Bible. We can tell what Jesus did and said in our stories.

Have children act out telling about Jesus. Shuffle the four *Who, What, When, Where* cards from page 282. Display the four answer cards on a wall. Let a child or pairs of children take turns drawing a question card and acting out who, what, when, or where they are telling about Jesus. They can use the answer cards to give them ideas. The rest of the group will guess what they are acting out.

What kinds of things do we say when we tell about Jesus? (what Jesus did or said) **What are some things Jesus has done? What are some things Jesus has said? Who can tell? What can we tell? Where can we tell?**

Option: Groups of 2 to 4 children can play a concentration game with cards from page 281. Copy the page twice for each group. Lay the cards face down in four rows. Take turns picking two cards, looking for a question and its answer. Keep cards that match; put back cards that don't match.

▼ Bible Project ▲

Purpose
Tell about Jesus.

Materials
materials to make sandwich boards (unit page 267)
paper
pencils

Before class, make a sandwich board to demonstrate this way to tell about Jesus.

We're going to make a fun way to tell about Jesus—sandwich boards. When we wear the sandwich boards, we can talk about Jesus to the people who read our signs.

Explain/demonstrate what a sandwich board is. Walk among the children and let them ask you about your sign. Then help the children plan and design their boards. Use the questions listed in Bible and Me to get them started. Have the children print or dictate to you their plans. Make sure they put their names on their papers. Save the plans to use during the next lesson.

▼ Bible Sharing ▲

Purpose
Share how Jesus' miracles help you to tell about Him.

Materials
a snack of pork barbecue, fruit, and drink
CD or cassette of songs about Jesus
CD or cassette player

Let the children share what they know about Jesus as you eat your snack. Then sing favorite songs about Jesus. For each song, ask **What does this song tell us about Jesus?**

To close the session, ask the children to think of people in their families or in their neighborhoods who need to know about Jesus. Ask for volunteers to pray for God's help to tell about Jesus.

Jesus Feeds 5,000

Matthew 14:13-21; Mark 6:32-44; Luke 9:10-17; John 6:1-14

Lesson Goals
- Tell what miracle Jesus did near the town of Bethsaida.
- Tell what the people said when they saw Jesus do this miracle.
- Recite Luke 8:38, 39.
- Tell the difference between telling and not telling about Jesus.
- Tell about Jesus.

Memory Block

"The man that Jesus had healed begged to go with him. But Jesus sent him away, saying, 'Go back home and tell people what God did for you.' So the man went all over town telling how much Jesus had done for him" (Luke 8:38, 39).

▼ Bible Search ▲

Before the session, cut apart the four cards on page 283.

In our story, Jesus does a miracle to help a hungry crowd. Four followers of Jesus wrote about this miracle in the Bible: Matthew, Mark, Luke, and John!

Group the children into four search teams. Give each team a card from page 283. Guide the children to search for two common facts in the four narratives of this story.

Report answers to the questions on the cards. **How many loaves of bread did Jesus' followers have? How many fish did they have? How many baskets of uneaten food were left? What miracle did Jesus do?**

Purpose
Tell what miracle Jesus did near the town of Bethsaida.

Materials
Bibles
copy of page 283
pencils
scissors

▼ Bible Story ▲

Before the session, print the six story facts listed in the review on six slips of paper. Slit six buns on one side. With a table knife, push a folded slip of paper into each bun. Each child can open a bun and eat it as they work to put the facts in order. Make one set for each six children.

Display picnic basket. **What do you need for a great picnic?** (green grass, food, bugs, people) **Listen to see which things are in the story!**

"Jesus Feeds 5,000"

The spring breeze on Lake Galilee felt cool in our faces as we sailed across the water. We were headed for a quiet place near my hometown of Bethsaida. The other apostles and I had just finished a preaching trip. We were eager to tell Jesus all we had done and taught. But so many people were coming and going around us…well, we didn't even have a chance to eat. So Jesus took us in a boat across the lake to get some rest.

Surprise! When we dropped anchor near Bethsaida, there was no place or time to rest! People had heard where we were headed. They had raced on foot around the lake to meet us. In His usual kind way, Jesus welcomed them. He healed sick people and taught the crowd about God.

Late in the afternoon, the other apostles and I began to feel a little worried. The crowd had grown to 5,000 men, plus women and children. Their stomachs were starting to growl hungrily. So we told Jesus, "No one lives in this place. It's already very late. Send the people away. They need to go away." Jesus knew what He was going to do, but first He asked me, "Philip, where can we buy bread for these people to eat?"

Purpose
Tell what the people said when they saw Jesus do this miracle.

Materials
a picnic basket, small buns (one for each child)
table knife
slips of paper
marker

I was from Bethsaida, so I knew there was no place around to get all the food we would need. We told Jesus, "We can't buy enough bread to feed all these! We would all have to work a month to earn enough money to buy that much bread."

Jesus asked, "How many loaves of bread do you have now? Go and see."

When we returned, Andrew said, "Here is one boy with five loaves of barley and two small fish. But that is not enough for so many people." However, it was enough for Jesus.

We spread out through the crowd and asked everyone to sit in groups of fifty on the new green grass. As Jesus took the boy's lunch, He looked up to Heaven and thanked God for the food. Then He began to divide the bread into baskets. He filled one basket, then another, then another and another and another. As quickly as Jesus filled the baskets, we carried them to each group of people. Again and again Jesus divided the bread until there was bread for every group! And then we watched with amazement as He did the same with those two little fish. Jesus divided the fish again and again and again and again until everyone in the crowd had fish to eat.

All of the 5,000 men, plus the women, plus the children, ate as much as they wanted. When everyone had enough, Jesus said, "Gather the pieces of fish and bread that were not eaten. Don't waste anything." When we came back from gathering leftovers, we had filled twelve large baskets with broken pieces of bread and fish. The people who saw this miracle said, "Jesus must be a prophet from God."

Use the prepared set of buns with these facts to put in order:
A crowd of people race around the lake to meet Jesus when He lands.
Apostles want to send the people away at the end of the day.
A boy gives his five loaves and two fish to Andrew.
Jesus thanks God for the food and divides it for the people.
The followers take the food to all the people.
The followers gather up twelve baskets of food that were left.

Summary questions: **What miracle did Jesus do? What could the people tell about Jesus?** (He fed 5,000 people with 5 loaves and 2 fish; Jesus was a prophet.)

▼ Bible Verse ▲

Purpose
Recite Luke 8:38, 39.

Materials
Bibles
copies of page 281 cut into triangles

Doctor Luke wrote a book to tell many things Jesus did and said. He wrote the verses we are learning.

Let the children find and read Luke 8:38, 39. Guide the children to put the triangles from page 281 in order on a wall. Then play "Bible, Bible, Verse" to help them memorize the verses. As the children sit in a circle, one child goes around the outside, patting heads and saying, "Bible, Bible, (and so on), Verse." Everyone but the person he pats when he says "verse" gets to read (or recite) the verses aloud. The person he patted on "verse" trades places and is next to say "Bible, Bible, Verse."

Where can we find the verses? What happened first? (man begged) **What happened second?** (Jesus sent him away.) **What happened next?** (Jesus said to go, tell.) **What happened last?** (man told) **Who will say the verses with a friend?**

▼ Bible and Me ▲

Before the session, print on half of the index cards statements or songs that tell about Jesus: Jesus fed 5,000 people; Jesus loves me; Jesus is God's Son; Jesus called Peter and Andrew to follow Him; and so on. On the other cards, print statements or songs that do not tell about Jesus: I Have Decided to Follow Jesus; God made the world; Church is a fun place; and so on. Be sure to include songs your children are familiar with on the cards to help them learn the difference between telling and not telling about Jesus. Tape a length of yarn to each index card. Drop the cards into a sack, but let the yarn hang outside the sack.

Telling about Jesus means talking about the things Jesus did or said in the Bible. We can tell what Jesus did and said in a song, poem, picture, or story. Let's see if the words or songs on these cards do or do not tell about Jesus.

The children can take turns pulling out a card from the sack. For each card, they must decide if it does or does not tell something Jesus did or said.

What kinds of things do we say when we tell about Jesus? (What He did or said.) **Does this card tell something Jesus did? What? Does this card tell something Jesus said? What? What is your favorite thing to tell about Jesus? What is your favorite song to sing about Jesus?**

Option: Provide a CD or cassette of songs your children are familiar with. Play a "name that tune" game. Play part of each song until the children can identify the title. Then decide as a group whether the song does or does not tell about something Jesus said or did.

Purpose
Tell the difference between telling and not telling about Jesus.

Materials
index cards
marker
yarn
tape

▼ Bible Project ▲

Telling about Jesus means talking about the things Jesus did or said in the Bible. Our sandwich boards will help us talk about Jesus to the people who read our signs.

Distribute the planning papers the children started last week. Guide the children to transfer their designs to poster board. You may want to use an overhead projector to enlarge and copy the designs. See unit page 267. Give help and encouragement as needed. The children should include on the sandwich boards amazing things Jesus did, what Jesus said, or who Jesus is. One side of the sandwich could even say, "Ask me about Jesus!"

Purpose
Tell about Jesus.

Materials
materials to make sandwich boards (unit page 267)
planning papers children made in Lesson 44

▼ Bible Sharing ▲

Let the children share what they know about Jesus by pantomime. Divide the children into pairs. Each pair will think of an amazing thing Jesus did. Give suggestions if needed. When ready, each pair will pantomime the amazing thing for the rest of the group to guess.

Purpose
Share how Jesus' miracles help you tell about Him.

Materials
a snack of fish sticks (to go with the bread from the story review)

Jesus Heals a Man at a Pool

John 5:1-15

Memory Block

"The man that Jesus had healed begged to go with him. But Jesus sent him away, saying, 'Go back home and tell people what God did for you.' So the man went all over town telling how much Jesus had done for him" (Luke 8:38, 39).

Purpose
Tell what miracle Jesus did at the Bethesda pool.

Materials
Bibles
copies of page 285
pencils

Purpose
Tell what the man did after Jesus healed him.

Materials
a small tablet with at least thirty-eight pages
marker

Lesson Goals

- Tell what miracle Jesus did at the Bethesda pool.
- Tell what the man did after Jesus healed him.
- Recite and explain Luke 8:38, 39.
- Tell why we want to tell about Jesus.
- Tell about Jesus.

▼ Bible Search ▲

In our story, Jesus does a miracle to help a man who was sick a long time.

Guide the children to find John 5:3 in their Bibles. Distribute copies of page 285 and let the children complete the page using their Bibles. They will also need to find verses 5 and 8 to complete the page.

What kinds of sick people were at the pool? What kind of sick person did Jesus help? How long had this man been sick? What did Jesus tell the man?

▼ Bible Story ▲

Print one year on each page of the small tablet beginning with the year thirty-eight years before the current one.

What is the longest time you know of someone being sick? The man in our story was sick thirty-eight years. Count and tear off thirty-eight pages of the small tablet (1, 2, 3, and so on). **Listen to see what Jesus told the man to do.**

"Jesus Heals a Man at a Pool"

The pool of water near the sheep gate in Jerusalem wasn't a swimming pool. This pool stored water for people to use in their homes. But many people wanted to get in the pool, including me. I had been sick for thirty-eight years. Someone told me if I could be the first one to get into the pool when the water was moving, I would be healed. But I could never move fast enough to get in first.

One Sabbath day, I was still lying there with lots of other people who were blind, crippled, or paralyzed. We were under the five porches around the pool, watching and waiting for the water to move. But the only thing that was moving was the crowd around us. One man came over to me.

Somehow He knew I had been sick for a very long time. He asked me a question I wasn't expecting, "Do you want to be well?" I tried to explain that I had no one to help me get in the pool so I could get well. But that wasn't want He wanted to know. He wanted to help me, but first He wanted to know if I really did want to walk. His next words showed that He knew I truly did want to walk. He told me simply, "Stand up. Pick up your mat and walk." To my surprise, I could do it! I was well! I could walk! Immediately I stood up. I tucked my mat under my arm and took my first steps. I didn't know how it happened, but now I could use my legs for walking! From the tips of my toes up to the top of my head I was quivering with excitement.

But the Jews in the crowd were not excited. They had special rules about what we should not do on a Sabbath. Their frowning voices complained, "Today is the Sabbath. It is against our law for you to do work, like carrying your mat, on the Sabbath day."

So I explained how the man who made me well had told me, "Pick up your mat and walk." My smile must have showed them how happy I was. But they didn't care about being happy with me. They didn't care that I could walk! Instead they demanded to know, "Who told you to pick up your mat and walk?" I had no idea who He was. There were too many people in that busy place to find Him. It looked like He was gone!

I was so excited to be able to walk. I walked down the street. I stopped by the temple. There, the man who told me to pick up my mat found me again. That's when I learned He was Jesus. Jesus had used His power from God to heal me. Jesus urged me to do what was right. He said, "You are well now. Stop sinning or something worse may happen to you." Now that I knew who had healed me, I took off walking again. I couldn't wait to tell the Jews it was Jesus who made me well. Jesus had done a miracle for me.

Invite a child to be the man at the pool and ask you questions about the story. The other children can tell if you have a right or wrong answer to each question. Possible questions follow with right and wrong answers:

Where was I lying? (by a pool; on a porch roof)
How long had I been sick? (38 years; 38 days)
What did Jesus ask me? (Want to get well? Want to go home?)
What did Jesus tell me? (Stand up; sit down and listen.)
What did the Jews ask me? (Who told you to walk? Where do you live?)
What did I tell the Jews? (Jesus did it; a priest did it.)
Summary questions: **What miracle did Jesus do?** (helped a man walk) **What did the healed man tell the Jews?** (Jesus made me well.)

▼ Bible Verse ▲

Doctor Luke wrote a book to tell many things Jesus did and said. The verses he wrote in Luke 8:38, 39 help us remember how a man from Gadara told people what Jesus had done and said. Let's take turns being Doctor Luke!

Let the children find and read Luke 8:38, 39. Ask for volunteers to say the verses with a friend or by themselves. If needed, give pairs of children a verse pyramid (page 281) to help them practice saying the verses from memory.

Allow children who can recite the verses to take turns being and interviewing Doctor Luke. Give each interviewer a question card from page 286. In the interviews, Luke can sit at a table, pretending to write his book about Jesus with a pretend scroll and quill.

Who do you think Jesus is? Why are you writing a book about Jesus? (to tell what Jesus did, what He said) **What are you writing in Luke 8:38, 39? What do want us to remember when we read these verses?**

Purpose
Recite and explain Luke 8:38, 39.

Materials
interview questions printed at the top of page 286
scroll (rolled paper)
quill (feather tied to a pen)
verse pyramid from page 281 (optional)

▼ Bible and Me ▲

Telling about Jesus is talking about things Jesus did or said in the Bible. The man in our verses told what Jesus had done because he was excited about what had happened and because he wanted to obey Jesus. Let's learn one more reason why we tell.

Form a circle around a child. Together, do the rap on page 286 to remember why we tell about Jesus. At the end of the rap, the child in the center chooses someone to answer: **1. Why do we tell about Jesus? 2. What can you tell about Jesus?** (Give each child at least one turn to be in the center.)

What kinds of things do we say when we tell about Jesus? (what He did or said) **Why do we tell about Jesus? What is your favorite thing to tell about Jesus?**

Purpose
Tell why we want to tell about Jesus.

Materials
copies of page 286

▼ Bible Project ▲

Telling about Jesus means talking about the things Jesus did or said in the Bible. Our sandwich boards will be a fun way to talk about Jesus to other people.

Help the children color and finish their designs on poster board. As each child finishes his boards, cut equal lengths of string or cord to tie the boards together over the child's shoulders. Make two holes in each piece of poster board large enough for the string to go through. See the illustration on page 267. Tie the boards together and try the sandwich on the child. Adjust as necessary. If you have time, let the children practice wearing the boards and talking to each other about Jesus.

Purpose
Tell about Jesus.

Materials
materials to make sandwich boards (unit page 267)

▼ Bible Sharing ▲

Squirt cheese on crackers or ask the children to whisper things from this unit to "squirt" on a cracker ("38," a happy face, a sad face, and so on). Each child can tell a friend something Jesus did or said using what is on her cracker or give the friend that cracker.

Let the snack be a great time of sharing about Jesus. Then sing favorite songs about Jesus.

Purpose
Share how Jesus' miracles help you tell about Him.

Materials
a snack of crackers and squirt cheese
CD or cassette of songs about Jesus
CD or cassette player

Jesus Brings Lazarus Back Alive

John 11:1-45

Lesson Goals

- Tell what miracle Jesus did when He went to Bethany.
- Tell why Jesus made Lazarus come back alive.
- Recite and explain Luke 8:38, 39.
- Tell what makes it easy to talk about Jesus.
- Tell about Jesus.

▼ Bible Search ▲

In our story, Jesus does a miracle to help two sisters who were very sad. Let's find out how other people in this story felt.

Group the children into four search teams. Guide each team to find its Scripture verse in John and answer the question. Then let each team report.

Who was worried? Who was crying? Who was sad? Who was glad to be alive? Since Jesus is the Son of God, what did He do to help these people?

▼ Bible Story ▲

Display a stone. The land where Bible people lived had lots of stones—big ones, little ones, all sizes. Listen to see what stones were used for in this story.

"Jesus Brings Lazarus Back Alive"

"Come quickly," the messenger panted. "Lazarus, the one you love, is sick. His sisters beg you to come and help him." But when Jesus heard the message, He waited two more days before He decided to visit His dear friends.

When Jesus said He was ready to go, His followers began to feel worried. Bethany was usually a happy place to visit. But not now. Jews near Bethany had just tried to kill Jesus with stones. If Jesus went back, they might try again to kill Him. Jesus' followers didn't want Jesus to go. So Jesus told them that Lazarus was dead. He wanted to go to Bethany to bring Lazarus back alive. This would help people believe that Jesus was from God.

When Jesus and His followers arrived outside Bethany, Lazarus had been dead, in a tomb, four days. Many Jews in Bethany were showing their sadness with Mary and Martha. When Martha heard Jesus had come, she hurried to meet Him. As she ran, her sad heart wished Jesus had come sooner. When she reached Jesus, she said, "If You had been here, my brother would not have died. But I know that even now God will give You anything You ask."

Jesus reassured her, "Your brother will rise and live again." But Martha thought Jesus was talking about living in Heaven.

Martha went back to tell Mary that Jesus had come and wanted to see her. When Mary jumped up, the Jews in the house thought she was going to the tomb to cry. But instead, she hurried out of town to find her Teacher. With tears in her eyes she fell at Jesus' feet and spoke the same words as Martha, "Lord, if You had been here, my brother would not have died."

Memory Block
"The man that Jesus had healed begged to go with him. But Jesus sent him away, saying, 'Go back home and tell people what God did for you.' So the man went all over town telling how much Jesus had done for him" (Luke 8:38, 39).

Purpose
Tell what miracle Jesus did when He went to Bethany.

Materials
Bibles
copies of page 287
pencils

Purpose
Tell why Jesus made Lazarus come back alive.

Materials
a stone
copies of page 288 cut apart

When Jesus saw Mary and the Jews crying, He began to feel deep sadness also. He thought about how much He loved His good friend Lazarus. Finally He was able to ask, "Where have you laid him?" As they told Jesus to come and see, tears came to Jesus' eyes and Jesus cried too. Some Jews who saw Jesus crying said, "See how much He loved him." Others just wondered why He hadn't saved Lazarus from dying.

As the sad group of people walked up to Lazarus' tomb, they could see the large stone blocking the entrance. When Jesus asked them to move the stone away, Martha spoke quickly, "But, Lord, it has been four days since he died. There will be a bad smell." So Jesus reminded Martha that if she believed, they could see what God's power can do.

After they moved the stone, Jesus looked up and spoke to God, "Father, thank You for always hearing me pray. I want the people around me to believe that You sent me." Then in His loud voice, Jesus gave a strong command, "Lazarus, come out!" With their eyes clouded with tears, the Jews, Mary, and Martha waited and watched the darkened entrance to the tomb. And then they began to cry again. Only this time they were crying tears of joy because Lazarus was standing in the opening of the tomb! He was still wrapped with burial cloths around his hands and feet and face. Joyfully, Jesus spoke again, "Take the cloth off of him and let him go!" Lazarus was alive!

State the words (on eight stones, page 288) in order and let the children make a sentence about the story with each word. Then shuffle the cards and let the children work together to put them in order. They can use the cards to tell you the story.

Summary questions: **What miracle did Jesus do?** (He made Lazarus alive again.) **Why did Jesus make Lazarus come back alive?** (to show Jesus is from God)

▼ Bible Verse ▲

Purpose
Recite and explain Luke 8:38, 39.

Materials
Bibles
six index cards
six empty two-liter bottles
tape
ball
verse pyramid from page 281
   (optional)

Before class, print the following questions, one per index card: Where can you read about a man from Gadara who told about Jesus? Who wrote the book where you can find the Bible verses? Print the following questions two times, one question on each of two cards: What does Luke 8:38, 39 say? What does Luke 8:38, 39 help us remember to do?

Doctor Luke wrote a book to tell what Jesus did and said. In our verses, a man from Gadara told people all over town what Jesus did and said. We can be like Luke and the man from Gadara when we tell about Jesus.

Let the children find and read Luke 8:38, 39. Ask for volunteers to say the verses with a friend or by themselves. If needed, give pairs of children a set of the triangle sides of the verse pyramid (page 281) to help them practice saying the verses from memory.

Play a game to help children recite and explain the verses. Tape the six cards to six empty two-liter bottles. The children can take turns rolling a ball toward the bottles and answering the question they knock down first.

▼ Bible and Me ▲

Put slips of paper with the following unfinished statements in balloons. 1) I like to tell about Jesus because He . . . ; 2) One thing I can tell about Jesus is . . . ; 3) One way I can tell about Jesus is . . . . Blow up at least 2-3 balloons per child. Keep the balloons in a large trash bag until the activity.

Telling about Jesus is talking about things Jesus did or said in the Bible. It's easy to do, because we have lots of things to say. We have lots of fun ways to say them. And we have our most special friend to talk about.

Use a balloon game to help children have fun telling about Jesus. The children can take turns popping balloons and finishing the sentence in each one. Each child should pop 2-3 balloons.

What kinds of things do we say when we tell about Jesus? (what He did or said) **Who do we tell about Jesus? What are all the ways we can tell about Jesus? What is your favorite thing to tell about Jesus?**

Purpose
Tell what makes it easy to talk about Jesus.

Materials
2-3 balloons for each child
slips of paper
marker
a large trash bag in which to keep balloons

▼ Bible Project ▲

Telling about Jesus is talking about things Jesus did or said in the Bible. It's easy to do, because we have lots of things to say. We have planned a fun way to talk about our most special friend.

If you have not planned to wear the sandwich boards during this session (at a mall or in a park or another place with many people), use this time to practice wearing the boards and to plan a time and place to wear them in your community. Make certain to obtain permission wherever you choose to wear them. Then have fun talking about Jesus!

Purpose
Tell about Jesus.

Materials
materials for making the sandwich boards if children still need supplies to complete the project

▼ Bible Sharing ▲

Offer the children a snack of wrapped candies. To get one, the child has to tell you, "Candy, come forth!" Then each can unwrap his candy when you say, "Unwrap them!" This will help the children remember one more amazing thing that Jesus did.

Play a game to share more things to tell about Jesus. The first child begins, "I am going to tell about Jesus, and I'm going to tell about (an amazing thing Jesus did or said)." The second child begins in the same way, telling what the first child said and adding another amazing thing to tell. Play the game until each child has had a turn to tell something. Make this another fun time to tell about Jesus!

To close, sing favorite songs the children have learned about Jesus.

Purpose
Share how Jesus' miracles help you tell about Him.

Materials
a snack of wrapped candies
CD or cassette of songs about Jesus
CD or cassette player

Bible Story

Cut apart the Bible story strips.
Link them together to make a chain.

glue	glue	glue	glue	glue	glue	glue	glue	glue	glue
Man lives in caves and breaks out of chains.	Jesus sails across the lake to Gadara.	Man runs and falls down before Jesus.	Jesus commands demons to leave.	Demons beg to live in some pigs.	2,000 pigs rush into the lake and drown.	People are afraid and ask Jesus to leave.	Man wants to go with Jesus.	Jesus asks the man to go and tell what God has done.	Jesus sails across the lake to Galilee.

UNIT 11, LESSON 44

Bible Verse

Find and read Luke 8:38, 39.
Number the sentences in the small triangles.
Cut apart and tape together the verse pyramid.
Learn the order of the sentences.

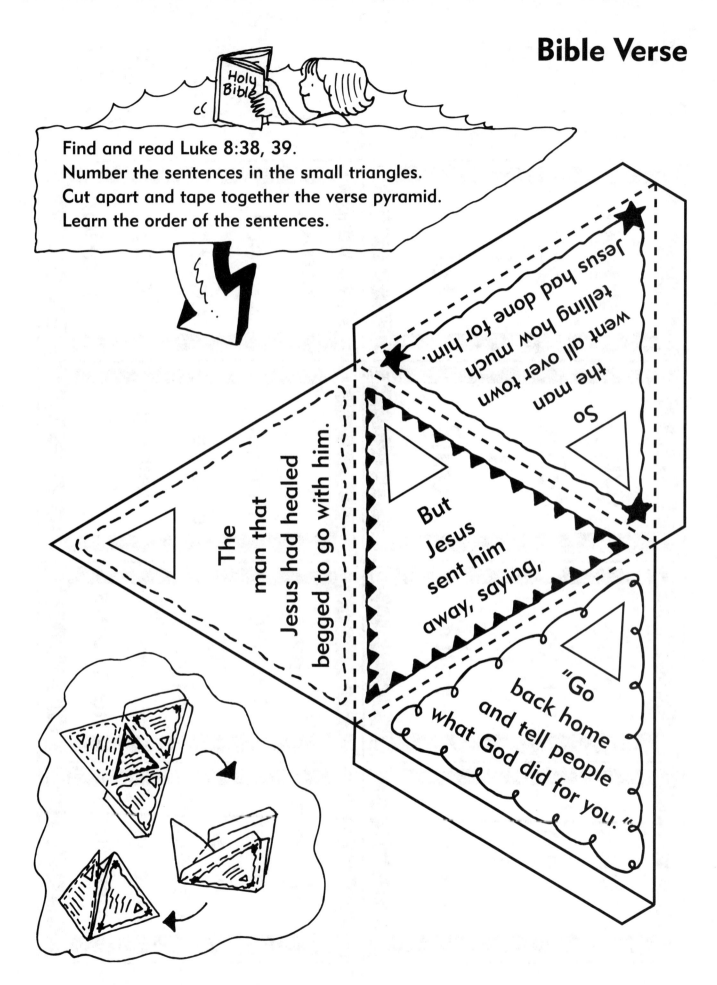

So
the man
went all over town
telling how much
Jesus had done for him.

The
man that
Jesus had healed
begged to go with him.

But
Jesus
sent him
away, saying,

"Go
back home
and tell people
what God did for you."

Bible and Me

Cut apart the cards.
Play a matching game with friends.

cut

Where can I tell?	home, school, church, play, vacation
When can I tell?	morning, afternoon, evening
Who can I tell?	my family, my friends, my neighbors
What can I tell?	Jesus can walk on water. Jesus said to remember Him.

 Unit 11, Lesson 44

Bible Search

Choose a Bible Search card.

Answer each question with a number.

cut

1. Find Matthew 14:17.
The followers had
_____ loaves of
bread and _____
fish.

2. Find Matthew 14:20.
There were _____
baskets of uneaten
food.

1. Find Mark 6:38.
The followers had
_____ loaves of
bread and _____
fish.

2. Find Mark 6:43.
There were _____
baskets of uneaten
food.

1. Find Luke 9:13.
The followers had
_____ loaves of
bread and _____
fish.

2. Find Luke 9:17.
There were _____
baskets of uneaten
food.

1. Find John 6:9.
The followers had
_____ loaves of
bread and _____
fish.

2. Find John 6:13.
There were _____
baskets of eaten food.

Bible Project

Use these words to make a sandwich board.
Or design your own sandwich board.

Jesus ♥ is ♥ Alive

UNIT 11, LESSON 45

Bible Search

Find John 5:3, 5, 8 in your Bible.
Color the wrong words in the sentences
below with a dark color.

John 5:3

Many [sick] [well] people
were [sitting] [lying] on
the [porches] [chairs] beside
the [river] [pool] .

John 5:5

There was a [boy] [man] who
had been sick for [38] [83] years.

John 5:8

Jesus told him to [stand] [sit]
and [stay] [go] .

UNIT 11, LESSON 46 ▼ 285

Bible Verse

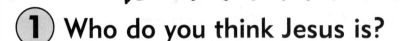

Use these questions to interview Doctor Luke.

1. Who do you think Jesus is?

2. Why are you writing a book about Jesus?

3. What are you writing in Luke 8:38, 39?

4. What do you want us to remember when we read these verses?

Bible and Me

Learn this rhyme to remember to tell about Jesus.

Use these verses about the unit stories to add to the rhyme.

We tell about Jesus because He is God's Son. We know many things to tell. You can tell us one!

Jesus made the demons leave; He helped the Gadarene man. We can tell this amazing thing. We can tell it— yes, we can!

Jesus used a small boy's lunch to feed 5,000 men. Jesus does amazing things. Let's tell this one again.

Jesus healed a man at a pool. He helped him stand and walk. Just another amazing thing to make our mouths talk.

Jesus is the Son of God. He brought Lazarus back alive. Jesus does amazing things. This makes four; tell five!

 Unit 11, Lesson 46

Bible Search

Find and read verses about people in the Bible story. How did they feel?

Read John 11:8.

Read John 11:33.

Who was worried?

Who was crying?

Who was sad?

Who was glad to be alive?

Read John 11:38.

Read John 11:44.

Bible Story

Cut out the stones.
Use them to tell the Bible story.

sick

two
more
days

come
out

Bethany

four
days

believe

Jesus
cried

stone

 UNIT 11, LESSON 47

Jesus' Resurrection is Good News for Me to Tell

Lessons 48–52

Unit Memory Block

"Jesus said to the followers, 'Go everywhere in the world. Tell the Good News to everyone'" (Mark 16:15).

Memory Challenge

"Then Jesus came to them and said, "All power in heaven and on earth is given to me. So go and make followers of all people in the world. Baptize them in the name of the Father and the Son and the Holy Spirit. Teach them to obey everything that I have told you. You can be sure that I will be with you always. I will continue with you until the end of the world.'" (Matthew 28:18-20).

48 Jesus Is Killed on a Cross
Matthew 26:36, 37, 57-66; 27:45; John 18:28—19:22, 38-42
The sad part of Jesus' Good News is that Jesus died on a cross. Jesus wants us to tell His Good News.

49 Jesus Is Alive
Matthew 28:1-11; Mark 16:1-7
The happy part of Jesus' Good News is that Jesus came back alive. Jesus wants us to tell His Good News.

50 Jesus Appears on the Emmaus Road
Luke 24:13-35
Two men learned the happy part of Jesus' Good News. He is alive! Jesus wants us to tell His Good News.

51 Jesus Appears by Lake Galilee
John 21:1-19
Jesus helped His followers catch fish and showed them He was alive. That's His Good News! Jesus wants us to tell His Good News.

52 Jesus' Command: Go, Tell
Matthew 28:16-20; Mark 16:15, 16, 19, 20; Luke 24:50-53; Acts 1:6-12
Jesus told His followers to tell the Good News to everyone. That means Jesus wants us to tell His Good News also.

By the end of the unit, the leaders and learners will

KNOW After Jesus died, He came back alive. Now we can live forever! That's the Good News.

FEEL excited about Jesus' Good News!

DO Tell Jesus' Good News!

Unit Value

Jesus has Good News for us to tell everyone: we can live forever! Of all the good things we can do in life, helping people know and respond to Jesus' Good News is the most significant. The stories in this unit will help children be able to follow Jesus' command to tell His Good News. The first story is the sad part of Jesus' Good News, His death. The second story is the happy part of Jesus' Good News, His resurrection. The next two stories prove the Good News, that Jesus came back alive. The last story and the unit memory block give us the command to tell Jesus' Good News wherever we go.

In Unit 11, the children worked on a project to help them feel eager to tell what Jesus has done and said. This unit builds on that ability to tell. It focuses on telling the most special things Jesus did: His death and resurrection. First the children will learn what Jesus' Good News is. Then they will work on the difference between telling about Jesus and telling Jesus' Good News. As the unit progresses, they will discover why it is important to tell the Good News and why we can have a positive attitude about this important job. The ages-old story of "Jesus and Me" comes to its proper conclusion when the children can say to their friends, "I want to tell you about 'Jesus and me,' so you can live forever with Him too!"

▼ Bible Project ▲

Good News Banners

Prepare the burlap ahead of time. Decide on the size of the banners, cut the burlap, and fringe three sides. Turn the top edge under, leaving a pocket to insert a small dowel, and sew in place. Secure the fringed edges by sewing with a large stitch. Enlarge the patterns on this page and on pages 309-311 by tracing them on transparency sheets and projecting them onto poster board. You will be able to make a variety of sizes using this method. If possible, make a sample banner to show the children.

The learners will design and make burlap and felt banners illustrating Jesus' Good News. Each child can work on a separate banner or you may ask children to work in pairs or larger teams. Make personal banners for the children to hang in their homes and/or work on large banners to hang in the church building. Perhaps the adult leaders could work on one large banner to keep in the classroom to remind the children to tell Jesus' Good News.

Show children the sample banner, the banner picture on this page, and the poster board patterns you made to give them ideas of what to include on their banners. Children can design their banner and then trace the patterns they choose onto the felt. Use sharp scissors to cut the felt and use Tacky® glue to attach it quickly to the burlap. Supervise closely (the glue is not recommended for children but dries quickly).

Week 1: Design banners. Provide patterns to inspire ideas.
Week 2: Trace designs onto felt.
Week 3: Cut designs; use no glue yet.
Week 4: Glue final designs.
Week 5: Add details to complete banners (perhaps glitter or rickrack). Display and tell Jesus' Good News. Tell how they will use the banner to tell family and friends Jesus' Good News.

Materials
patterns on this page
copies of pages 309-311
markers
poster board
scissors
felt
Tacky® glue
items to decorate banners
    (glitter or rickrack)
burlap
small dowels
sewing machine or needle and
    thread
transparency sheets and
    overhead projector
(optional)

Jesus Is Killed on a Cross

Matthew 26:36, 37, 57-66; 27:45; John 18:28–19:22, 38-42

Lesson Goals
- Tell the sad part of Jesus' Good News.
- Tell why God planned for Jesus to die.
- Begin to memorize Mark 16:15.
- Tell what Jesus' Good News is.
- Tell Jesus' Good News.

> **Memory Block**
> "Jesus said to the followers, 'Go everywhere in the world. Tell the Good News to everyone'" (Mark 16:15).

▼ Bible Search ▲

In our story, more than one person was part of Jesus' death. Let's search in our Bibles to see who was involved.

Give each pair of children page 306. Guide the children to search John 19:15, 16, 18 for people involved in Jesus' death. Let them work together to find the Scripture verses, answer the questions, and check their answers.

Who wanted to have Jesus killed? What did they say? Who gave permission for Jesus to be killed? Who put Jesus on the cross to die? What is the sad part of these verses? (Jesus died.)

> **Purpose**
> Tell the sad part of Jesus' Good News.
>
> **Materials**
> Bibles
> copies of page 306
> colored pencils

▼ Bible Story ▲

What's the worst punishment for you? Display reminders: TV listings guide (no TV), chair in corner (sit in chair), calendar (miss a trip). **How would it feel if someone said, "I'll take your punishment for you?" Listen to what happened to Jesus when He was punished, even though He had done no wrong.**

> **Purpose**
> Tell why God planned for Jesus to die.
>
> **Materials**
> a TV listings guide
> chair
> a calendar

"Jesus Is Killed on a Cross"

On a dark, dark night for Jesus, He went to pray in a garden named Gethsemane. He asked Peter, James, and John to be near Him. Then, in the darkness, people came with swords and clubs to arrest Jesus and take Him away to the house of Caiaphas, the High Priest. Trembling with fear, Peter followed and waited outside the house to see what would happen.

Inside the house, the Jewish leaders tried to find a reason to kill Jesus. All through the night, they listened to people make up lies about Jesus, but no one said anything that was bad enough for them to kill Jesus. Finally Caiaphas commanded Jesus to tell if He was the Christ, the Son of God. When Jesus said, "Yes I am," Caiaphas said that was enough reason to kill Jesus! Caiaphas thought anyone who said he was from God should die. The other Jews agreed, "He is guilty and must die." Some spit at Him and watched it drip down His face. Others stung Him with slaps of their hands. But Jesus never hit back or said anything unkind.

In the early morning, the Jews tied Jesus and led Him to the palace of Pilate, the Roman Governor. Pilate had to give his permission before the Jews could kill Jesus. When Pilate came out to ask what Jesus had done wrong, the Jews said, "He is a criminal. That's why we brought him to you." So Pilate took Jesus inside, but he found no reason to kill Him. Pilate tried to get the Jews to let Jesus go free.

But the Jews would not change their minds.

So Pilate ordered the Roman soldiers to take Jesus away and whip Him. The soldiers used thorns to make a crown. When they pushed it down into Jesus' head, blood ran down His face. They put a purple robe around Him and pretended to make Him a king. "Hail, King of the Jews." They laughed and slapped Him in the face.

When the soldiers were through, Pilate brought Jesus back to the Jews. The priests and guards shouted, "Kill Him on a cross. Kill Him on a cross." But Pilate was afraid to kill a man who had done no wrong. Again he tried to get the Jews to let Jesus go free. But the Jews said if Pilate let Jesus go free, then Pilate was not a friend of Caesar—the highest Roman leader. They argued until late in the morning. Then, in exasperation, Pilate sat down to give his decision. He said, "Here is your king." The people screamed in anger, "Take Him away! Take Him away! Kill Him on a cross!" So Pilate gave Jesus to them to be killed on a cross.

Pilate's soldiers made Jesus carry a rough, wood cross part of the way to a hill outside Jerusalem. There, the soldiers pounded nails through Jesus' hands and feet to hang Him on the cross. Pilate put a sign on the cross: JESUS OF NAZARETH, THE KING OF THE JEWS. As Jesus hung there, right in the middle of the day it turned dark for three hours. And then, Jesus died.

Later, two of Jesus' friends, Nicodemus and Joseph of Arimethea, laid His body in a new, dark tomb. The whole day was a dark time for Jesus' followers.

Jesus did not deserve to die. But it was God's plan for Jesus to die to take our punishment! That is the sad part of Jesus' Good News.

Ask "Who am I?" for each review riddle.
I went to Gethsemane to pray. (Jesus)
People brought Jesus to my house at night. (Caiaphas, High Priest)
We tried to find a reason to kill Jesus. (Jewish leaders)
I tried to get the Jews to let Jesus go free. (Pilate)
We made fun of Jesus with a crown of thorns and a purple robe. (soldiers)
We told Pilate, "Take Him away. Kill Him on the cross." (Jews)
We nailed Jesus to a cross. (soldiers)
We laid Jesus' body in a new tomb. (Joseph and Nicodemus)
Summary questions: **What is the sad part of Jesus' Good News?** (Jesus died on the cross.) **Why did God plan for Jesus to die?** (to take our punishment: Good News!)

▼ Bible Verse ▲

Purpose
Begin to memorize Mark 16:15.

Materials
Bibles
copies of page 307
scissors

At the end of Jesus' life on earth, He gave His followers an important job. One of Jesus' followers named Mark wrote the instructions in his book.

Let the children find and read Mark 16:15. Find the page number for Mark in the table of contents. Then find a big number 16 for the chapter and a small number 15 for the verse.

Use page 307 to let pairs of children do a globe jigsaw puzzle of the verse. Guide children to cut out the puzzle pieces of the globe and assemble the puzzle. After they read the verse, they can remove a piece, say the verse, remove a piece, say the verse, and so on, to begin memorizing it.

Use the following questions to talk about Mark 16:15. **Who wrote down the words in this verse? Who spoke the words in this verse? What are some places in the world you know about? What is the sad part of the Good News in our story?** (Jesus died.)

▼ Bible and Me ▲

Jesus' Good News has one sad part and two happy parts. In our story we learned the sad part—Jesus died. The happy parts are that Jesus came back alive and now we can live forever. That's the Good News!

Small groups can use molding dough (or art materials) to make symbols of the three parts of Jesus' Good News (examples: a cross, an empty tomb, and a mansion). While they work, play songs about Jesus' Good News.

Guide the children to use their symbols to tell what Jesus' Good News is. **What is the sad part of Jesus' Good News? What is one happy part of Jesus' Good News? What is the other happy part of Jesus' Good News? Who can tell me all three parts of Jesus' Good News?**

Purpose
Tell what Jesus' Good News is.

Materials
molding dough or a variety of art materials
CD or cassette with songs about Jesus' Good News (His death and resurrection)
CD or cassette player

▼ Bible Project ▲

See the instructions on page 290 for preparing the burlap banners.
Jesus' Good News has three parts: Jesus died, He came back alive, and He lives in Heaven where we can live too. We are going to make banners to help us tell Jesus' Good News.

Share with enthusiasm details of the unit project. Show children the sample banner you made or the picture of a banner on page 290. When you have explained about the banners, guide the children to design on paper what they want to include in their banners. Each banner should include words or symbols that tell about Jesus' Good News. Display the poster board patterns you made from page 290 and pages 309-311 to give the children ideas.

Purpose
Tell Jesus' Good News.

Materials
materials to make banners (listed on page 290)
patterns and pictures (from pages 290 and 309-311, enlarged if possible)
sketch paper
pencils
erasers

▼ Bible Sharing ▲

What part of Jesus' Good News do our snacks remind us of? (Jesus died on a cross.) **What are the other two parts of Jesus' Good News?**

Let each child share with the large group how he designed his banner. Then sing songs about Jesus' Good News used during Bible and Me.

Purpose
Share why Jesus' resurrection is Good News for you to tell.

Materials
a snack of tradition bread called "Hot Cross Buns" (bun with currants or raisins and a cross on top formed with icing)
CD or cassette used during Bible and Me
CD or cassette player

Jesus Is Alive

Matthew 28:1-11; Mark 16:1-7

Memory Block
"Jesus said to the followers, 'Go everywhere in the world. Tell the Good News to everyone'" (Mark 16:15).

Lesson Goals
- Tell the happy part of Jesus' Good News.
- Tell what the women did when they left the empty tomb.
- Memorize Mark 16:15.
- Tell the difference between telling about Jesus and telling Jesus' Good News.
- Tell Jesus' Good News.

▼ Bible Search ▲

In our story, there is a lot of happy news. Let's find some!
Guide the children to find Matthew 28:5-7 in their Bibles. Read the verses slowly as the children follow along. Then discuss the verses.

How did the angel think the women felt? Who were the women looking for? What had happened to Jesus? What did the angel tell the women to do? What did the angel tell the woman to say? What is the happy part of Jesus' Good News? (He is alive.)

Allow the children to act out the verses, playing the part of the women and the angel. The angel can read his part from the Bible verses.

Purpose
Tell the happy part of Jesus' Good News.

Materials
Bibles
Bibles times costumes (optional)

▼ Bible Story ▲

Before the session, cut out four copies of the tomb on page 311 and glue or tape it to index cards. Print the following phrases on the cards: earthquake, angel rolls away stone, women come to tomb, angel speaks to women to go and tell.

Display the light bulb. **What is the brightest light you can think of? Listen to see what the brightest thing in this story is.**

"Jesus Is Alive"

Very early in the morning, our footsteps pattered quietly on the street as we hurried outside the walls of Jerusalem. It was the first day of the week, the day after our Sabbath. Our faces were sad because our best friend, Jesus, had been killed on a cross on Friday. Two of Jesus' followers had laid Him in a new tomb, but now we wanted to get there as soon as possible to finish preparing His body to be buried. There were three of us—Mary, the mother of James, Salome, and myself, Mary Magdalene. As light began to show on the edge of the sky, we talked quietly about what we must do. "There is a large stone covering the entrance of the tomb. Who will move the stone for us?"

But before we got to the tomb, all of our sadness turned to fear when the ground under us began moving. It was an earthquake! And then, at the entrance to the tomb, we saw an angel of the Lord come down from Heaven. After rolling the stone away from the entrance, he sat down on the stone. The brightness of the angel was enough to blind us. He was shining as bright as lightning, and his clothes were as white as snow. Around him the guards who had been at the tomb had become like dead men with fear frozen on their faces.

Our question about the stone was answered, but now we had even more ques-

Purpose
Tell what the women did when they left the empty tomb.

Materials
a light bulb
four copies of page 311
index cards
glue or tape
scissors
marker

tions. What was happening? Why was the angel here? What should we do now? Since that huge stone was moved, it was possible to go inside. We wanted to see Jesus, so carefully, cautiously we entered. But Jesus was not there. Instead there was an angel wearing a white robe, sitting on the right side of the tomb. We were scared.

Before we could run away, the angel spoke, "Don't be afraid. I know that you are looking for Jesus, the one who was killed on the cross. But He is not here. He has risen from death as He said He would. Come and see the place where His body was. And go quickly and tell His followers. Say to them, 'Jesus has risen from death.'"

What did the angel say? Did he say Jesus was alive? But how? And when? And why? Our fears wanted to turn to joy, but it was all too confusing. Shaking and trembling, we turned and ran from the tomb. Our first thought was to find other followers of Jesus and tell them what we had seen. But suddenly, as we were running someone met us and said, "Good Morning." When we looked up into His face, we knew immediately it was Jesus! Oh, it was our Jesus. Tears filled our eyes as we fell before Him and worshiped Him. Could it really be? Was it really true? Our fears must have still shown on our faces. For Jesus said, "Don't be afraid. Go and tell my brothers to go to Galilee. They will see me there." Oh, it had to be true. Jesus had died but now He was back alive. We ran to tell the Good News.

Give the phrases you printed on index cards to the children. Let them work together to put the phrases in order. Then act out the story.

Summary questions: **What is the happy part of Jesus' Good News?** (Jesus is alive.) **What did the women do when they learned the Good News?** (told the followers)

▼ Bible Verse ▲

Jesus gave His followers a very important command in our Bible verse. One of Jesus' followers named Mark wrote it in his book.

Let the children find and read Mark 16:15. Then pairs of children can use clothespins to attach the verse puzzle pieces in order on yarn tied between two chairs. Because clothespins are heavier than the puzzle pieces, put the pins under the yarn and the puzzle pieces above the yarn. The children can remove a piece, say the verse, remove a piece, say the verse, and so on, to help them memorize it. For variety, use a stopwatch to see how long it takes each group to get their puzzle pieces in order.

Use these questions to talk about Mark 16:15. **Who spoke the words in this verse? What is the sad part of the Good News?** (Jesus died.) **What is a happy part of the Good News from our story?** (Jesus is alive.) **Where in the world could you tell Jesus' Good News?**

Purpose
Memorize Mark 16:15.

Materials
Bibles, verse puzzles from page 307 used in Lesson 48
spring-type clothespins
yarn or string
stopwatch

▼ Bible and Me ▲

Before the session, prepare the "Twist & Tell" game. Use the masking tape to outline four rows of four 10" x 10" squares on the floor. Tape a symbol (from pages 310-312) in each square. Copy the game cards from page 309. If you have more than eight children, make more grids on the floor so everyone can have a turn to play.

We know that telling about Jesus means talking about what Jesus did and said. But when we tell Jesus' Good News, we are talking about the most special thing Jesus did: He died and came back alive so we can live forever. That is Good News! There are three parts of this Good News.

Purpose
Tell the difference between telling about Jesus and telling Jesus' Good News.

Materials
copies of pages 309-311
scissors
masking tape

1) A cross reminds us He died. 2) An empty tomb reminds us He is alive. 3) Heaven reminds us we can live forever.

Play Twist & Tell (variation of Twister). Players can remove their shoes. The first four players stand on each side of the grid and follow the leader's directions for where to place their hands and feet. If the leader says, "Put your right hand on Good News to tell," players put their right hands only on a symbol of Good News. If the leader says, "Put your left foot on anything Jesus did or said," the players put their left feet on any symbol. The goal is to follow the directions of the leader eight times without falling down. Then switch places. Players who fall down get to tell the leader the difference between telling about Jesus and telling about Jesus' Good News.

Summarize the activity with questions. **What is the sad part of Jesus' Good News? What are the two happy parts of Jesus' Good News? Who can tell me all three parts of Jesus' Good News? What is the difference between telling about Jesus and telling Jesus' Good News?** (Telling about Jesus is talking about what He did or said. The Good News is the most important thing Jesus did. It is what He commanded us to tell.)

▼ Bible Project ▲

We know Jesus' Good News is the most special thing Jesus did: He died and came back alive so we can live forever. That's Good News!

Guide the children to transfer their sketched designs onto felt. Children may use the poster board patterns you made, or they may use their own sketches. They should trace around the designs on felt with a fine tipped black marker. To avoid seeing black lines, place the design on the felt upside down. Provide assistance as necessary.

Purpose
Tell Jesus' Good News.

Materials
materials to work on banners
(listed on page 290)
fine-tipped black markers

▼ Bible Sharing ▲

Children get three jelly beans if they can tell the three parts of Jesus' Good News. They get one more for every other thing they can tell that Jesus did or said.

Sing songs that tell Jesus' Good News. Guide the children to thank God for Jesus' Good News. "Thank You for Jesus' death. Thank You for Jesus' resurrection! We are so glad Jesus lives! Help us tell Jesus' Good News. In Jesus' name, amen."

Purpose
Share why Jesus' resurrection is Good News for you to tell.

Materials
a snack of jelly beans
CD or cassette of songs that
tell Jesus' Good News
CD or cassette player

Jesus Appears on the Emmaus Road

Luke 24:13-35

Lesson Goals

- Tell who saw Jesus on the Emmaus Road.
- Tell what the two men did when they realized it was Jesus.
- Recite Mark 16:15.
- Tell why it is important for people to know Jesus' Good News.
- Tell Jesus' Good News.

Memory Block
"Jesus said to the followers, 'Go everywhere in the world. Tell the Good News to everyone'" (Mark 16:15).

▼ Bible Search ▲

On the day Jesus came back alive, He walked with Cleopas and another man on the road to Emmaus. Jesus did lots of things to prove to them He really was alive.

Give the children copies of page 312. Guide them to find Luke 24 in their Bibles. Together find each verse listed on the page and complete the activity to discover what Jesus did to show He was alive.

Who saw Jesus on the Emmaus road? What kinds of things did Jesus do to show He was alive?

Purpose
Tell who saw Jesus on the Emmaus road.

Materials
Bibles
copies of page 312
pencils

▼ Bible Story ▲

Display the map. **Have you ever walked seven miles? How long do you think it takes to walk seven miles? Two times in our story, two men walked seven miles. Listen to see which trip took the least amount of time.**

"Jesus Appears on the Emmaus Road"

"I just don't understand," I told my friend Cleopas. "I know Jesus was dead. But they said the tomb was empty this morning." We shuffled sadly down the seven-mile road to Emmaus. We planned to reach there by night, but it seemed like it was taking forever.

We were still talking sadly when another man joined us. We didn't know Him and we didn't ask His name. We just kept talking about all that had happened. The other man asked us, "What are these things you are talking about while you walk?" We stopped in the middle of the road, and with deep sadness, Cleopas answered, "You must be the only man in Jerusalem who does not know what just happened here."

We explained we were talking about Jesus of Nazareth. We said, "He was a prophet from God to the people. He did many powerful things. But the Jewish leaders and leading priests judged Him and let Him be killed. They nailed Him to a cross. It has been three days since He died. But this morning, the first day of the week, some women told us amazing things. They went early to the tomb where Jesus had been laid. When they arrived, they did not find the body there. Instead they saw angels who said that Jesus was alive! Some of our friends went to the tomb and found just what the women said. They did not see Jesus either."

We continued our sad walk to Emmaus. Then in a very special way, the other man began to explain how the prophets in the Old Testament had written that

Purpose
Tell what the two men did when they realized it was Jesus.

Materials
a map of your area with a distance of seven miles highlighted or print the number 7 on paper
copies of page 313
pencils

these things would happen to Jesus. He started with what Moses said and went through all the things the other prophets said about Jesus.

The time flew by and too soon, we came to the house in Emmaus where we were going to stay. The other man was going on, so we invited Him, "Stay with us, it is late; it is almost night." He came inside to eat the evening meal with us. After we sat down, He took some bread, gave thanks for the food, and divided it among us. At that moment, Cleopas and I realized who He was. It was Jesus! Our arms and legs tingled with excitement as we realized He really was alive. But then He was gone! Our words tumbled out, "When Jesus talked to us on the road, it felt like a fire burning in us. It was exciting when He explained the true meaning of the Scriptures."

Now we understood that God had planned for Jesus to die and come back alive. We jumped up and headed back to Jerusalem. Even the darkness of the night didn't stop us. We had Good News to share. Jesus was alive and we had seen Him. Back in Jerusalem we found the eleven apostles and others gathered together. They told us, "The Lord really has risen from death. He showed himself to Simon!" We responded with the same joy, "Yes, He met us on the road. We recognized Him when He divided the bread for our meal. Good News! He is alive! Jesus is alive!"

Give children copies of page 313. Guide them to answer the seven questions along the path of the maze. Each right answer gets the men one more mile closer to Jerusalem.

Summary questions: **Who saw Jesus on the Emmaus road?** (two men) **What did the two men do when they realized it was Jesus?** (went to tell the apostles in Jerusalem)

Option: Make a life-sized maze in your classroom. Print the questions and statements on the maze on separate pieces of construction paper and tape them to the floor in an arrangement similar to the maze on page 313. Make an "Emmaus" and "Jerusalem" sign and post them at the beginning and end of the maze. Let the children work together to walk the maze and answer the questions to get from Emmaus to Jerusalem.

▼ Bible Verse ▲

Purpose
Recite Mark 16:15.

Materials
Bibles
verse puzzles from page 307
  used in the last two lessons
pushpins
yarn
stopwatch

Jesus gave His followers His last command in our Bible verse. This command was the work they would do after Jesus was gone.

Let the children find and read Mark 16:15. Ask for volunteers to say the verse with a friend or by themselves. If needed, give pairs of children a globe puzzle (page 307) to do to help them memorize the verse.

For children who know the verse, attach the verse puzzle pieces to a bulletin board in random order with pushpins. Fasten a length of yarn to the first word of the verse. Let pairs of children work together to connect the verse pieces in order by wrapping the yarn around the pushpin on each puzzle piece. Option: Use a stopwatch to see if each group can improve its time.

Use these questions to talk about Mark 16:15. **What is the sad part of the Good News?** (Jesus died.) **What are the happy parts of the Good News?** (Jesus is alive; we live, too.) **Where in the world can we tell Jesus' Good News? Who can say this verse by himself? Who can do this verse?**

▼ Bible and Me ▲

Before the session, record the following words to the tune "Oh, How I Love Jesus."

I'll tell Jesus' Good News. (Repeat twice.)
That Jesus died for me. (stanza 1)
That Jesus is alive. (stanza 2)
That Jesus is God's Son. (stanza 3)
That Jesus lives in Heaven. (stanza 4)

Only people who know Jesus' Good News will get to live in Heaven. If we don't tell the Good News, then people won't know! If they don't know the Good News, then they can't choose if they want to live in Heaven.

Together, listen to the song "I'll Tell Jesus' Good News." Sing the stanzas that tell the three parts of the Good News (1, 2, and 4). Sing through the song several times to become familiar with its message. Then do a rap to reinforce why it is important to tell Jesus' Good News.

Leader in the middle asks: Why is it important for (name) to know the Good News? Group answers: If we don't (clap-clap-clap), then they won't (clap-clap-clap), KNOW! (shout and clap at same time).

The leader gets three turns to ask the question and supply a name. Then the leader chooses someone else to be the leader. At the end, sing "I'll Tell Jesus' Good News."

What is Jesus' Good News? What is the difference between telling about Jesus and telling Jesus' Good News? Why is it important to tell people Jesus' Good News?

Option: Play "Twist & Tell." See the instructions in Lesson 49, Bible and Me.

Purpose
Tell why it is important for people to know Jesus' Good News.

Materials
blank cassette
cassette player

▼ Bible Project ▲

We know that Jesus' Good News is the most special thing Jesus did: He died and came back alive so we can live forever. That is Good News!

Guide the children to finish tracing the designs on the felt and cut their traced felt designs. Provide assistance and close supervision while children use sharp scissors to cut the felt.

Review what Jesus' Good News is as the children work. **What are the three parts of Jesus' Good News? Which part is sad? Which part is happy?**

Purpose
Tell Jesus' Good News.

Materials
materials to work on banners (listed on page 290)
sharp scissors

▼ Bible Sharing

The number of bears the children receive should equal the number of names of people they can name to tell Jesus' Good News.

Play a song about Jesus' Good News or sing "I'll Tell Jesus' Good News" from Bible and Me, with the last line "I'll tell His Good News." After each time singing the song, ask three children to stand and tell the three parts of Jesus' Good News. Sing until each child has a turn to tell at least one part of the Good News. Then sing other songs about Jesus' Good News.

Purpose
Share why Jesus' resurrection is Good News for you to tell.

Materials
a snack of bear-shaped graham crackers
CD or cassette of songs that tell Jesus' Good News
CD or cassette player

Jesus Appears by Lake Galilee

John 21:1-19

Memory Block
"Jesus said to the followers, 'Go everywhere in the world. Tell the Good News to everyone'" (Mark 16:15).

Purpose
Tell who saw Jesus by the seashore.

Materials
Bibles
copies of the top of page 314
pencils

Purpose
Tell what Peter did when he saw it was Jesus.

Materials
a copy of pages 78, 79, and 315
scissors
magnetic strips
a tin cookie sheet

Lesson Goals

- Tell who saw Jesus by the seashore.
- Tell what Peter did when he saw it was Jesus.
- Recite and explain Mark 16:15.
- Tell what makes it easy to tell Jesus' Good News.
- Tell Jesus' Good News.

▼ Bible Search ▲

Seven men who had been fishing in Lake Galilee saw Jesus after He came back alive. Let's find the names of as many as possible.

Guide the children to search for names of followers who saw Jesus by Lake Galilee. Help them locate John 21:2 in their Bibles. Read the verse together. Find the names of five followers and two more mentioned. Read Matthew 4:21 to find the names of the sons of Zebedee. Work to fit the names in the crossword puzzle in order: John, Nathanael, James, Peter, Thomas.

How many men saw Jesus this time? (seven) **What were five of their names?**

▼ Bible Story ▲

Before the session, cut out the fish on page 315 and attach a magnetic strip on each fish where indicated. Place the fish on the cookie sheet.

Display the picture of the apostles from pages 78 and 79. **Which five of the apostles are in our story?** Let children report. **Listen for what they were doing when Jesus came.**

"Jesus Appears by Lake Galilee"

"I'm going fishing," I told the other six men. I was talking to James, John, Thomas, Nathanael, and two more men. They chimed in, "We'll go, too!" So we gathered some fishing gear and got a boat on Lake Galilee. It was like old times, before we ever followed Jesus. And just like old times sometimes, we caught nothing. In fact we fished all night and still caught nothing.

Early the next morning, we saw someone standing on the shore, but we didn't know who it was. He called out to us, "Friends, have you caught any fish?" It was kind of embarrassing to have to tell Him we didn't even have one fish! Then He hollered back, "Throw your net into the water on the right side of the boat, and you will find some." It was worth a try. Maybe He saw one jump out of the water over there. So we heaved the net over the side.

As the net hit the lake, the water began splashing and churning. In amazement, we watched huge fish jumping around in our net. In fact, there were so many fish that all of us together could not pull the net back into the boat. What was happening?

John figured it out first. He shouted with joy, "It is the Lord!" When I heard John say that, my whole body sprang into action. I grabbed my coat and wrapped it around me as I jumped into the water. With all my energy I swam to the shore to see my Lord, my Jesus. I loved fishing, but I loved Jesus even more. I just wanted to be near Him.

In the boat, the other men dragged the net full of fish about 100 yards toward the shore where Jesus was waiting. In the sand, Jesus was cooking fish and bread for breakfast over a fire of hot coals. Jesus asked us to bring some of the fish we had caught. So I went out to the boat to help pull the net to shore. We found out the reason it was so heavy was because it was full of 153 huge fish. We were amazed that even with so many fish pulling and stretching the net, the net did not tear in even one place. The smell of the fish and bread cooking for breakfast made us realize how hungry we were. When Jesus invited us to eat, none of us needed to ask Him who He was. We knew for sure it was Jesus. It was so wonderful to be with Him again.

After we finished eating, Jesus talked to us. Three times Jesus asked me, "Peter, do you love me?" Each time I told Him that I did. But I was beginning to wonder why He kept asking the same question. I guess He wanted me to remember His next words. And I have never forgotten them. He said simply, "Follow me." On that day, Jesus showed me He was alive. And I showed Jesus that I was going to follow His commands and tell His Good News.

Display the fish on the cookie sheet and tell children they are going fishing, but they are looking for fish with questions on them. Let pairs of children take turns choosing a fish. When they answer the question on the fish they choose, they may keep the fish. If the fish has no question, they return it to the cookie sheet.

Summary questions: **Who saw Jesus by the seashore after He came back alive?** (seven followers) **What did Peter do because he was so excited to see Jesus?** (swam to shore)

▼ Bible Verse ▲

Before the session, glue the spinner board and spinner on page 314 to poster board and cut them out. Attach the spinner to the board with a paper fastener. Make a spinner for every 3 to 4 children.

Our verse in Mark is Jesus' last command to His followers. It tells what Jesus' followers must do until Jesus comes back for them!

Let the children find and read Mark 16:15. Ask for volunteers to say the verse with a friend or by themselves. If needed, give pairs of children a set of their verse puzzle pieces (page 307) to help them practice saying the verse from memory. Then use the spinner and board (page 314) to help groups of 3-4 children take turns saying and explaining the verse to each other.

Use these questions to talk about Mark 16:15. **What is the sad part of the Good News?** (Jesus died.) **What are the happy parts of the Good News?** (Jesus is alive; we live, too.) **Where in the world can we tell Jesus' Good News? Who can say this verse by herself? Who can do this verse?**

Purpose
Recite and explain Mark 16:15.

Materials
Bibles, copies of the verse puzzle from page 307 used the last three lessons
copies of the bottom of page 314
scissors
glue
poster board
paper fasteners

▼ Bible and Me ▲

Before Jesus went up to Heaven He promised always to be with us when we tell His Good News. That helps us! And it's fun to help people know the Good News so they can live in Heaven forever too.

Make badges to help tell the Good News. Children should choose one or two of the badges on page 316 to color and cut out. Then they can glue the badges to poster board circles and decorate them with glitter or beads. Help the children use masking tape to attach a safety pin to the backs of their completed badges.

Let the children wear the badges and practice having partners ask each other the following questions: **What's the Good News? What's so important about Jesus being alive?**

Use these questions to review what they are learning about the Good News. **What is Jesus' Good News? What is the difference between telling about Jesus and telling Jesus' Good News? Why is it important? What makes it easier?** (Jesus said He would be with us.)

▼ Bible Project ▲

We know that Jesus' Good News is the most special thing Jesus did: He died and came back alive so we can live forever. That is Good News!

Guide the children to glue their designs to the prepared burlap pieces. Help each child lay pieces on the burlap, positioning them without glue. Then glue. If you are using glue not recommended for children, supervise closely!

Review what Jesus' Good News is as the children work.

▼ Bible Sharing ▲

Ask the children to help you count out 153 crackers and then divide them among the children.

Use this time to review the unit memory block. With the children sitting in a circle, say the first word of the verse. The child to your left says the second word. The child to his left says the next word, and so on, until the verse is complete. The next person tells the three parts of Jesus' Good News. Repeat several times.

Close by singing favorite songs that tell Jesus' Good News.

Purpose
Tell what makes it easy to tell Jesus' Good News.

Materials
copies of page 316
poster board cut into 3-inch circles
glue sticks
safety pins
masking tape
markers and colored pencils
glitter or beads

Purpose
Tell Jesus' Good News.

Materials
materials to work on banners (listed on page 290)
fast-drying glue

Purpose
Share why Jesus' resurrection is Good News for you to tell.

Materials
a snack of fish crackers
CD or cassette of songs about Jesus' Good News
CD or cassette player

Jesus' Command: Go, Tell

Matthew 28:16-20; Mark 16:15, 16, 19, 20; Luke 24:50-53; Acts 1:6-12

Lesson Goals
- Tell what Jesus asked His followers to do.
- Tell who saw Jesus go up into Heaven.
- Recite and explain Mark 16:15.
- Report times and ways they are telling Jesus' Good News.

▼ Bible Search ▲

Jesus wanted His followers to know for sure He was alive. Two more places He showed He was alive were on a mountain in Galilee and on the Mount of Olives near Bethany. Let's search for what He told His followers.

Guide the children to find the Scriptures listed on page 317. Read the verses aloud. Work together to fill in the blanks on the page.

Where are two more places Jesus' followers saw that He was alive? What kinds of things did Jesus tell His followers at those two places? What did Jesus want His followers to be sure to do after He was gone?

▼ Bible Story ▲

Display a picture of clouds or look out the window to see clouds. **What do clouds make you think of? Listen to see what Jesus' followers may have thought about when they saw clouds.** (Jesus will come back in a cloud!)

"Jesus' Command: Go, Tell"

Some of Jesus' followers still didn't believe that He was alive! Time was running out. Jesus knew that soon He would go up to Heaven. So He did many things to help people believe He was alive. One time, Jesus said He would meet us on a mountain in Galilee. We eleven apostles walked to Galilee, climbed up the mountain, and waited for Jesus to come. On the mountain all of us saw Jesus and heard Him give us an important message. He said, "Go and make followers of all people in the world. Baptize them. Teach them to obey everything I have told you. You can be sure that I will be with you always." As we walked back down the mountain, some of us were wondering how we would be able to do this job for Jesus after He was gone.

Another time, forty days after He came back alive, Jesus was with us in Jerusalem. Together we walked down the streets, out of town, and almost to Bethany. Jesus led us to a high place named the Mount of Olives, a place where groves of olive trees were growing. Jesus knew this was the last time we would see Him until He came back. With love in His eyes, He looked one last time at each of us apostles. Then, with authority, Jesus gave us His final command, "Go everywhere in the world. Tell the Good News to everyone." It was a big job and Jesus knew we would need help. So He promised He would send the Holy Spirit to help us speak first in Jerusalem, then in Judea, Samaria, and every part of the world. As He raised His hands to bless us, Jesus was lifted from the ground, up into the air, up higher in the sky, up higher into a cloud. Even after the cloud hid Him, we

Memory Block
"Jesus said to the followers, 'Go everywhere in the world. Tell the Good News to everyone'" (Mark 16:15).

Purpose
Tell what Jesus asked His followers to do.

Materials
Bibles
copies of the top of page 317
pencils

Purpose
Tell who saw Jesus go up into Heaven.

Materials
a picture of clouds
copies of the bottom of page 317
nine cotton balls for each child

kept watching and hoping to see Jesus one more time.

We were still looking up when suddenly two angels stood beside us. The angels asked, "Men of Galilee, why are you standing here looking into the sky? You saw Jesus taken away from you into Heaven. He will come back in the same way you saw Him go." The angel's message reminded us that this was both a sad and happy day. Along with the sadness of saying goodbye to Jesus, we were joyful because we knew Jesus would come back for us.

Back in Jerusalem, some of us went to the temple to praise God for what we had seen and heard. One week, then eight days, then nine days passed. On the tenth day, the Holy Spirit came just as Jesus promised. Then we knew it was time to tell Jesus' Good News to people everywhere in the world. On that very day, we began to do exactly what Jesus asked. With the Lord's help, we began to tell Jesus' Good News to everyone: "Jesus died, but He came back alive. He is in Heaven now. And we can go to Heaven too!"

Give each child a copy of the bottom of page 317 to review the story. Let children take turns answering the questions. Every time a question is answered correctly, they place a cotton ball on the cloud. Continue until all clouds are filled. If you have time, let children work in pairs to ask each other questions and complete their own Cotton Ball Bingo cards.

Summary questions: **Who saw Jesus go up into Heaven?** (apostles) **What did Jesus ask His followers to do?** (go, tell)

▼ Bible Verse ▲

<table>
<tr><td>

Purpose
Recite and explain Mark 16:15.

Materials
Bibles, a cotton ball
CD or cassette of songs that
   tell Jesus' Good News
CD or cassette player

</td></tr>
</table>

Mark 16:15 is Jesus' last command to His followers. It tells what Jesus wants you and me to do until He comes back for us!

Let the children find and read Mark 16:15. Then play "Cotton, Cotton" to recite and explain the verse. The children will pass a cotton ball around the circle while you sing or play a favorite Good News song. Whenever the music stops, whoever has the cotton must say the verse and then ask someone else in the circle to explain what this verse helps them to do.

Use these questions if you need to help the children explain the verse. **What is the sad part of the Good News?** (Jesus died.) **What are the happy parts of the Good News?** (Jesus is alive; we live, too.) **Where in the world can we tell Jesus' Good News?**

▼ Bible and Me ▲

We've been working on obeying Jesus' command to tell His Good News. Let's play a game to celebrate what we have been doing!

Play the game on page 318. Children should take turns tossing a button onto the number circle on the board. Move a game marker (penny, bean) the number of spaces indicated, and read the question on that space. If a player cannot answer the question, the game marker goes back where it was. Provide one game for every 3 to 4 children so they can have frequent turns to play.

Use these questions if you need more help to review or evaluate what the children have learned about telling Jesus' Good News. **What is Jesus' Good News? What is the difference between telling about Jesus and telling Jesus' Good News? Why is it important? What makes it easier?**

Option: Make a Good News obstacle course. Set up a path in your room, around, under, and above. At stations along the way, place a card on which you have printed a question from page 317. Children may only advance when they have answered the question. Let children go through the course in pairs while the group cheers them on and gives help as needed. For an extra challenge, time the children to see who can complete the course the quickest.

Purpose
Report times and ways they are telling Jesus' Good News.

Materials
copies of page 318
buttons to toss
pennies or beans for game markers

▼ Bible Project ▲

We know that telling Jesus' Good News is the most special thing Jesus did: He died and came back alive so we can live forever. That is Good News!

Guide the children to complete banners. Add any special details (perhaps rickrack, glitter, or yarn). Attach dowels and string to hang banners. Help each child prepare to display and tell about her banner in the Bible Sharing time. If you can, invite parents to attend the end of the session; children can display the banners for their family and friends.

Review what Jesus' Good News is as the children work.

Purpose
Tell Jesus' Good News.

Materials
materials to complete banners (listed on page 290)

▼ Bible Sharing ▲

As you eat the snack, talk about the Good News. **What are the three parts of the Good News about Jesus? Why is Jesus' resurrection such Good News for us to tell?** (It means we will live with Him in Heaven someday.)

Ask volunteers to display and tell about their completed banners. If possible, plan a time to display the banners in other parts of the church building and tell Jesus' Good News. Encourage the children to use the banners at home to tell family and friends Jesus' Good News.

Sing songs you have learned about telling the Good News.

Purpose
Share why Jesus' resurrection is Good News for you to tell.

Materials
a snack of cotton candy
banners
CD or cassette of songs about Jesus' Good News
CD or cassette player

Bible Search

More than one person was a part of
   Jesus' death.
Find and read about some of them.

1. Read John 19:15 in your Bible.
   Who wanted to have Jesus killed? _____

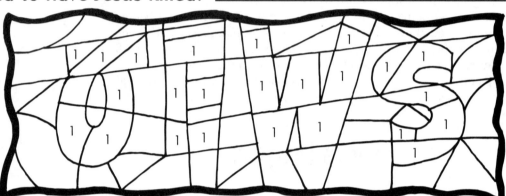

Check
your answer by
coloring in all the
shapes with **1** in
them the same
color.

2. Read John 19:16 in your Bible.
   Who gave Jesus to the Jews to be killed? _____

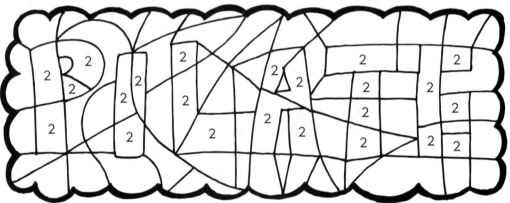

Check
your answer by
coloring in all the
shapes with **2** in
them the same
color.

3. Read John 19:16, 18 in your Bible.
   Who put Jesus on the cross? _____

Check
your answer by
coloring in all the
shapes with **3** in
them the same
color.

UNIT 12, LESSON 48

Bible Verse

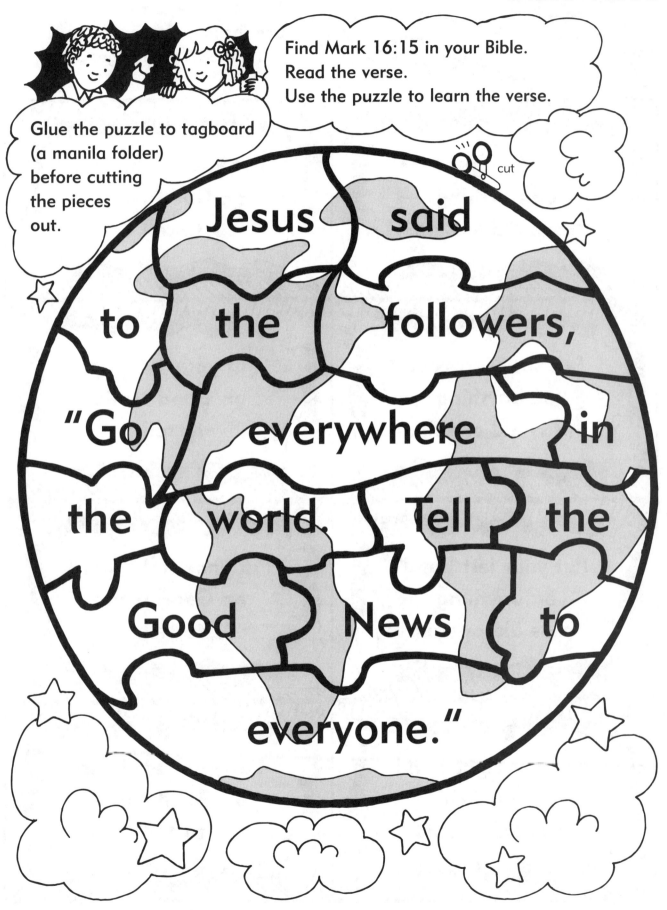

Find Mark 16:15 in your Bible.
Read the verse.
Use the puzzle to learn the verse.

Glue the puzzle to tagboard (a manila folder) before cutting the pieces out.

cut

Jesus said to the followers, "Go everywhere in the world. Tell the Good News to everyone."

Bible and Me

cut

Cut apart the cards.
Use them to play Twist and Tell.
You will also need pages 309-311.

Put your right foot
on anything
Jesus did or said.

Put your right foot
on Good News
to tell.

Put your left foot
on anything
Jesus did or said.

Put your left foot
on Good News
to tell.

Put your left hand
on anything
Jesus did or said.

Put your right hand
on Good News
to tell.

Put your right hand
on anything
Jesus did or said.

Put your left hand
on Good News
to tell.

308 ▲

Copy this page three times.
Use the pictures to play Twist and Tell.

Bible and Me

Sample layout for Twist and Tell.

Share.

I'll help.

Be still.

Bible and Me

Cut apart the pictures.
Use them to play Twist and Tell.

 UNIT 12, LESSON 49

Cut apart the pictures.
Use them to play Twist and Tell.

Share.

Be still.

I'll help.

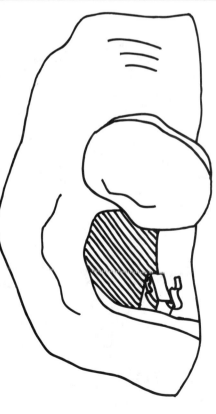

Use this tomb pattern to make review questions for Lesson 49 Bible Story. Use 3- by 5-inch cards.

Bible Search

Find Luke 24 in your Bible. Answer the questions about what Jesus did.

A B C D E F G H I J K L M N O P Q R S T U V W X Y Z

Jesus did many things to show He was really alive. What did He do on the road to Emmaus?

Write the letter that comes next in ABC order.

1 Find Luke 24:15.

V		K	J	D	C

Jesus | | A | | | | | .

2 Find Luke 24:27.

S		K	J	D	C

Jesus | | A | | | | | .

3 Find Luke 24:29.

R	S		X	D	C

Jesus | | | A | | | | with them.

4 Find Luke 24:30.

R		S			C	N	V	M

Jesus | | A | | | | | | | .

S	G		M	J	R

Jesus gave | | | A | | | | for food.

C	H	U	H	C	D	C

Jesus | | | | | | | | the bread.

UNIT 12, LESSON 50

Follow the maze from Emmaus to Jerusalem.
Answer each question to take
the men back to Jerusalem.

Bible Story

Emmaus

1 mile

Who walked from Jerusalem to Emmaus?

2 miles

How did the men feel on the road to Emmaus?

Dead end. Go back.

3 miles

What happened on the road?

When did they recognize Jesus?

Bridge out. Go back.

4 miles

What happened when they got to Emmaus?

5 miles

Rock slide. Road blocked.

6 miles

What did the men decide to do?

How did the men feel on the way back to Jerusalem?

7 miles

Jerusalem

Bible Search

Find John 21:2 in your Bible.
Who saw Jesus by Lake Galilee?
Put their names in the puzzle. (The sons of Zebedee are named in Matthew 4:21.)

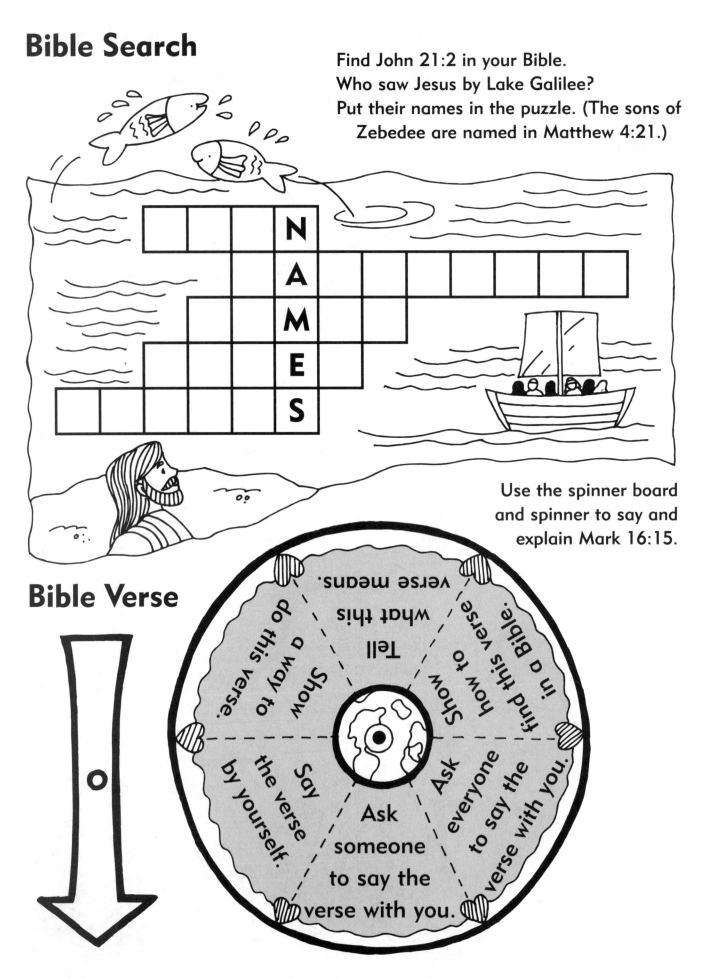

N
A
M
E
S

Use the spinner board and spinner to say and explain Mark 16:15.

Bible Verse

Show a way to do this verse.

Tell what this verse means.

Show how to find this verse in a Bible.

Say the verse by yourself.

Ask someone to say the verse with you.

Ask everyone to say the verse with you.

Unit 12, Lesson 51

Bible Story

Copy and cut apart the fish.
Attach a magnetic strip to each one.
Use the questions to review the Bible Story.

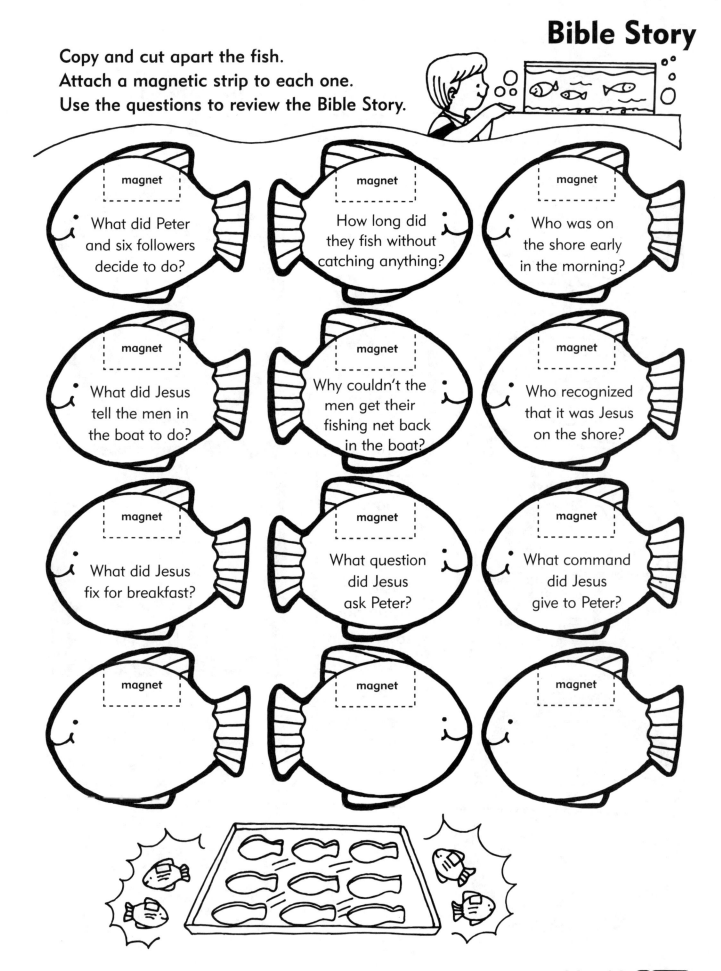

magnet
What did Peter and six followers decide to do?

magnet
How long did they fish without catching anything?

magnet
Who was on the shore early in the morning?

magnet
What did Jesus tell the men in the boat to do?

magnet
Why couldn't the men get their fishing net back in the boat?

magnet
Who recognized that it was Jesus on the shore?

magnet
What did Jesus fix for breakfast?

magnet
What question did Jesus ask Peter?

magnet
What command did Jesus give to Peter?

magnet

magnet

magnet

Bible and Me

Make badges to help you tell the Good News!

JESUS is ALIVE!

I have GOOD NEWS

Good News! Jesus is Alive!

Cut out a badge. Color it. Mount it on poster board.

Tape a safety pin to the back so you can wear your badge.

Ask me about Good News!

Jesus died, but now He lives!

I know Jesus' Good News!

 UNIT 12, LESSON 51

Bible Search

Find the verses in your Bible.
What did Jesus tell His followers to do?

Matthew 28:19

Jesus told His followers to ___ ___

and make ___ ___ ___ ___ ___ ___ ___ ___ ___ ___.

Mark 16:15

Jesus told His followers to ___ ___

And tell the ___ ___ ___ ___ ___ ___ ___ ___ ___.

Bible Story

Name one place Jesus showed His apostles He was alive.

Put a cotton cloud on each question you answer.

How many days after Jesus came back alive did He go up to Heaven?

Where did Jesus tell His followers to go after He was gone?

What did Jesus ask His followers to tell everyone?

How long did Jesus' followers watch Jesus go up?

How many apostles saw Jesus on the mountain in Galilee?

What did the angels tell the followers?

When did the followers start telling the Good News?

Who helped the followers tell Jesus' Good News?

Bible and Me

CELEBRATE!

Play a game to celebrate telling Jesus' Good News!

START

Name a place you did or could tell Jesus' Good News.

What Bible verse helps you remember to tell Jesus' Good News?

Name a time you did or could tell Jesus' Good News.

1 or 2

2

1

Why is it important for people to know Jesus' Good News?

JESUS IS ALIVE

Name a person you did or could tell Jesus' Good News.

What are the three parts of Jesus' Good News?

Name a way you did or could tell Jesus' Good News.

What does Mark 16:15 help you remember to do?

Go back 3 spaces.

Name a place you did or could tell Jesus' Good News.

What's the difference between telling about Jesus and telling Jesus' Good News?

What Bible verse helps you remember to tell Jesus' Good News?

Name a person you did or could tell Jesus' Good News.

What makes it easier to tell Jesus' Good News?

What final command did Jesus give His followers?

If you don't know, go back to start!

FINISH

What is your favorite song about telling Jesus' Good News?

If you don't know, go back to start!

 UNIT 12, LESSON 52

Route 52 Road Map

Year 1 | **Year 2**

Ages 3, 4

DISCOVER GOD'S LOVE (42071)
- God Is Great
- God Is Love
- God Is Good
- God Sends His Son, Jesus
- God's Son, Jesus, Grows Up
- God's Son, Jesus
- We Can Know Jesus Is Our Friend
- We Can Know Jesus Is Close to Us
- We Can Be Jesus' Helpers
- We Can Learn to Help
- We Can Learn to Share
- We Can Learn to Love God

DISCOVER GOD'S WORD (42075)
- God Made the World
- God Made People
- God Cares for Me
- Jesus Is Born
- Jesus Is God's Son
- Jesus Loves Us
- Be Thankful
- Help Jesus
- Discover About Myself
- Learn from the Bible
- Talk to God
- Help Others

Ages 4-6

EXPLORE BIBLE PEOPLE (42072)
- Learning That I Am Special (Joseph)
- Learning to Trust God (Gideon)
- Learning to Do What Is Right (Nehemiah)
- Learning to Be Brave (Esther)
- Learning to Pray Always (Daniel)
- Learning to Obey God (Jonah)
- Learning to Love People
- Learning to Be Happy
- Learning to Be Thankful
- Learning to Share
- Learning to Help Others
- Learning to Follow Jesus

EXPLORE BIBLE STORIES (42076)
- Learning About God's Creation
- Learning That God Keeps His Promises
- Learning About God's Care
- Learning About Baby Jesus
- Learning to Be a Friend Like Jesus
- Learning to Follow Jesus
- Learning About Jesus' Power
- Learning That Jesus Is the Son of God
- Learning About the Church
- Learning to Do Right
- Learning That God Is Powerful
- Learning That God Hears My Prayers

Ages 6-8

FOLLOW THE BIBLE (42073)
- The Bible Helps Me Worship God
- The Bible Teaches That God Helps People
- The Bible Helps Me Obey God
- The Bible Teaches That God Answers Prayer
- The Bible Teaches That Jesus Is the Son of God
- The Bible Teaches That Jesus Does Great Things
- The Bible Helps Me Obey Jesus
- The Bible Tells How Jesus Helped People
- The Bible Teaches Me to Tell About Jesus
- The Bible Tells How Jesus' Church Helps People

FOLLOW JESUS (42077)
- Jesus' Birth Helps Me Worship
- Jesus Was a Child Just Like Me
- Jesus Wants Me to Follow Him
- Jesus Teaches Me to Have His Attitude
- Jesus' Stories Help Me Follow Him
- Jesus Helps Me Worship
- Jesus Helps Me Be a Friend
- Jesus Helps Me Bring Friends to Him
- Jesus Helps Me Love My Family
- Jesus' Power Helps Me Worship Him
- Jesus' Miracles Help Me Tell About Him
- Jesus' Resurrection Is Good News for Me to Tell

Ages 8-12

GROW THROUGH THE BIBLE (42074)
- God's Word
- God's World
- God's Chosen People
- God's Great Nation
- The Promised Land
- The Kings of Israel
- The Kingdom Divided, Conquered
- From Jesus' Birth to His Baptism
- Jesus, the Lord
- Jesus, the Savior
- The Church Begins
- The Church Grows
- Reviewing God's Plan for His People

STUDY GOD'S PLAN (42078)
- The Bible Teaches Us How to Please God
- Books of Law Tell Us How God's People Were Led
- History and Poetry Tell About Choices God's People Made
- Prophets Reveal That God Does What He Says
- God Planned, Promised, and Provided Salvation
- Gospels Teach Us What Jesus Did
- Gospels Teach Us What Jesus Said
- Gospels Teach Us That Jesus Is Our Savior
- Acts Records How the Church Began and Grew
- Letters Instruct the Church in Right Living
- OT People and Events Prepare for God's Plan
- NT People and Events Spread God's Plan

Ages 8-12

GROW UP IN CHRIST (42080)
- Growing in Faith
- Growing in Obedience
- Growing in Attitude
- Growing in Worship
- Growing in Discipleship
- Growing in Prayer
- Growing in Goodness
- Growing in Love for Christ
- Growing in Devotion to the Church
- Growing in Grace
- Growing in Confidence
- Growing in Hope

STUDY JESUS' TEACHINGS (42079)
- Jesus Teaches Us About Who God Is
- Jesus Teaches Us That God Loves Us
- Jesus Teaches Us How to Love God
- Jesus Teaches Us About Himself
- Jesus Teaches Us to Do God's Will
- Jesus Teaches Us to Love Others
- Jesus Teaches Us About God's Kingdom
- Jesus Teaches Us How to Live Right
- Jesus Teaches Us the Truth
- Jesus Teaches Us About Forgiveness
- Jesus Teaches Us About God's Power
- Jesus Teaches Us About God's Word

Look for these and other excellent Christian education products by Standard Publishing at your local Christian bookstore or order directly from Standard Publishing by calling 1-800-543-1353.

www.standardpub.com

A 52-Week Bible Journey . . . Just for Kids!

Ages 3 to 4

Discover God's Love

Help young children discover what God has done, thank Him for what He made, celebrate Jesus, begin to follow Jesus, and practice doing what God's Word says.

Product code: 42071

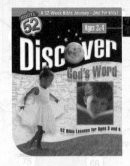

Discover God's Word

Help young children discover what God's Word says about the world, who God is, what He wants them to do, and Bible people who loved God.

Product code: 42075

Ages 4 to 6

Explore Bible People

Stories of Bible people will help children learn that they are special, how to trust God and choose to do right, how to love and obey Jesus, and how to help and share with others.

Product code: 42072

Explore Bible Stories

Bible stories will help children learn about creation, God's promises, power and care, who Jesus is and what He did, and how to follow Jesus' example and teaching.

Product code: 42076

Ages 6 to 8

Follow the Bible

Young readers will learn to follow Bible teachings as they look up Bible verses, experience basic Bible stories, and practice beginning Bible study skills.

Product code: 42073

Follow Jesus

Young learners will learn to follow Jesus as they experience stories from the Gospels. Through a variety of activities, children will worship, follow, and tell about Jesus.

Product code: 42077

Ages 8 to 12

Grow Through the Bible

Kids will grow in their understanding of God's Word as they investigate the Bible from Genesis through Paul's journeys and letters.

Product code: 42074

Grow Up in Christ

Kids will grow up in Christ as they explore New Testament truths about growing in faith, obedience, worship, goodness, prayer, love, devotion, grace, confidence, and hope.

Product code: 42080

Study God's Plan

Kids will study God's plan for salvation by exploring Bible people and events, Bible divisions and eras, and Bible themes and content, all while practicing Bible study skills.

Product code: 42078

Study Jesus' Teachings

Kids will study what Jesus teaches about who God is, His love, how to love God and others, about God's kingdom, truth, forgiveness, power, God's Word, and doing His will.

Product code: 42079